Praise for the second edition of *The Pragmatic Programmer*

Some say that with *The Pragmatic Programmer*, Andy and Dave captured lightning in a bottle; that it's unlikely anyone will soon write a book that can move an entire industry as it did. Sometimes, though, lightning does strike twice, and this book is proof. The updated content ensures that it will stay at the top of "best books in software development" lists for another 20 years, right where it belongs.

➤ **VM (Vicky) Brasseur**
   Director of Open Source Strategy, Juniper Networks

If you want your software to be easy to modernize and maintain, keep a copy of *The Pragmatic Programmer* close. It's filled with practical advice, both technical and professional, that will serve you and your projects well for years to come.

➤ **Andrea Goulet**
   CEO, Corgibytes; Founder, LegacyCode.Rocks

The Pragmatic Programmer is the one book I can point to that completely dislodged the existing trajectory of my career in software and pointed me in the direction of success. Reading it opened my mind to the possibilities of being a craftsman, not just a cog in a big machine. One of the most significant books in my life.

➤ **Obie Fernandez**
   Author, *The Rails Way*

First-time readers can look forward to an enthralling induction into the modern world of software practice, a world that the first edition played a major role in shaping. Readers of the first edition will rediscover here the insights and practical wisdom that made the book so significant in the first place, expertly curated and updated, along with much that's new.

➤ **David A. Black**
   Author, *The Well-Grounded Rubyist*

I have an old paper copy of the original *Pragmatic Programmer* on my bookshelf. It has been read and re-read and a long time ago it changed everything about how I approached my job as a programmer. In the new edition everything and nothing has changed: I now read it on my iPad and the code examples use modern programming languages—but the underlying concepts, ideas, and attitudes are timeless and universally applicable. Twenty years later, the book is as relevant as ever. It makes me happy to know that current and future developers will have the same opportunity to learn from Andy and Dave's profound insights as I did back in the day.

➤ **Sandy Mamoli**
   Agile coach, author of *How Self-Selection Lets People Excel*

Twenty years ago, the first edition of *The Pragmatic Programmer* completely changed the trajectory of my career. This new edition could do the same for yours.

➤ **Mike Cohn**
   Author of *Succeeding with Agile, Agile Estimating and Planning*, and *User Stories Applied*

The Pragmatic Programmer
your journey to mastery

20th Anniversary Edition

Dave Thomas
Andy Hunt

♦♦ Addison-Wesley

Boston · Columbus · New York · San Francisco · Amsterdam · Cape Town
Dubai · London · Madrid · Milan · Munich · Paris · Montreal · Toronto · Delhi · Mexico City
São Paulo · Sydney · Hong Kong · Seoul · Singapore · Taipei · Tokyo

For information about buying this title in bulk quantities, or for special sales opportunities (which may include electronic versions; custom cover designs; and content particular to your business, training goals, marketing focus, or branding interests), please contact our corporate sales department at corpsales@pearsoned.com or (800) 382-3419.

For government sales inquiries, please contact governmentsales@pearsoned.com.

For questions about sales outside the U.S., please contact intlcs@pearson.com.

Visit us on the Web: informit.com/aw

Library of Congress Control Number: 2019944178

Copyright © 2020 Pearson Education, Inc.

Cover images: Mihalec/Shutterstock, Stockish/Shutterstock

ISBN-13: 978-0-13-595705-9
ISBN-10: 0-13-595705-2

1 2019   d   d

We made some difficult decisions. We dropped the *Resources* appendix, both because it would be impossible to keep up-to-date and because it's easier to search for what you want. We reorganized and rewrote topics to do with concurrency, given the current abundance of parallel hardware and the dearth of good ways of dealing with it. We added content to reflect changing attitudes and environments, from the agile movement which we helped launch, to the rising acceptance of functional programming idioms and the growing need to consider privacy and security.

Interestingly, though, there was considerably less debate between us on the content of this edition than there was when we wrote the first. We both felt that the stuff that was important was easier to identify.

Anyway, this book is the result. Please enjoy it. Maybe adopt some new practices. Maybe decide that some of the stuff we suggest is wrong. Get involved in your craft. Give us feedback.

But, most important, remember to make it fun.

How the Book Is Organized

This book is written as a collection of short topics. Each topic is self-contained, and addresses a particular theme. You'll find numerous cross references, which help put each topic in context. Feel free to read the topics in any order—this isn't a book you need to read front-to-back.

Occasionally you'll come across a box labeled *Tip nn* (such as Tip 1, *Care About Your Craft*, on page xxi). As well as emphasizing points in the text, we feel the tips have a life of their own—we live by them daily. You'll find a summary of all the tips on a pull-out card inside the back cover.

We've included exercises and challenges where appropriate. Exercises normally have relatively straightforward answers, while the challenges are more open-ended. To give you an idea of our thinking, we've included our answers to the exercises in an appendix, but very few have a single *correct* solution. The challenges might form the basis of group discussions or essay work in advanced programming courses.

There's also a short bibliography listing the books and articles we explicitly reference.

Preface to the Second Edition

Back in the 1990s, we worked with companies whose projects were having problems. We found ourselves saying the same things to each: maybe you should test that before you ship it; why does the code only build on Mary's machine? Why didn't anyone ask the users?

To save time with new clients, we started jotting down notes. And those notes became *The Pragmatic Programmer*. To our surprise the book seemed to strike a chord, and it has continued to be popular these last 20 years.

But 20 years is many lifetimes in terms of software. Take a developer from 1999 and drop them into a team today, and they'd struggle in this strange new world. But the world of the 1990s is equally foreign to today's developer. The book's references to things such as CORBA, CASE tools, and indexed loops were at best quaint and more likely confusing.

At the same time, 20 years has had no impact whatsoever on common sense. Technology may have changed, but people haven't. Practices and approaches that were a good idea then remain a good idea now. Those aspects of the book aged well.

So when it came time to create this 20th *Anniversary Edition*, we had to make a decision. We could go through and update the technologies we reference and call it a day. Or we could reexamine the assumptions behind the practices we recommended in the light of an additional two decades' worth of experience.

In the end, we did both.

As a result, this book is something of a *Ship of Theseus*.[1] Roughly one-third of the topics in the book are brand new. Of the rest, the majority have been rewritten, either partially or totally. Our intent was to make things clearer, more relevant, and hopefully somewhat timeless.

---

1. If, over the years, every component of a ship is replaced as it fails, is the resulting vessel the same ship?

As a relative newcomer, it's easy to be overwhelmed not by the act of programming but the process of becoming a programmer. There is an entire mindset shift that needs to happen—a change in habits, behaviors, and expectations. The process of becoming a better programmer doesn't just happen because you know how to code; it must be met with intention and deliberate practice. This book is a guide to becoming a better programmer efficiently.

But make no mistake—it doesn't tell you how programming should be. It's not philosophical or judgmental in that way. It tells you, plain and simple, what a Pragmatic Programmer is—how they operate, and how they approach code. They leave it up to you to decide if you want to be one. If you feel it's not for you, they won't hold it against you. But if you decide it is, they're your friendly neighbors, there to show you the way.

▶ *Saron Yitbarek*
  Founder & CEO of CodeNewbie
  Host of Command Line Heroes

But the second is what makes this release truly exciting. After writing the first edition, they had the chance to reflect on what they were trying to say, what they wanted their readers to take away, and how it was being received. They got feedback on those lessons. They saw what stuck, what needed refining, what was misunderstood. In the twenty years that this book has made its way through the hands and hearts of programmers all over the world, Dave and Andy have studied this response and formulated new ideas, new concepts.

They've learned the importance of agency and recognized that developers have arguably more agency than most other professionals. They start this book with the simple but profound message: "it's your life." It reminds us of our own power in our code base, in our jobs, in our careers. It sets the tone for everything else in the book—that it's more than just another technical book filled with code examples.

What makes it truly stand out among the shelves of technical books is that it understands what it means to be a programmer. Programming is about trying to make the future less painful. It's about making things easier for our teammates. It's about getting things wrong and being able to bounce back. It's about forming good habits. It's about understanding your toolset. Coding is just part of the world of being a programmer, and this book explores that world.

I spend a lot of time thinking about the coding journey. I didn't grow up coding; I didn't study it in college. I didn't spend my teenage years tinkering with tech. I entered the coding world in my mid-twenties and had to learn what it meant to be a programmer. This community is very different from others I'd been a part of. There is a unique dedication to learning and practicality that is both refreshing and intimidating.

For me, it really does feel like entering a new world. A new town, at least. I had to get to know the neighbors, pick my grocery store, find the best coffee shops. It took a while to get the lay of the land, to find the most efficient routes, to avoid the streets with the heaviest traffic, to know when traffic was likely to hit. The weather is different, I needed a new wardrobe.

The first few weeks, even months, in a new town can be scary. Wouldn't it be wonderful to have a friendly, knowledgeable neighbor who'd been living there a while? Who can give you a tour, show you those coffee shops? Someone who'd been there long enough to know the culture, understand the pulse of the town, so you not only feel at home, but become a contributing member as well? Dave and Andy are those neighbors.

Foreword

I remember when Dave and Andy first tweeted about the new edition of this book. It was big news. I watched as the coding community responded with excitement. My feed buzzed with anticipation. After twenty years, *The Pragmatic Programmer* is just as relevant today as it was back then.

It says a lot that a book with such history had such a reaction. I had the privilege of reading an unreleased copy to write this foreword, and I understood why it created such a stir. While it's a technical book, calling it that does it a disservice. Technical books often intimidate. They're stuffed with big words, obscure terms, convoluted examples that, unintentionally, make you feel stupid. The more experienced the author, the easier it is to forget what it's like to learn new concepts, to be a beginner.

Despite their decades of programming experience, Dave and Andy have conquered the difficult challenge of writing with the same excitement of people who've just learned these lessons. They don't talk down to you. They don't assume you are an expert. They don't even assume you've read the first edition. They take you as you are—programmers who just want to be better. They spend the pages of this book helping you get there, one actionable step at a time.

To be fair, they'd already done this before. The original release was full of tangible examples, new ideas, and practical tips to build your coding muscles and develop your coding brain that still apply today. But this updated edition makes two improvements on the book.

The first is the obvious one: it removes some of the older references, the out-of-date examples, and replaces them with fresh, modern content. You won't find examples of loop invariants or build machines. Dave and Andy have taken their powerful content and made sure the lessons still come through, free of the distractions of old examples. It dusts off old ideas like DRY (don't repeat yourself) and gives them a fresh coat of paint, really making them shine.

9. **Pragmatic Projects**   263
    Topic 49.   Pragmatic Teams 264
    Topic 50.   Coconuts Don't Cut It 270
    Topic 51.   Pragmatic Starter Kit 273
    Topic 52.   Delight Your Users 280
    Topic 53.   Pride and Prejudice 282

    Postface   285

    Bibliography   289

    Possible Answers to the Exercises   293

    Index   307

4.	**Pragmatic Paranoia**	**103**
Topic 23.	Design by Contract	104
Topic 24.	Dead Programs Tell No Lies	112
Topic 25.	Assertive Programming	115
Topic 26.	How to Balance Resources	118
Topic 27.	Don't Outrun Your Headlights	125

5.	**Bend, or Break**	**129**
Topic 28.	Decoupling	130
Topic 29.	Juggling the Real World	137
Topic 30.	Transforming Programming	147
Topic 31.	Inheritance Tax	158
Topic 32.	Configuration	166

6.	**Concurrency**	**169**
Topic 33.	Breaking Temporal Coupling	170
Topic 34.	Shared State Is Incorrect State	174
Topic 35.	Actors and Processes	181
Topic 36.	Blackboards	187

7.	**While You Are Coding**	**191**
Topic 37.	Listen to Your Lizard Brain	192
Topic 38.	Programming by Coincidence	197
Topic 39.	Algorithm Speed	203
Topic 40.	Refactoring	209
Topic 41.	Test to Code	214
Topic 42.	Property-Based Testing	224
Topic 43.	Stay Safe Out There	231
Topic 44.	Naming Things	238

8.	**Before the Project**	**243**
Topic 45.	The Requirements Pit	244
Topic 46.	Solving Impossible Puzzles	252
Topic 47.	Working Together	256
Topic 48.	The Essence of Agility	259

Contents

Foreword		xi
Preface to the Second Edition		xv
From the Preface to the First Edition		xix

1. A Pragmatic Philosophy   **1**

Topic 1.	It's Your Life	2
Topic 2.	The Cat Ate My Source Code	3
Topic 3.	Software Entropy	6
Topic 4.	Stone Soup and Boiled Frogs	8
Topic 5.	Good-Enough Software	11
Topic 6.	Your Knowledge Portfolio	13
Topic 7.	Communicate!	19

2. A Pragmatic Approach   **27**

Topic 8.	The Essence of Good Design	28
Topic 9.	DRY—The Evils of Duplication	30
Topic 10.	Orthogonality	39
Topic 11.	Reversibility	47
Topic 12.	Tracer Bullets	50
Topic 13.	Prototypes and Post-it Notes	56
Topic 14.	Domain Languages	59
Topic 15.	Estimating	65

3. The Basic Tools   **73**

Topic 16.	The Power of Plain Text	74
Topic 17.	Shell Games	78
Topic 18.	Power Editing	81
Topic 19.	Version Control	84
Topic 20.	Debugging	88
Topic 21.	Text Manipulation	97
Topic 22.	Engineering Daybooks	100

For Juliet and Ellie,
Zachary and Elizabeth,
Henry and Stuart

What's in a Name?

"When I use a word," Humpty Dumpty said, in rather a scornful tone, "it means just what I choose it to mean—neither more nor less."

> ➤ Lewis Carroll, *Through the Looking-Glass*

Scattered throughout the book you'll find various bits of jargon—either perfectly good English words that have been corrupted to mean something technical, or horrendous made-up words that have been assigned meanings by computer scientists with a grudge against the language. The first time we use each of these jargon words, we try to define it, or at least give a hint to its meaning. However, we're sure that some have fallen through the cracks, and others, such as *object* and *relational database,* are in common enough usage that adding a definition would be boring. If you *do* come across a term you haven't seen before, please don't just skip over it. Take time to look it up, perhaps on the web, or maybe in a computer science textbook. And, if you get a chance, drop us an email and complain, so we can add a definition to the next edition.

Having said all this, we decided to get revenge against the computer scientists. Sometimes, there are perfectly good jargon words for concepts, words that we've decided to ignore. Why? Because the existing jargon is normally restricted to a particular problem domain, or to a particular phase of development. However, one of the basic philosophies of this book is that most of the techniques we're recommending are universal: modularity applies to code, designs, documentation, and team organization, for instance. When we wanted to use the conventional jargon word in a broader context, it got confusing—we couldn't seem to overcome the baggage the original term brought with it. When this happened, we contributed to the decline of the language by inventing our own terms.

Source Code and Other Resources

Most of the code shown in this book is extracted from compilable source files, available for download from our website.[2]

There you'll also find links to resources we find useful, along with updates to the book and news of other Pragmatic Programmer developments.

---

2. https://pragprog.com/titles/tpp20

Send Us Feedback

We'd appreciate hearing from you. Email us at ppbook@pragprog.com.

Second Edition Acknowledgments

We have enjoyed literally thousands of interesting conversations about programming over the last 20 years, meeting people at conferences, at courses, and sometimes even on the plane. Each one of these has added to our understanding of the development process, and has contributed to the updates in this edition. Thank you all (and keep telling us when we're wrong).

Thanks to the participants in the book's beta process. Your questions and comments helped us explain things better.

Before we went beta, we shared the book with a few folks for comments. Thanks to VM (Vicky) Brasseur, Jeff Langr, and Kim Shrier for your detailed comments, and to José Valim and Nick Cuthbert for your technical reviews.

Thanks to Ron Jeffries for letting us use the Sudoku example.

Much gratitude to the folks at Pearson who agreed to let us create this book our way.

A special thanks to the indispensable Janet Furlow, who masters whatever she takes on and keeps us in line.

And, finally, a shout out to all the Pragmatic Programmers out there who have been making programming better for everyone for the last twenty years. Here's to twenty more.

From the Preface to the First Edition

This book will help you become a better programmer.

You could be a lone developer, a member of a large project team, or a consultant working with many clients at once. It doesn't matter; this book will help you, as an individual, to do better work. This book isn't theoretical—we concentrate on practical topics, on using your experience to make more informed decisions. The word *pragmatic* comes from the Latin *pragmaticus*—"skilled in business"—which in turn is derived from the Greek πραγματικός, meaning "fit for use."

This is a book about doing.

Programming is a craft. At its simplest, it comes down to getting a computer to do what you want it to do (or what your user wants it to do). As a programmer, you are part listener, part advisor, part interpreter, and part dictator. You try to capture elusive requirements and find a way of expressing them so that a mere machine can do them justice. You try to document your work so that others can understand it, and you try to engineer your work so that others can build on it. What's more, you try to do all this against the relentless ticking of the project clock. You work small miracles every day.

It's a difficult job.

There are many people offering you help. Tool vendors tout the miracles their products perform. Methodology gurus promise that their techniques guarantee results. Everyone claims that their programming language is the best, and every operating system is the answer to all conceivable ills.

Of course, none of this is true. There are no easy answers. There is no *best* solution, be it a tool, a language, or an operating system. There can only be systems that are more appropriate in a particular set of circumstances.

This is where pragmatism comes in. You shouldn't be wedded to any particular technology, but have a broad enough background and experience base to allow you to choose good solutions in particular situations. Your background stems from an understanding of the basic principles of computer science, and your experience comes from a wide range of practical projects. Theory and practice combine to make you strong.

You adjust your approach to suit the current circumstances and environment. You judge the relative importance of all the factors affecting a project and use your experience to produce appropriate solutions. And you do this continuously as the work progresses. Pragmatic Programmers get the job done, and do it well.

Who Should Read This Book?

This book is aimed at people who want to become more effective and more productive programmers. Perhaps you feel frustrated that you don't seem to be achieving your potential. Perhaps you look at colleagues who seem to be using tools to make themselves more productive than you. Maybe your current job uses older technologies, and you want to know how newer ideas can be applied to what you do.

We don't pretend to have all (or even most) of the answers, nor are all of our ideas applicable in all situations. All we can say is that if you follow our approach, you'll gain experience rapidly, your productivity will increase, and you'll have a better understanding of the entire development process. And you'll write better software.

What Makes a Pragmatic Programmer?

Each developer is unique, with individual strengths and weaknesses, preferences and dislikes. Over time, each will craft their own personal environment. That environment will reflect the programmer's individuality just as forcefully as his or her hobbies, clothing, or haircut. However, if you're a Pragmatic Programmer, you'll share many of the following characteristics:

Early adopter/fast adapter
> You have an instinct for technologies and techniques, and you love trying things out. When given something new, you can grasp it quickly and integrate it with the rest of your knowledge. Your confidence is born of experience.

Inquisitive
> You tend to ask questions. *That's neat—how did you do that? Did you have problems with that library? What's this quantum computing I've heard about? How are symbolic links implemented?* You are a pack rat for little facts, each of which may affect some decision years from now.

Critical thinker

You rarely take things as given without first getting the facts. When colleagues say "because that's the way it's done," or a vendor promises the solution to all your problems, you smell a challenge.

Realistic

You try to understand the underlying nature of each problem you face. This realism gives you a good feel for how difficult things are, and how long things will take. Deeply understanding that a process *should* be difficult or *will* take a while to complete gives you the stamina to keep at it.

Jack of all trades

You try hard to be familiar with a broad range of technologies and environments, and you work to keep abreast of new developments. Although your current job may require you to be a specialist, you will always be able to move on to new areas and new challenges.

We've left the most basic characteristics until last. All Pragmatic Programmers share them. They're basic enough to state as tips:

Tip 1	Care About Your Craft

We feel that there is no point in developing software unless you care about doing it well.

Tip 2	Think! About Your Work

In order to be a Pragmatic Programmer, we're challenging you to think about what you're doing while you're doing it. This isn't a one-time audit of current practices—it's an ongoing critical appraisal of every decision you make, every day, and on every project. Never run on auto-pilot. Constantly be thinking, critiquing your work in real time. The old IBM corporate motto, *THINK!*, is the Pragmatic Programmer's mantra.

If this sounds like hard work to you, then you're exhibiting the *realistic* characteristic. This is going to take up some of your valuable time—time that is probably already under tremendous pressure. The reward is a more active involvement with a job you love, a feeling of mastery over an increasing range of subjects, and pleasure in a feeling of continuous improvement. Over the long term, your time investment will be repaid as you and your team become more efficient, write code that's easier to maintain, and spend less time in meetings.

Individual Pragmatists, Large Teams

Some people feel that there is no room for individuality on large teams or complex projects. "Software is an engineering discipline," they say, "that breaks down if individual team members make decisions for themselves."

We strongly disagree.

There *should* be engineering in software construction. However, this doesn't preclude individual craftsmanship. Think about the large cathedrals built in Europe during the Middle Ages. Each took thousands of person-years of effort, spread over many decades. Lessons learned were passed down to the next set of builders, who advanced the state of structural engineering with their accomplishments. But the carpenters, stonecutters, carvers, and glass workers were all craftspeople, interpreting the engineering requirements to produce a whole that transcended the purely mechanical side of the construction. It was their belief in their individual contributions that sustained the projects: *We who cut mere stones must always be envisioning cathedrals.*

Within the overall structure of a project there is always room for individuality and craftsmanship. This is particularly true given the current state of software engineering. One hundred years from now, our engineering may seem as archaic as the techniques used by medieval cathedral builders seem to today's civil engineers, while our craftsmanship will still be honored.

It's a Continuous Process

A tourist visiting England's Eton College asked the gardener how he got the lawns so perfect. "That's easy," he replied, "You just brush off the dew every morning, mow them every other day, and roll them once a week."

"Is that all?" asked the tourist. "Absolutely," replied the gardener. "Do that for 500 years and you'll have a nice lawn, too."

Great lawns need small amounts of daily care, and so do great programmers. Management consultants like to drop the word *kaizen* in conversations. "Kaizen" is a Japanese term that captures the concept of continuously making many small improvements. It was considered to be one of the main reasons for the dramatic gains in productivity and quality in Japanese manufacturing and was widely copied throughout the world. Kaizen applies to individuals, too. Every day, work to refine the skills you have and to add new tools to your repertoire. Unlike the Eton lawns, you'll start seeing results in a matter of days. Over the years, you'll be amazed at how your experience has blossomed and how your skills have grown.

## CHAPTER 1

A Pragmatic Philosophy

This book is about you.

Make no mistake, it is *your* career, and more importantly, *It's Your Life*. You own it. You're here because you know you can become a better developer and help others become better as well. You can become a *Pragmatic Programmer*.

What distinguishes Pragmatic Programmers? We feel it's an attitude, a style, a philosophy of approaching problems and their solutions. They think beyond the immediate problem, placing it in its larger context and seeking out the bigger picture. After all, without this larger context, how can you be pragmatic? How can you make intelligent compromises and informed decisions?

Another key to their success is that Pragmatic Programmers take responsibility for everything they do, which we discuss in *The Cat Ate My Source Code*. Being responsible, Pragmatic Programmers won't sit idly by and watch their projects fall apart through neglect. In *Software Entropy*, we tell you how to keep your projects pristine.

Most people find change difficult, sometimes for good reasons, sometimes because of plain old inertia. In *Stone Soup and Boiled Frogs*, we look at a strategy for instigating change and (in the interests of balance) present the cautionary tale of an amphibian that ignored the dangers of gradual change.

One of the benefits of understanding the context in which you work is that it becomes easier to know just how good your software has to be. Sometimes near-perfection is the only option, but often there are trade-offs involved. We explore this in *Good-Enough Software*.

Of course, you need to have a broad base of knowledge and experience to pull all of this off. Learning is a continuous and ongoing process. In *Your Knowledge Portfolio*, we discuss some strategies for keeping the momentum up.

Finally, none of us works in a vacuum. We all spend a large amount of time interacting with others. *Communicate!* lists ways we can do this better.

Pragmatic programming stems from a philosophy of pragmatic thinking. This chapter sets the basis for that philosophy.

It's Your Life

I'm not in this world to live up to your expectations and you're not in this world to live up to mine.

➤ Bruce Lee

It is *your* life. You own it. You run it. You create it.

Many developers we talk to are frustrated. Their concerns are varied. Some feel they're stagnating in their job, others that technology has passed them by. Folks feel they are under appreciated, or underpaid, or that their teams are toxic. Maybe they want to move to Asia, or Europe, or work from home.

And the answer we give is always the same.

"Why can't you change it?"

Software development must appear close to the top of any list of careers where you have control. Our skills are in demand, our knowledge crosses geographic boundaries, we can work remotely. We're paid well. We really can do just about anything we want.

But, for some reason, developers seem to resist change. They hunker down, and hope things will get better. They look on, passively, as their skills become dated and complain that their companies don't train them. They look at ads for exotic locations on the bus, then step off into the chilling rain and trudge into work.

So here's the most important tip in the book.

Tip 3	You Have Agency

Does your work environment suck? Is your job boring? Try to fix it. But don't try forever. As Martin Fowler says, "you can change your organization or change your organization."[1]

---

1.   http://wiki.c2.com/?ChangeYourOrganization

If technology seems to be passing you by, make time (in your own time) to study new stuff that looks interesting. You're investing in yourself, so doing it while you're off-the-clock is only reasonable.

Want to work remotely? Have you asked? If they say no, then find someone who says yes.

This industry gives you a remarkable set of opportunities. Be proactive, and take them.

Related Sections Include

- Topic 4, *Stone Soup and Boiled Frogs*, on page 8
- Topic 6, *Your Knowledge Portfolio*, on page 13

The Cat Ate My Source Code

The greatest of all weaknesses is the fear of appearing weak.

> ➤ *J.B. Bossuet, Politics from Holy Writ, 1709*

One of the cornerstones of the pragmatic philosophy is the idea of taking responsibility for yourself and your actions in terms of your career advancement, your learning and education, your project, and your day-to-day work. Pragmatic Programmers take charge of their own career, and aren't afraid to admit ignorance or error. It's not the most pleasant aspect of programming, to be sure, but it will happen—even on the best of projects. Despite thorough testing, good documentation, and solid automation, things go wrong. Deliveries are late. Unforeseen technical problems come up.

These things happen, and we try to deal with them as professionally as we can. This means being honest and direct. We can be proud of our abilities, but we must own up to our shortcomings—our ignorance and our mistakes.

Team Trust

Above all, your team needs to be able to trust and rely on you—and you need to be comfortable relying on each of them as well. Trust in a team is absolutely essential for creativity and collaboration according to the research literature.[2] In a healthy environment based in trust, you can safely speak your mind,

---

2. See, for example, a good meta-analysis at *Trust and team performance: A meta-analysis of main effects, moderators, and covariates,* http://dx.doi.org/10.1037/apl0000110

present your ideas, and rely on your team members who can in turn rely on you. Without trust, well...

Imagine a high-tech, stealth ninja team infiltrating the villain's evil lair. After months of planning and delicate execution, you've made it on site. Now it's your turn to set up the laser guidance grid: "Sorry, folks, I don't have the laser. The cat was playing with the red dot and I left it at home."

That sort of breach of trust might be hard to repair.

Take Responsibility

Responsibility is something you actively agree to. You make a commitment to ensure that something is done right, but you don't necessarily have direct control over every aspect of it. In addition to doing your own personal best, you must analyze the situation for risks that are beyond your control. You have the right *not* to take on a responsibility for an impossible situation, or one in which the risks are too great, or the ethical implications too sketchy. You'll have to make the call based on your own values and judgment.

When you *do* accept the responsibility for an outcome, you should expect to be held accountable for it. When you make a mistake (as we all do) or an error in judgment, admit it honestly and try to offer options.

Don't blame someone or something else, or make up an excuse. Don't blame all the problems on a vendor, a programming language, management, or your coworkers. Any and all of these may play a role, but it is up to *you* to provide solutions, not excuses.

If there was a risk that the vendor wouldn't come through for you, then you should have had a contingency plan. If your mass storage melts—taking all of your source code with it—and you don't have a backup, it's your fault. Telling your boss "the cat ate my source code" just won't cut it.

Tip 4	Provide Options, Don't Make Lame Excuses

Before you approach anyone to tell them why something can't be done, is late, or is broken, stop and listen to yourself. Talk to the rubber duck on your monitor, or the cat. Does your excuse sound reasonable, or stupid? How's it going to sound to your boss?

Run through the conversation in your mind. What is the other person likely to say? Will they ask, "Have you tried this..." or "Didn't you consider that?" How will you respond? Before you go and tell them the bad news, is there anything else you can try? Sometimes, you just *know* what they are going to say, so save them the trouble.

Instead of excuses, provide options. Don't say it can't be done; explain what *can* be done to salvage the situation. Does code have to be deleted? Tell them so, and explain the value of refactoring (see Topic 40, *Refactoring*, on page 209).

Do you need to spend time prototyping to determine the best way to proceed (see Topic 13, *Prototypes and Post-it Notes*, on page 56)? Do you need to introduce better testing (see Topic 41, *Test to Code*, on page 214, and *Ruthless and Continuous Testing*, on page 275) or automation to prevent it from happening again?

Perhaps you need additional resources to complete this task. Or maybe you need to spend more time with the users? Or maybe it's just you: do you need to learn some technique or technology in greater depth? Would a book or a course help? Don't be afraid to ask, or to admit that you need help.

Try to flush out the lame excuses before voicing them aloud. If you must, tell your cat first. After all, if little Tiddles is going to take the blame....

Related Sections Include

- Topic 49, *Pragmatic Teams*, on page 264

Challenges

- How do you react when someone—such as a bank teller, an auto mechanic, or a clerk—comes to you with a lame excuse? What do you think of them and their company as a result?

- When you find yourself saying, "I don't know," be sure to follow it up with "—but I'll find out." It's a great way to admit what you don't know, but then take responsibility like a pro.

Software Entropy

While software development is immune from almost all physical laws, the inexorable increase in *entropy* hits us hard. *Entropy* is a term from physics that refers to the amount of "disorder" in a system. Unfortunately, the laws of thermodynamics guarantee that the entropy in the universe tends toward a maximum. When disorder increases in software, we call it "software rot." Some folks might call it by the more optimistic term, "technical debt," with the implied notion that they'll pay it back someday. They probably won't.

Whatever the name, though, both debt and rot can spread uncontrollably.

There are many factors that can contribute to software rot. The most important one seems to be the psychology, or culture, at work on a project. Even if you are a team of one, your project's psychology can be a very delicate thing. Despite the best-laid plans and the best people, a project can still experience ruin and decay during its lifetime. Yet there are other projects that, despite enormous difficulties and constant setbacks, successfully fight nature's tendency toward disorder and manage to come out pretty well.

What makes the difference?

In inner cities, some buildings are beautiful and clean, while others are rotting hulks. Why? Researchers in the field of crime and urban decay discovered a fascinating trigger mechanism, one that very quickly turns a clean, intact, inhabited building into a smashed and abandoned derelict.[3]

A broken window.

One broken window, left unrepaired for any substantial length of time, instills in the inhabitants of the building a sense of abandonment—a sense that the powers that be don't care about the building. So another window gets broken. People start littering. Graffiti appears. Serious structural damage begins. In a relatively short span of time, the building becomes damaged beyond the owner's desire to fix it, and the sense of abandonment becomes reality.

Why would that make a difference? Psychologists have done studies[4] that show hopelessness can be contagious. Think of the flu virus in close quarters. Ignoring a clearly broken situation reinforces the ideas that perhaps *nothing*

---

3. See *The police and neighborhood safety* [WH82]
4. See *Contagious depression: Existence, specificity to depressed symptoms, and the role of reassurance seeking* [Joi94]

can be fixed, that no one cares, all is doomed; all negative thoughts which can spread among team members, creating a vicious spiral.

| Tip 5 | Don't Live with Broken Windows |

Don't leave "broken windows" (bad designs, wrong decisions, or poor code) unrepaired. Fix each one as soon as it is discovered. If there is insufficient time to fix it properly, then *board it up.* Perhaps you can comment out the offending code, or display a "Not Implemented" message, or substitute dummy data instead. Take *some* action to prevent further damage and to show that you're on top of the situation.

We've seen clean, functional systems deteriorate pretty quickly once windows start breaking. There are other factors that can contribute to software rot, and we'll touch on some of them elsewhere, but neglect *accelerates* the rot faster than any other factor.

You may be thinking that no one has the time to go around cleaning up all the broken glass of a project. If so, then you'd better plan on getting a dumpster, or moving to another neighborhood. Don't let entropy win.

First, Do No Harm

Andy once had an acquaintance who was obscenely rich. His house was immaculate, loaded with priceless antiques, *objets d'art,* and so on. One day, a tapestry that was hanging a little too close to a fireplace caught on fire. The fire department rushed in to save the day—and his house. But before they dragged their big, dirty hoses into the house, they stopped—with the fire raging—to roll out a mat between the front door and the source of the fire.

They didn't want to mess up the carpet.

Now that sounds pretty extreme. Surely the fire department's first priority is to put out the fire, collateral damage be damned. But they clearly had assessed the situation, were confident of their ability to manage the fire, and were careful not to inflict unnecessary damage to the property. That's the way it must be with software: don't cause collateral damage just because there's a crisis of some sort. One broken window is one too many.

One broken window—a badly designed piece of code, a poor management decision that the team must live with for the duration of the project—is all it takes to start the decline. If you find yourself working on a project with quite a few broken windows, it's all too easy to slip into the mindset of "All the rest of this code is crap, I'll just follow suit." It doesn't matter if the project has been fine up to this point. In the original experiment leading to the "Broken Window Theory," an abandoned car sat for a week untouched. But once a single window was broken, the car was stripped and turned upside down within *hours*.

By the same token, if you find yourself on a project where the code is pristinely beautiful—cleanly written, well designed, and elegant—you will likely take extra special care not to mess it up, just like the firefighters. Even if there's a fire raging (deadline, release date, trade show demo, etc.), *you* don't want to be the first one to make a mess and inflict additional damage.

Just tell yourself, "No broken windows."

Related Sections Include

- Topic 10, *Orthogonality*, on page 39
- Topic 40, *Refactoring*, on page 209
- Topic 44, *Naming Things*, on page 238

Challenges

- Help strengthen your team by surveying your project neighborhood. Choose two or three broken windows and discuss with your colleagues what the problems are and what could be done to fix them.

- Can you tell when a window first gets broken? What is your reaction? If it was the result of someone else's decision, or a management edict, what can you do about it?

Stone Soup and Boiled Frogs

The three soldiers returning home from war were hungry. When they saw the village ahead their spirits lifted—they were sure the villagers would give them a meal. But when they got there, they found the doors locked and the windows closed. After many years of war, the villagers were short of food, and hoarded what they had.

Undeterred, the soldiers boiled a pot of water and carefully placed three stones into it. The amazed villagers came out to watch.

"This is stone soup," the soldiers explained. "Is that all you put in it?" asked the villagers. "Absolutely—although some say it tastes even better with a few carrots..." A villager ran off, returning in no time with a basket of carrots from his hoard.

A couple of minutes later, the villagers again asked "Is that it?"

"Well," said the soldiers, "a couple of potatoes give it body." Off ran another villager.

Over the next hour, the soldiers listed more ingredients that would enhance the soup: beef, leeks, salt, and herbs. Each time a different villager would run off to raid their personal stores.

Eventually they had produced a large pot of steaming soup. The soldiers removed the stones, and they sat down with the entire village to enjoy the first square meal any of them had eaten in months.

There are a couple of morals in the stone soup story. The villagers are tricked by the soldiers, who use the villagers' curiosity to get food from them. But more importantly, the soldiers act as a catalyst, bringing the village together so they can jointly produce something that they couldn't have done by themselves—a synergistic result. Eventually everyone wins.

Every now and then, you might want to emulate the soldiers.

You may be in a situation where you know exactly what needs doing and how to do it. The entire system just appears before your eyes—you know it's right. But ask permission to tackle the whole thing and you'll be met with delays and blank stares. People will form committees, budgets will need approval, and things will get complicated. Everyone will guard their own resources. Sometimes this is called "start-up fatigue."

It's time to bring out the stones. Work out what you *can* reasonably ask for. Develop it well. Once you've got it, show people, and let them marvel. Then say "of course, it *would* be better if we added..." Pretend it's not important. Sit back and wait for them to start asking you to add the functionality you originally wanted. People find it easier to join an ongoing success. Show them a glimpse of the future and you'll get them to rally around.[5]

Tip 6	Be a Catalyst for Change

---

5. While doing this, you may be comforted by the line attributed to Rear Admiral Dr. Grace Hopper: "It's easier to ask forgiveness than it is to get permission."

The Villagers' Side

On the other hand, the stone soup story is also about gentle and gradual deception. It's about focusing too tightly. The villagers think about the stones and forget about the rest of the world. We all fall for it, every day. Things just creep up on us.

We've all seen the symptoms. Projects slowly and inexorably get totally out of hand. Most software disasters start out too small to notice, and most project overruns happen a day at a time. Systems drift from their specifications feature by feature, while patch after patch gets added to a piece of code until there's nothing of the original left. It's often the accumulation of small things that breaks morale and teams.

> **Tip 7**   Remember the Big Picture

We've never tried this—honest. But "they" say that if you take a frog and drop it into boiling water, it will jump straight back out again. However, if you place the frog in a pan of cold water, then gradually heat it, the frog won't notice the slow increase in temperature and will stay put until cooked.

Note that the frog's problem is different from the broken windows issue discussed in Topic 3, *Software Entropy*, on page 6. In the Broken Window Theory, people lose the will to fight entropy because they perceive that no one else cares. The frog just doesn't notice the change.

Don't be like the fabled frog. Keep an eye on the big picture. Constantly review what's happening around you, not just what you personally are doing.

Related Sections Include

- Topic 1, *It's Your Life*, on page 2
- Topic 38, *Programming by Coincidence*, on page 197

Challenges

- While reviewing a draft of the first edition, John Lakos raised the following issue: The soldiers progressively deceive the villagers, but the change they catalyze does them all good. However, by progressively deceiving the frog, you're doing it harm. Can you determine whether you're making stone soup or frog soup when you try to catalyze change? Is the decision subjective or objective?

- Quick, without looking, how many lights are in the ceiling above you? How many exits in the room? How many people? Is there anything out of context, anything that looks like it doesn't belong? This is an exercise in *situational awareness*, a technique practiced by folks ranging from Boy and Girl Scouts to Navy SEALs. Get in the habit of really looking and noticing your surroundings. Then do the same for your project.

---

5 ▶ Good-Enough Software

Striving to better, oft we mar what's well.

> ➤ *Shakespeare, King Lear 1.4*

There's an old(ish) joke about a company that places an order for 100,000 ICs with a Japanese manufacturer. Part of the specification was the defect rate: one chip in 10,000. A few weeks later the order arrived: one large box containing thousands of ICs, and a small one containing just ten. Attached to the small box was a label that read: "These are the faulty ones."

If only we really had this kind of control over quality. But the real world just won't let us produce much that's truly perfect, particularly not bug-free software. Time, technology, and temperament all conspire against us.

However, this doesn't have to be frustrating. As Ed Yourdon described in an article in *IEEE Software, When good-enough software is best [You95],* you can discipline yourself to write software that's good enough—good enough for your users, for future maintainers, for your own peace of mind. You'll find that you are more productive and your users are happier. And you may well find that your programs are actually better for their shorter incubation.

Before we go any further, we need to qualify what we're about to say. The phrase "good enough" does not imply sloppy or poorly produced code. All systems must meet their users' requirements to be successful, and meet basic performance, privacy, and security standards. We are simply advocating that users be given an opportunity to participate in the process of deciding when what you've produced is good enough for their needs.

Involve Your Users in the Trade-Off

Normally you're writing software for other people. Often you'll remember to find out what they want.[6] But do you ever ask them *how good* they want their

---

6. That was supposed to be a joke!

software to be? Sometimes there'll be no choice. If you're working on pacemakers, an autopilot, or a low-level library that will be widely disseminated, the requirements will be more stringent and your options more limited.

However, if you're working on a brand-new product, you'll have different constraints. The marketing people will have promises to keep, the eventual end users may have made plans based on a delivery schedule, and your company will certainly have cash-flow constraints. It would be unprofessional to ignore these users' requirements simply to add new features to the program, or to polish up the code just one more time. We're not advocating panic: it is equally unprofessional to promise impossible time scales and to cut basic engineering corners to meet a deadline.

The scope and quality of the system you produce should be discussed as part of that system's requirements.

Tip 8	Make Quality a Requirements Issue

Often you'll be in situations where trade-offs are involved. Surprisingly, many users would rather use software with some rough edges *today* than wait a year for the shiny, bells-and-whistles version (and in fact what they will need a year from now may be completely different anyway). Many IT departments with tight budgets would agree. Great software today is often preferable to the fantasy of perfect software tomorrow. If you give your users something to play with early, their feedback will often lead you to a better eventual solution (see Topic 12, *Tracer Bullets*, on page 50).

Know When to Stop

In some ways, programming is like painting. You start with a blank canvas and certain basic raw materials. You use a combination of science, art, and craft to determine what to do with them. You sketch out an overall shape, paint the underlying environment, then fill in the details. You constantly step back with a critical eye to view what you've done. Every now and then you'll throw a canvas away and start again.

But artists will tell you that all the hard work is ruined if you don't know when to stop. If you add layer upon layer, detail over detail, *the painting becomes lost in the paint.*

Don't spoil a perfectly good program by overembellishment and overrefinement. Move on, and let your code stand in its own right for a while. It may not be perfect. Don't worry: it could never be perfect. (In Chapter 7, *While You Are*

Coding, on page 191, we'll discuss philosophies for developing code in an imperfect world.)

Related Sections Include

- Topic 45, *The Requirements Pit*, on page 244
- Topic 46, *Solving Impossible Puzzles*, on page 252

Challenges

- Look at the software tools and operating systems that you use regularly. Can you find any evidence that these organizations and/or developers are comfortable shipping software they know is not perfect? As a user, would you rather (1) wait for them to get all the bugs out, (2) have complex software and accept some bugs, or (3) opt for simpler software with fewer defects?

- Consider the effect of modularization on the delivery of software. Will it take more or less time to get a tightly coupled monolithic block of software to the required quality compared with a system designed as very loosely coupled modules or microservices? What are the advantages or disadvantages of each approach?

- Can you think of popular software that suffers from *feature bloat*? That is, software containing far more features than you would ever use, each feature introducing more opportunity for bugs and security vulnerabilities, and making the features you *do* use harder to find and manage. Are you in danger of falling into this trap yourself?

Your Knowledge Portfolio

An investment in knowledge always pays the best interest.

➤ *Benjamin Franklin*

Ah, good old Ben Franklin—never at a loss for a pithy homily. Why, if we could just be early to bed and early to rise, we'd be great programmers—right? The early bird might get the worm, but what happens to the early worm?

In this case, though, Ben really hit the nail on the head. Your knowledge and experience are your most important day-to-day professional assets.

Unfortunately, they're *expiring assets.*[7] Your knowledge becomes out of date as new techniques, languages, and environments are developed. Changing market forces may render your experience obsolete or irrelevant. Given the ever-increasing pace of change in our technological society, this can happen pretty quickly.

As the value of your knowledge declines, so does your value to your company or client. We want to prevent this from ever happening.

Your ability to learn new things is your most important strategic asset. But how do you learn *how* to learn, and how do you know *what* to learn?

Your Knowledge Portfolio

We like to think of all the facts programmers know about computing, the application domains they work in, and all their experience as their *knowledge portfolios*. Managing a knowledge portfolio is very similar to managing a financial portfolio:

1. Serious investors invest regularly—as a habit.
2. Diversification is the key to long-term success.
3. Smart investors balance their portfolios between conservative and high-risk, high-reward investments.
4. Investors try to buy low and sell high for maximum return.
5. Portfolios should be reviewed and rebalanced periodically.

To be successful in your career, you must invest in your knowledge portfolio using these same guidelines.

The good news is that managing this kind of investment is a skill just like any other—it can be learned. The trick is to make yourself do it initially and form a habit. Develop a routine which you follow until your brain internalizes it. At that point, you'll find yourself sucking up new knowledge automatically.

Building Your Portfolio

Invest regularly

Just as in financial investing, you must invest in your knowledge portfolio *regularly*, even if it's just a small amount. The habit is as important as the sums, so plan to use a consistent time and place, away from interruptions. A few sample goals are listed in the next section.

---

7. An *expiring asset* is something whose value diminishes over time. Examples include a warehouse full of bananas and a ticket to a ball game.

Diversify

The more *different* things you know, the more valuable you are. As a baseline, you need to know the ins and outs of the particular technology you are working with currently. But don't stop there. The face of computing changes rapidly—hot technology today may well be close to useless (or at least not in demand) tomorrow. The more technologies you are comfortable with, the better you will be able to adjust to change. And don't forget all the *other* skills you need, including those in non-technical areas.

Manage risk

Technology exists along a spectrum from risky, potentially high-reward to low-risk, low-reward standards. It's not a good idea to invest all of your money in high-risk stocks that might collapse suddenly, nor should you invest all of it conservatively and miss out on possible opportunities. Don't put all your technical eggs in one basket.

Buy low, sell high

Learning an emerging technology before it becomes popular can be just as hard as finding an undervalued stock, but the payoff can be just as rewarding. Learning Java back when it was first introduced and unknown may have been risky at the time, but it paid off handsomely for the early adopters when it became an industry mainstay later.

Review and rebalance

This is a very dynamic industry. That hot technology you started investigating last month might be stone cold by now. Maybe you need to brush up on that database technology that you haven't used in a while. Or perhaps you could be better positioned for that new job opening if you tried out that other language....

Of all these guidelines, the most important one is the simplest to do:

Tip 9	Invest Regularly in Your Knowledge Portfolio

Goals

Now that you have some guidelines on what and when to add to your knowledge portfolio, what's the best way to go about acquiring intellectual capital with which to fund your portfolio? Here are a few suggestions:

Learn at least one new language every year

Different languages solve the same problems in different ways. By learning several different approaches, you can help broaden your thinking and avoid getting stuck in a rut. Additionally, learning many languages is easy thanks to the wealth of freely available software.

Read a technical book each month

While there's a glut of short-form essays and occasionally reliable answers on the web, for deep understanding you need long-form books. Browse the booksellers for technical books on interesting topics related to your current project.[8] Once you're in the habit, read a book a month. After you've mastered the technologies you're currently using, branch out and study some that *don't* relate to your project.

Read nontechnical books, too

It is important to remember that computers are used by *people*—people whose needs you are trying to satisfy. You work with people, are employed by people, and get hacked by people. Don't forget the human side of the equation, as that requires an entirely different skill set (we ironically call these *soft* skills, but they are actually quite hard to master).

Take classes

Look for interesting courses at a local or online college or university, or perhaps at the next nearby trade show or conference.

Participate in local user groups and meetups

Isolation can be deadly to your career; find out what people are working on outside of your company. Don't just go and listen: actively participate.

Experiment with different environments

If you've worked only in Windows, spend some time with Linux. If you've used only makefiles and an editor, try a sophisticated IDE with cutting-edge features, and vice versa.

Stay current

Read news and posts online on technology different from that of your current project. It's a great way to find out what experiences other people are having with it, the particular jargon they use, and so on.

It's important to continue investing. Once you feel comfortable with some new language or bit of technology, move on. Learn another one.

It doesn't matter whether you ever use any of these technologies on a project, or even whether you put them on your resume. The process of learning will expand your thinking, opening you to new possibilities and new ways of doing things. The cross-pollination of ideas is important; try to apply the lessons

---

8. We may be biased, but there's a fine selection available at https://pragprog.com.

you've learned to your current project. Even if your project doesn't use that technology, perhaps you can borrow some ideas. Get familiar with object orientation, for instance, and you'll write procedural programs differently. Understand the functional programming paradigm and you'll write object-oriented code differently, and so on.

Opportunities for Learning

So you're reading voraciously, you're on top of all the latest breaking developments in your field (not an easy thing to do), and somebody asks you a question. You don't have the faintest idea what the answer is, and freely admit as much.

Don't let it stop there. Take it as a personal challenge to find the answer. Ask around. Search the web—the scholarly parts too, not just the consumer parts.

If you can't find the answer yourself, find out who *can*. Don't let it rest. Talking to other people will help build your personal network, and you may surprise yourself by finding solutions to other, unrelated problems along the way. And that old portfolio just keeps getting bigger....

All of this reading and researching takes time, and time is already in short supply. So you need to plan ahead. Always have something to read in an otherwise dead moment. Time spent waiting for doctors and dentists can be a great opportunity to catch up on your reading—but be sure to bring your own e-reader with you, or you might find yourself thumbing through a dog-eared 1973 article about Papua New Guinea.

Critical Thinking

The last important point is to think *critically* about what you read and hear. You need to ensure that the knowledge in your portfolio is accurate and unswayed by either vendor or media hype. Beware of the zealots who insist that their dogma provides the *only* answer—it may or may not be applicable to you and your project.

Never underestimate the power of commercialism. Just because a web search engine lists a hit first doesn't mean that it's the best match; the content provider can pay to get top billing. Just because a bookstore features a book prominently doesn't mean it's a good book, or even popular; they may have been paid to place it there.

| Tip 10 | Critically Analyze What You Read and Hear |

Critical thinking is an entire discipline unto itself, and we encourage you to read and study all you can about it. In the meantime, here's a head start with a few questions to ask and think about.

Ask the "Five Whys"

A favorite consulting trick: ask "why?" at least five times. Ask a question, and get an answer. Dig deeper by asking "why?" Repeat as if you were a petulant four-year old (but a polite one). You might be able to get closer to a root cause this way.

Who does this benefit?

It may sound cynical, but *follow the money* can be a very helpful path to analyze. The benefits to someone else or another organization may be aligned with your own, or not.

What's the context?

Everything occurs in its own context, which is why "one size fits all" solutions often don't. Consider an article or book touting a "best practice." Good questions to consider are "best for who?" What are the prerequisites, what are the consequences, short and long term?

When or Where would this work?

Under what circumstances? Is it too late? Too early? Don't stop with first-order thinking (*what will happen next*), but use second-order thinking: *what will happen after that?*

Why is this a problem?

Is there an underlying model? How does the underlying model work?

Unfortunately, there are very few simple answers anymore. But with your extensive portfolio, and by applying some critical analysis to the torrent of technical articles you will read, you can understand the *complex* answers.

Related Sections Include

- Topic 1, *It's Your Life*, on page 2
- Topic 22, *Engineering Daybooks*, on page 100

Challenges

- Start learning a new language this week. Always programmed in the same old language? Try Clojure, Elixir, Elm, F#, Go, Haskell, Python, R, ReasonML, Ruby, Rust, Scala, Swift, TypeScript, or anything else that appeals and/or looks as if you might like it.[9]

- Start reading a new book (but finish this one first!). If you are doing very detailed implementation and coding, read a book on design and architecture. If you are doing high-level design, read a book on coding techniques.

- Get out and talk technology with people who aren't involved in your current project, or who don't work for the same company. Network in your company cafeteria, or maybe seek out fellow enthusiasts at a local meetup.

---

7 Communicate!

I believe that it is better to be looked over than it is to be overlooked.

> *Mae West, Belle of the Nineties, 1934*

Maybe we can learn a lesson from Ms. West. It's not just what you've got, but also how you package it. Having the best ideas, the finest code, or the most pragmatic thinking is ultimately sterile unless you can communicate with other people. A good idea is an orphan without effective communication.

As developers, we have to communicate on many levels. We spend hours in meetings, listening and talking. We work with end users, trying to understand their needs. We write code, which communicates our intentions to a machine and documents our thinking for future generations of developers. We write proposals and memos requesting and justifying resources, reporting our status, and suggesting new approaches. And we work daily within our teams to advocate our ideas, modify existing practices, and suggest new ones. A large part of our day is spent communicating, so we need to do it well.

Treat English (or whatever your native tongue may be) as just another programming language. Write natural language as you would write code: honor the DRY principle, ETC, automation, and so on. (We discuss the DRY and ETC design principles in the next chapter.)

---

9. Never heard of any of these languages? Remember, knowledge is an expiring asset, and so is popular technology. The list of hot new and experimental languages was very different for the first edition, and is probably different again by the time you read this. All the more reason to keep learning.

> | Tip 11 | English is Just Another Programming Language |

We've put together a list of additional ideas that we find useful.

Know Your Audience

You're communicating only if you're conveying what you mean to convey—just talking isn't enough. To do that, you need to understand the needs, interests, and capabilities of your audience. We've all sat in meetings where a development geek glazes over the eyes of the vice president of marketing with a long monologue on the merits of some arcane technology. This isn't communicating: it's just talking, and it's annoying.[10]

Say you want to change your remote monitoring system to use a third-party message broker to disseminate status notifications. You can present this update in many different ways, depending on your audience. End users will appreciate that their systems can now interoperate with other services that use the broker. Your marketing department will be able to use this fact to boost sales. Development and operations managers will be happy because the care and maintenance of that part of the system is now someone else's problem. Finally, developers may enjoy getting experience with new APIs, and may even be able to find new uses for the message broker. By making the appropriate pitch to each group, you'll get them all excited about your project.

As with all forms of communication, the trick here is to gather feedback. Don't just wait for questions: ask for them. Look at body language, and facial expressions. One of the Neuro Linguistic Programming presuppositions is "The meaning of your communication is the response you get." Continuously improve your knowledge of your audience as you communicate.

Know What You Want to Say

Probably the most difficult part of the more formal styles of communication used in business is working out exactly what it is you want to say. Fiction writers often plot out their books in detail before they start, but people writing technical documents are often happy to sit down at a keyboard, enter:

1. Introduction

and start typing whatever comes into their heads next.

---

10. The word *annoy* comes from the Old French *enui*, which also means "to bore."

Plan what you want to say. Write an outline. Then ask yourself, "Does this communicate what I want to express to my audience in a way that works for them?" Refine it until it does.

This approach works for more than just documents. When you're faced with an important meeting or a chat with a major client, jot down the ideas you want to communicate, and plan a couple of strategies for getting them across.

Now that you know what your audience wants, let's deliver it.

Choose Your Moment

It's six o'clock on Friday afternoon, following a week when the auditors have been in. Your boss's youngest is in the hospital, it's pouring rain outside, and the commute home is guaranteed to be a nightmare. This probably isn't a good time to ask her for a memory upgrade for your laptop.

As part of understanding what your audience needs to hear, you need to work out what their priorities are. Catch a manager who's just been given a hard time by her boss because some source code got lost, and you'll have a more receptive listener to your ideas on source code repositories. Make what you're saying relevant in time, as well as in content. Sometimes all it takes is the simple question, "Is this a good time to talk about...?"

Choose a Style

Adjust the style of your delivery to suit your audience. Some people want a formal "just the facts" briefing. Others like a long, wide-ranging chat before getting down to business. What is their skill level and experience in this area? Are they experts? Newbies? Do they need hand-holding or just a quick tl;dr? If in doubt, ask.

Remember, however, that you are half of the communication transaction. If someone says they need a paragraph describing something and you can't see any way of doing it in less than several pages, tell them so. Remember, that kind of feedback is a form of communication, too.

Make It Look Good

Your ideas are important. They deserve a good-looking vehicle to convey them to your audience.

Too many developers (and their managers) concentrate solely on content when producing written documents. We think this is a mistake. Any chef (or watcher of the Food Network) will tell you that you can slave in the kitchen for hours only to ruin your efforts with poor presentation.

There is no excuse today for producing poor-looking printed documents. Modern software can produce stunning output, regardless of whether you're writing using Markdown or using a word processor. You need to learn just a few basic commands. If you're using a word processor, use its style sheets for consistency. (Your company may already have defined style sheets that you can use.) Learn how to set page headers and footers. Look at the sample documents included with your package to get ideas on style and layout. *Check the spelling,* first automatically and then by hand. After awl, their are spelling miss steaks that the chequer can knot ketch.

Involve Your Audience

We often find that the documents we produce end up being less important than the process we go through to produce them. If possible, involve your readers with early drafts of your document. Get their feedback, and pick their brains. You'll build a good working relationship, and you'll probably produce a better document in the process.

Be a Listener

There's one technique that you must use if you want people to listen to you: *listen to them.* Even if this is a situation where you have all the information, even if this is a formal meeting with you standing in front of 20 suits—if you don't listen to them, they won't listen to you.

Encourage people to talk by asking questions, or ask them to restate the discussion in their own words. Turn the meeting into a dialog, and you'll make your point more effectively. Who knows, you might even learn something.

Get Back to People

If you ask someone a question, you feel they're impolite if they don't respond. But how often do you fail to get back to people when they send you an email or a memo asking for information or requesting some action? In the rush of everyday life, it's easy to forget. Always respond to emails and voicemails, even if the response is simply "I'll get back to you later." Keeping people informed makes them far more forgiving of the occasional slip, and makes them feel that you haven't forgotten them.

> **Tip 12**   It's Both What You Say and the Way You Say It

Unless you work in a vacuum, you need to be able to communicate. The more effective that communication, the more influential you become.

Documentation

Finally, there's the matter of communicating via documentation. Typically, developers don't give much thought to documentation. At best it is an unfortunate necessity; at worst it is treated as a low-priority task in the hope that management will forget about it at the end of the project.

Pragmatic Programmers embrace documentation as an integral part of the overall development process. Writing documentation can be made easier by not duplicating effort or wasting time, and by keeping documentation close at hand—in the code itself. In fact, we want to apply *all* of our pragmatic principles to documentation as well as to code.

Tip 13	Build Documentation In, Don't Bolt It On

It's easy to produce good-looking documentation from the comments in source code, and we recommend adding comments to modules and exported functions to give other developers a leg up when they come to use it.

However, this doesn't mean we agree with the folks who say that *every* function, data structure, type declaration, etc., needs its own comment. This kind of mechanical comment writing actually makes it more difficult to maintain code: now there are two things to update when you make a change. So restrict your non-API commenting to discussing *why* something is done, its purpose and its goal. The code already shows *how* it is done, so commenting on this is redundant—and is a violation of the DRY principle.

Commenting source code gives you the perfect opportunity to document those elusive bits of a project that can't be documented anywhere else: engineering trade-offs, why decisions were made, what other alternatives were discarded, and so on.

Summary

- Know what you want to say.
- Know your audience.
- Choose your moment.
- Choose a style.
- Make it look good.
- Involve your audience.
- Be a listener.
- Get back to people.
- Keep code and documentation together.

Related Sections Include

- Topic 15, *Estimating*, on page 65
- Topic 18, *Power Editing*, on page 81
- Topic 45, *The Requirements Pit*, on page 244
- Topic 49, *Pragmatic Teams*, on page 264

Challenges

- There are several good books that contain sections on communications within teams, including *The Mythical Man-Month: Essays on Software Engineering [Bro96]* and *Peopleware: Productive Projects and Teams [DL13]*. Make it a point to try to read these over the next 18 months. In addition, *Dinosaur Brains: Dealing with All Those Impossible People at Work [BR89]* discusses the emotional baggage we all bring to the work environment.

- The next time you have to give a presentation, or write a memo advocating some position, try working through the advice in this section before you start. Explicitly identify the audience and what you need to communicate. If appropriate, talk to your audience afterward and see how accurate your assessment of their needs was.

Online Communication

Everything we've said about communicating in writing applies equally to email, social media posts, blogs, and so on. Email in particular has evolved to the point where it is a mainstay of corporate communications; it's used to discuss contracts, to settle disputes, and as evidence in court. But for some reason, people who would never send out a shabby paper document are happy to fling nasty-looking, incoherent emails around the world.

Our tips are simple:

- Proofread before you hit SEND.

- Check your spelling and look for any accidental auto-correct mishaps.

- Keep the format simple and clear.

- Keep quoting to a minimum. No one likes to receive back their own 100-line email with "I agree" tacked on.

- If you're quoting other people's email, be sure to attribute it, and quote it inline (rather than as an attachment). Same when quoting on social media platforms.

- Don't flame or act like a troll unless you want it to come back and haunt you later. If you wouldn't say it to someone's face, don't say it online.

- Check your list of recipients before sending. It's become a cliché to criticize the boss over departmental email without realizing that the boss is on the cc list. Better yet, don't criticize the boss over email.

As countless large corporations and politicians have discovered, email and social media posts are forever. Try to give the same attention and care to email as you would to any written memo or report.

## CHAPTER 2

A Pragmatic Approach

There are certain tips and tricks that apply at all levels of software development, processes that are virtually universal, and ideas that are almost axiomatic. However, these approaches are rarely documented as such; you'll mostly find them written down as odd sentences in discussions of design, project management, or coding. But for your convenience, we'll bring these ideas and processes together here.

The first and maybe most important topic gets to the heart of software development: *The Essence of Good Design*. Everything follows from this.

The next two sections, *DRY—The Evils of Duplication* and *Orthogonality*, are closely related. The first warns you not to duplicate knowledge throughout your systems, the second not to split any one piece of knowledge across multiple system components.

As the pace of change increases, it becomes harder and harder to keep our applications relevant. In *Reversibility*, we'll look at some techniques that help insulate your projects from their changing environment.

The next two sections are also related. In *Tracer Bullets*, we talk about a style of development that allows you to gather requirements, test designs, and implement code at the same time. It's the only way to keep up with the pace of modern life.

Prototypes and Post-it Notes shows you how to use prototyping to test architectures, algorithms, interfaces, and ideas. In the modern world, it's critical to test ideas and get feedback before you commit to them whole-heartedly.

As computer science slowly matures, designers are producing increasingly higher-level languages. While the compiler that accepts "make it so" hasn't yet been invented, in *Domain Languages* we present some more modest suggestions that you can implement for yourself.

Finally, we all work in a world of limited time and resources. You can survive these scarcities better (and keep your bosses or clients happier) if you get good at working out how long things will take, which we cover in *Estimating*.

Keep these fundamental principles in mind during development, and you'll write code that's better, faster, and stronger. You can even make it look easy.

8 The Essence of Good Design

The world is full of gurus and pundits, all eager to pass on their hard-earned wisdom when it comes to How to Design Software. There are acronyms, lists (which seem to favor five entries), patterns, diagrams, videos, talks, and (the internet being the internet) probably a cool series on the Law of Demeter explained using interpretive dance.

And we, your gentle authors, are guilty of this too. But we'd like to make amends by explaining something that only became apparent to us fairly recently. First, the general statement:

> Tip 14   Good Design Is Easier to Change Than Bad Design

A thing is well designed if it adapts to the people who use it. For code, that means it must adapt by changing. So we believe in the ETC principle: *Easier to Change. ETC.* That's it.

As far as we can tell, every design principle out there is a special case of ETC.

Why is decoupling good? Because by isolating concerns we make each easier to change. ETC.

Why is the single responsibility principle useful? Because a change in requirements is mirrored by a change in just one module. ETC.

Why is naming important? Because good names make code easier to read, and you have to read it to change it. ETC!

ETC Is a Value, Not a Rule

Values are things that help you make decisions: should I do this, or that? When it comes to thinking about software, ETC is a guide, helping you choose between paths. Just like all your other values, it should be floating just behind your conscious thought, subtly nudging you in the right direction.

But how do you make that happen? Our experience is that it requires some initial conscious reinforcement. You may need to spend a week or so deliberately asking yourself "did the thing I just did make the overall system easier or harder to change?" Do it when you save a file. Do it when you write a test. Do it when you fix a bug.

There's an implicit premise in ETC. It assumes that a person can tell which of many paths will be easier to change in the future. Much of the time, common sense will be correct, and you can make an educated guess.

Sometimes, though, you won't have a clue. That's OK. In those cases, we think you can do two things.

First, given that you're not sure what form change will take, you can always fall back on the ultimate "easy to change" path: try to make what you write replaceable. That way, whatever happens in the future, this chunk of code won't be a roadblock. It seems extreme, but actually it's what you should be doing all the time, anyway. It's really just thinking about keeping code decoupled and cohesive.

Second, treat this as a way to develop instincts. Note the situation in your engineering day book: the choices you have, and some guesses about change. Leave a tag in the source. Then, later, when this code has to change, you'll be able to look back and give yourself feedback. It might help the next time you reach a similar fork in the road.

The rest of the sections in this chapter have specific ideas on design, but all are motivated by this one principle.

Related Sections Include

- Topic 9, *DRY—The Evils of Duplication*, on page 30
- Topic 10, *Orthogonality*, on page 39
- Topic 11, *Reversibility*, on page 47
- Topic 14, *Domain Languages*, on page 59
- Topic 28, *Decoupling*, on page 130
- Topic 30, *Transforming Programming*, on page 147
- Topic 31, *Inheritance Tax*, on page 158

Challenges

- Think about a design principle you use regularly. Is it intended to make things easy-to-change?

- Also think about languages and programming paradigms (OO, FP, Reactive, and so on). Do any have either big positives or big negatives when it comes to helping you write ETC code? Do any have both?

  When coding, what can you do to eliminate the negatives and accentuate the positives?[1]

- Many editors have support (either built-in or via extensions) to run commands when you save a file. Get your editor to popup an *ETC?* message every time you save[2] and use it as a cue to think about the code you just wrote. Is it easy to change?

---

9 ▶ DRY—The Evils of Duplication

Giving a computer two contradictory pieces of knowledge was Captain James T. Kirk's preferred way of disabling a marauding artificial intelligence. Unfortunately, the same principle can be effective in bringing down *your* code.

As programmers, we collect, organize, maintain, and harness knowledge. We document knowledge in specifications, we make it come alive in running code, and we use it to provide the checks needed during testing.

Unfortunately, knowledge isn't stable. It changes—often rapidly. Your understanding of a requirement may change following a meeting with the client. The government changes a regulation and some business logic gets outdated. Tests may show that the chosen algorithm won't work. All this instability means that we spend a large part of our time in maintenance mode, reorganizing and reexpressing the knowledge in our systems.

Most people assume that maintenance begins when an application is released, that maintenance means fixing bugs and enhancing features. We think these people are wrong. Programmers are constantly in maintenance mode. Our understanding changes day by day. New requirements arrive and existing requirements evolve as we're heads-down on the project. Perhaps the environment changes. Whatever the reason, maintenance is not a discrete activity, but a routine part of the entire development process.

When we perform maintenance, we have to find and change the representations of things—those capsules of knowledge embedded in the application. The problem is that it's easy to duplicate knowledge in the specifications,

---

1. To paraphrase the old Arlen/Mercer song...
2. Or, perhaps, to keep your sanity, every 10th time...

processes, and programs that we develop, and when we do so, we invite a maintenance nightmare—one that starts well before the application ships.

We feel that the only way to develop software reliably, and to make our developments easier to understand and maintain, is to follow what we call the DRY principle:

Every piece of knowledge must have a single, unambiguous, authoritative representation within a system.

Why do we call it DRY?

Tip 15	DRY—Don't Repeat Yourself

The alternative is to have the same thing expressed in two or more places. If you change one, you have to remember to change the others, or, like the alien computers, your program will be brought to its knees by a contradiction. It isn't a question of whether you'll remember: it's a question of when you'll forget.

You'll find the DRY principle popping up time and time again throughout this book, often in contexts that have nothing to do with coding. We feel that it is one of the most important tools in the Pragmatic Programmer's tool box.

In this section we'll outline the problems of duplication and suggest general strategies for dealing with it.

DRY Is More Than Code

Let's get something out of the way up-front. In the first edition of this book we did a poor job of explaining just what we meant by *Don't Repeat Yourself*. Many people took it to refer to code only: they thought that DRY means "don't copy-and-paste lines of source."

That *is* part of DRY, but it's a tiny and fairly trivial part.

DRY is about the duplication of *knowledge*, of *intent*. It's about expressing the same thing in two different places, possibly in two totally different ways.

Here's the acid test: when some single facet of the code has to change, do you find yourself making that change in multiple places, and in multiple different formats? Do you have to change code and documentation, or a database schema and a structure that holds it, or...? If so, your code isn't DRY.

So let's look at some typical examples of duplication.

Duplication in Code

It may be trivial, but code duplication is oh, so common. Here's an example:

```
def print_balance(account)
  printf "Debits:  %10.2f\n", account.debits
  printf "Credits: %10.2f\n", account.credits
  if account.fees < 0
    printf "Fees:     %10.2f-\n", -account.fees
  else
    printf "Fees:     %10.2f\n", account.fees
  end
  printf "             ——-\n"
  if account.balance < 0
    printf "Balance: %10.2f-\n", -account.balance
  else
    printf "Balance: %10.2f\n", account.balance
  end
end
```

For now ignore the implication that we're committing the newbie mistake of storing currencies in floats. Instead see if you can spot duplications in this code. (We can see at least three things, but you might see more.)

What did you find? Here's our list.

First, there's clearly a copy-and-paste duplication of handling the negative numbers. We can fix that by adding another function:

```
def format_amount(value)
  result = sprintf("%10.2f", value.abs)
  if value < 0
    result + "-"
  else
    result + " "
  end
end

def print_balance(account)
  printf "Debits:  %10.2f\n", account.debits
  printf "Credits: %10.2f\n", account.credits
  printf "Fees:     %s\n",      format_amount(account.fees)
  printf "             ——-\n"
  printf "Balance: %s\n",      format_amount(account.balance)
end
```

Another duplication is the repetition of the field width in all the printf calls. We *could* fix this by introducing a constant and passing it to each call, but why not just use the existing function?

```ruby
def format_amount(value)
  result = sprintf("%10.2f", value.abs)
  if value < 0
    result + "-"
  else
    result + " "
  end
end

def print_balance(account)
  printf "Debits:  %s\n", format_amount(account.debits)
  printf "Credits: %s\n", format_amount(account.credits)
  printf "Fees:    %s\n", format_amount(account.fees)
  printf "            ----\n"
  printf "Balance: %s\n", format_amount(account.balance)
end
```

Anything more? Well, what if the client asks for an extra space between the labels and the numbers? We'd have to change five lines. Let's remove that duplication:

```ruby
def format_amount(value)
  result = sprintf("%10.2f", value.abs)
  if value < 0
    result + "-"
  else
    result + " "
  end
end

def print_line(label, value)
  printf "%-9s%s\n", label, value
end

def report_line(label, amount)
  print_line(label + ":", format_amount(amount))
end

def print_balance(account)
  report_line("Debits",  account.debits)
  report_line("Credits", account.credits)
  report_line("Fees",    account.fees)
  print_line("",         "----")
  report_line("Balance", account.balance)
end
```

If we have to change the formatting of amounts, we change format_amount. If we want to change the label format, we change report_line.

There's still an implicit DRY violation: the number of hyphens in the separator line is related to the width of the amount field. But it isn't an exact match: it's currently one character shorter, so any trailing minus signs extend beyond the column. This is the customer's intent, and it's a different intent to the actual formatting of amounts.

Not All Code Duplication Is Knowledge Duplication

As part of your online wine ordering application you're capturing and validating your user's age, along with the quantity they're ordering. According to the site owner, they should both be numbers, and both greater than zero. So you code up the validations:

```
def validate_age(value):
    validate_type(value, :integer)
    validate_min_integer(value, 0)

def validate_quantity(value):
    validate_type(value, :integer)
    validate_min_integer(value, 0)
```

During code review, the resident know-it-all bounces this code, claiming it's a DRY violation: both function bodies are the same.

They are wrong. The code is the same, but the knowledge they represent is different. The two functions validate two separate things that just happen to have the same rules. That's a coincidence, not a duplication.

Duplication in Documentation

Somehow the myth was born that you should comment all your functions. Those who believe in this insanity then produce something such as this:

```
# Calculate the fees for this account.
#
# * Each returned check costs $20
# * If the account is in overdraft for more than 3 days,
#   charge $10 for each day
# * If the average account balance is greater that $2,000
#   reduce the fees by 50%
def fees(a)
  f = 0
  if a.returned_check_count > 0
    f += 20 * a.returned_check_count
  end
  if a.overdraft_days > 3
    f += 10*a.overdraft_days
  end
  if a.average_balance > 2_000
    f /= 2
  end
  f
end
```

The intent of this function is given twice: once in the comment and again in the code. The customer changes a fee, and we have to update both. Given time, we can pretty much guarantee the comment and the code will get out of step.

Ask yourself what the comment adds to the code. From our point of view, it simply compensates for some bad naming and layout. How about just this:

```
def calculate_account_fees(account)
  fees  = 20 * account.returned_check_count
  fees += 10 * account.overdraft_days  if account.overdraft_days > 3
  fees /= 2                            if account.average_balance > 2_000
  fees
end
```

The name says what it does, and if someone needs details, they're laid out in the source. That's DRY!

DRY Violations in Data

Our data structures represent knowledge, and they can fall afoul of the DRY principle. Let's look at a class representing a line:

```
class Line {
  Point  start;
  Point  end;
  double length;
};
```

At first sight, this class might appear reasonable. A line clearly has a start and end, and will always have a length (even if it's zero). But we have duplication. The length is defined by the start and end points: change one of the points and the length changes. It's better to make the length a calculated field:

```
class Line {
  Point  start;
  Point  end;
  double length() { return start.distanceTo(end); }
};
```

Later on in the development process, you may choose to violate the DRY principle for performance reasons. Frequently this occurs when you need to cache data to avoid repeating expensive operations. The trick is to localize the impact. The violation is not exposed to the outside world: only the methods within the class have to worry about keeping things straight:

```
class Line {
  private double length;
  private Point  start;
  private Point  end;

  public Line(Point start, Point end) {
    this.start = start;
    this.end   = end;
    calculateLength();
  }
  // public
  void setStart(Point p) { this.start = p; calculateLength(); }
  void setEnd(Point p)   { this.end   = p; calculateLength(); }

  Point getStart()       { return start; }
  Point getEnd()         { return end;   }

  double getLength()     { return length; }

  private void calculateLength() {
    this.length = start.distanceTo(end);
  }
};
```

This example also illustrates an important issue: whenever a module exposes a data structure, you're coupling all the code that uses that structure to the implementation of that module. Where possible, always use accessor functions to read and write the attributes of objects. It will make it easier to add functionality in the future.

This use of accessor functions ties in with Meyer's *Uniform Access principle*, described in *Object-Oriented Software Construction [Mey97]*, which states that

> All services offered by a module should be available through a uniform notation, which does not betray whether they are implemented through storage or through computation.

Representational Duplication

Your code interfaces to the outside world: other libraries via APIs, other services via remote calls, data in external sources, and so on. And pretty much each time you do, you introduce some kind of DRY violation: your code has to have knowledge that is also present in the external *thing*. It needs to know the API, or the schema, or the meaning of error codes, or whatever. The duplication here is that two things (your code and the external entity) have to have knowledge of the representation of their interface. Change it at one end, and the other end breaks.

This duplication is inevitable, but can be mitigated. Here are some strategies.

Duplication Across Internal APIs

For internal APIs, look for tools that let you specify the API in some kind of neutral format. These tools will typically generate documentation, mock APIs, functional tests, and API clients, the latter in a number of different languages. Ideally the tool will store all your APIs in a central repository, allowing them to be shared across teams.

Duplication Across External APIs

Increasingly, you'll find that public APIs are documented formally using something like OpenAPI.[3] This allows you to import the API spec into your local API tools and integrate more reliably with the service.

If you can't find such a specification, consider creating one and publishing it. Not only will others find it useful; you may even get help maintaining it.

Duplication with Data Sources

Many data sources allow you to introspect on their data schema. This can be used to remove much of the duplication between them and your code. Rather than manually creating the code to contain this stored data, you can generate the containers directly from the schema. Many persistence frameworks will do this heavy lifting for you.

There's another option, and one we often prefer. Rather than writing code that represents external data in a fixed structure (an instance of a struct or class, for example), just stick it into a key/value data structure (your language might call it a map, hash, dictionary, or even object).

On its own this is risky: you lose a lot of the security of knowing just what data you're working with. So we recommend adding a second layer to this solution: a simple table-driven validation suite that verifies that the map you've created contains at least the data you need, in the format you need it. Your API documentation tool might be able to generate this.

Interdeveloper Duplication

Perhaps the hardest type of duplication to detect and handle occurs between different developers on a project. Entire sets of functionality may be inadvertently duplicated, and that duplication could go undetected for years, leading to maintenance problems. We heard firsthand of a U.S. state whose governmental computer systems were surveyed for Y2K compliance. The audit turned

---

3.   https://github.com/OAI/OpenAPI-Specification

up more than 10,000 programs that each contained a different version of Social Security Number validation code.

At a high level, deal with the problem by building a strong, tight-knit team with good communications.

However, at the module level, the problem is more insidious. Commonly needed functionality or data that doesn't fall into an obvious area of responsibility can get implemented many times over.

We feel that the best way to deal with this is to encourage active and frequent communication between developers.

Maybe run a daily scrum standup meeting. Set up forums (such as Slack channels) to discuss common problems. This provides a nonintrusive way of communicating—even across multiple sites—while retaining a permanent history of everything said.

Appoint a team member as the project librarian, whose job is to facilitate the exchange of knowledge. Have a central place in the source tree where utility routines and scripts can be deposited. And make a point of reading other people's source code and documentation, either informally or during code reviews. You're not snooping—you're learning from them. And remember, the access is reciprocal—don't get twisted about other people poring (pawing?) through *your* code, either.

> **Tip 16** Make It Easy to Reuse

What you're trying to do is foster an environment where it's easier to find and reuse existing stuff than to write it yourself. *If it isn't easy, people won't do it.* And if you fail to reuse, you risk duplicating knowledge.

Related Sections Include

- Topic 8, *The Essence of Good Design*, on page 28
- Topic 28, *Decoupling*, on page 130
- Topic 32, *Configuration*, on page 166
- Topic 38, *Programming by Coincidence*, on page 197
- Topic 40, *Refactoring*, on page 209

10 Orthogonality

Orthogonality is a critical concept if you want to produce systems that are easy to design, build, test, and extend. However, the concept of orthogonality is rarely taught directly. Often it is an implicit feature of various other methods and techniques you learn. This is a mistake. Once you learn to apply the principle of orthogonality directly, you'll notice an immediate improvement in the quality of systems you produce.

What Is Orthogonality?

"Orthogonality" is a term borrowed from geometry. Two lines are orthogonal if they meet at right angles, such as the axes on a graph. In vector terms, the two lines are *independent*. As the number 1 on the diagram moves north, it doesn't change how far east or west it is. The number 2 moves east, but not north or south.

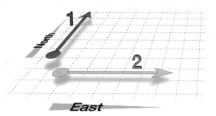

In computing, the term has come to signify a kind of independence or decoupling. Two or more things are orthogonal if changes in one do not affect any of the others. In a well-designed system, the database code will be orthogonal to the user interface: you can change the interface without affecting the database, and swap databases without changing the interface.

Before we look at the benefits of orthogonal systems, let's first look at a system that isn't orthogonal.

A Nonorthogonal System

You're on a helicopter tour of the Grand Canyon when the pilot, who made the obvious mistake of eating fish for lunch, suddenly groans and faints. Fortunately, he left you hovering 100 feet above the ground.

As luck would have it, you had read a Wikipedia page about helicopters the previous night. You know that helicopters have four basic controls. The *cyclic* is the stick you hold in your right hand. Move it, and the helicopter moves in the corresponding direction. Your left hand holds the *collective pitch lever*. Pull up on this and you increase the pitch on all the blades, generating lift. At the end of the pitch lever is the *throttle*. Finally you have two *foot pedals*, which vary the amount of tail rotor thrust and so help turn the helicopter.

"Easy!," you think. "Gently lower the collective pitch lever and you'll descend gracefully to the ground, a hero." However, when you try it, you discover that life isn't that simple. The helicopter's nose drops, and you start to spiral down to the left. Suddenly you discover that you're flying a system where every control input has secondary effects. Lower the left-hand lever and you need to add compensating backward movement to the right-hand stick and push the right pedal. But then each of these changes affects all of the other controls again. Suddenly you're juggling an unbelievably complex system, where every change impacts all the other inputs. Your workload is phenomenal: your hands and feet are constantly moving, trying to balance all the interacting forces.

Helicopter controls are decidedly not orthogonal.

Benefits of Orthogonality

As the helicopter example illustrates, nonorthogonal systems are inherently more complex to change and control. When components of any system are highly interdependent, there is no such thing as a local fix.

Tip 17	Eliminate Effects Between Unrelated Things

We want to design components that are self-contained: independent, and with a single, well-defined purpose (what Yourdon and Constantine call *cohesion* in *Structured Design: Fundamentals of a Discipline of Computer Program and Systems Design [YC79]*). When components are isolated from one another, you know that you can change one without having to worry about the rest. As long as you don't change that component's external interfaces, you can be confident that you won't cause problems that ripple through the entire system.

You get two major benefits if you write orthogonal systems: increased productivity and reduced risk.

Gain Productivity

- Changes are localized, so development time and testing time are reduced. It is easier to write relatively small, self-contained components than a single large block of code. Simple components can be designed, coded, tested, and then forgotten—there is no need to keep changing existing code as you add new code.

- An orthogonal approach also promotes reuse. If components have specific, well-defined responsibilities, they can be combined with new components in ways that were not envisioned by their original implementors. The more loosely coupled your systems, the easier they are to reconfigure and reengineer.

- There is a fairly subtle gain in productivity when you combine orthogonal components. Assume that one component does M distinct things and another does N things. If they are orthogonal and you combine them, the result does $M \times N$ things. However, if the two components are not orthogonal, there will be overlap, and the result will do less. You get more functionality per unit effort by combining orthogonal components.

Reduce Risk

An orthogonal approach reduces the risks inherent in any development.

- Diseased sections of code are isolated. If a module is sick, it is less likely to spread the symptoms around the rest of the system. It is also easier to slice it out and transplant in something new and healthy.

- The resulting system is less fragile. Make small changes and fixes to a particular area, and any problems you generate will be restricted to that area.

- An orthogonal system will probably be better tested, because it will be easier to design and run tests on its components.

- You will not be as tightly tied to a particular vendor, product, or platform, because the interfaces to these third-party components will be isolated to smaller parts of the overall development.

Let's look at some of the ways you can apply the principle of orthogonality to your work.

Design

Most developers are familiar with the need to design orthogonal systems, although they may use words such as *modular*, *component-based*, and *layered* to describe the process. Systems should be composed of a set of cooperating modules, each of which implements functionality independent of the others. Sometimes these components are organized into layers, each providing a level of abstraction. This layered approach is a powerful way to design orthogonal systems. Because each layer uses only the abstractions provided by the layers below it, you have great flexibility in changing underlying implementations without affecting code. Layering also reduces the risk of runaway dependencies between modules. You'll often see layering expressed in diagrams:

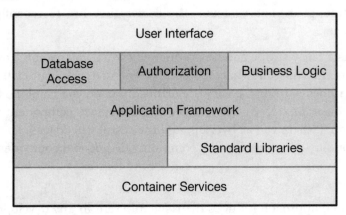

There is an easy test for orthogonal design. Once you have your components mapped out, ask yourself: *If I dramatically change the requirements behind a particular function, how many modules are affected?* In an orthogonal system, the answer should be "one."[4] Moving a button on a GUI panel should not require a change in the database schema. Adding context-sensitive help should not change the billing subsystem.

Let's consider a complex system for monitoring and controlling a heating plant. The original requirement called for a graphical user interface, but the requirements were changed to add a mobile interface that lets engineers monitor key values. In an orthogonally designed system, you would need to change only those modules associated with the user interface to handle this: the underlying logic of controlling the plant would remain unchanged. In fact, if you structure your system carefully, you should be able to support both interfaces with the same underlying code base.

Also ask yourself how decoupled your design is from changes in the real world. Are you using a telephone number as a customer identifier? What happens when the phone company reassigns area codes? Postal codes, Social Security Numbers or government IDs, email addresses, and domains are all external identifiers that you have no control over, and could change at any time for any reason. *Don't rely on the properties of things you can't control.*

---

4. In reality, this is naive. Unless you are remarkably lucky, most real-world requirements changes will affect multiple functions in the system. However, if you analyze the change in terms of functions, each functional change should still ideally affect just one module.

Toolkits and Libraries

Be careful to preserve the orthogonality of your system as you introduce third-party toolkits and libraries. Choose your technologies wisely.

When you bring in a toolkit (or even a library from other members of your team), ask yourself whether it imposes changes on your code that shouldn't be there. If an object persistence scheme is transparent, then it's orthogonal. If it requires you to create or access objects in a special way, then it's not. Keeping such details isolated from your code has the added benefit of making it easier to change vendors in the future.

The Enterprise Java Beans (EJB) system is an interesting example of orthogonality. In most transaction-oriented systems, the application code has to delineate the start and end of each transaction. With EJB, this information is expressed declaratively as annotations, outside the methods that do the work. The same application code can run in different EJB transaction environments with no change.

In a way, EJB is an example of the Decorator Pattern: adding functionality to things without changing them. This style of programming can be used in just about every programming language, and doesn't necessarily require a framework or library. It just takes a little discipline when programming.

Coding

Every time you write code you run the risk of reducing the orthogonality of your application. Unless you constantly monitor not just what you are doing but also the larger context of the application, you might unintentionally duplicate functionality in some other module, or express existing knowledge twice.

There are several techniques you can use to maintain orthogonality:

Keep your code decoupled
> Write shy code—modules that don't reveal anything unnecessary to other modules and that don't rely on other modules' implementations. Try the Law of Demeter, which we discuss in Topic 28, *Decoupling*, on page 130. If you need to change an object's state, get the object to do it for you. This way your code remains isolated from the other code's implementation and increases the chances that you'll remain orthogonal.

Avoid global data
> Every time your code references global data, it ties itself into the other components that share that data. Even globals that you intend only to

read can lead to trouble (for example, if you suddenly need to change your code to be multithreaded). In general, your code is easier to understand and maintain if you explicitly pass any required context into your modules. In object-oriented applications, context is often passed as parameters to objects' constructors. In other code, you can create structures containing the context and pass around references to them.

The Singleton pattern in *Design Patterns: Elements of Reusable Object-Oriented Software [GHJV95]* is a way of ensuring that there is only one instance of an object of a particular class. Many people use these singleton objects as a kind of global variable (particularly in languages, such as Java, that otherwise do not support the concept of globals). Be careful with singletons—they can also lead to unnecessary linkage.

Avoid similar functions

Often you'll come across a set of functions that all look similar—maybe they share common code at the start and end, but each has a different central algorithm. Duplicate code is a symptom of structural problems. Have a look at the Strategy pattern in *Design Patterns* for a better implementation.

Get into the habit of being constantly critical of your code. Look for any opportunities to reorganize it to improve its structure and orthogonality. This process is called *refactoring*, and it's so important that we've dedicated a section to it (see Topic 40, *Refactoring*, on page 209).

Testing

An orthogonally designed and implemented system is easier to test. Because the interactions between the system's components are formalized and limited, more of the system testing can be performed at the individual module level. This is good news, because module level (or unit) testing is considerably easier to specify and perform than integration testing. In fact, we suggest that these tests be performed automatically as part of the regular build process (see Topic 41, *Test to Code*, on page 214).

Writing unit tests is itself an interesting test of orthogonality. What does it take to get a unit test to build and run? Do you have to import a large percentage of the rest of the system's code? If so, you've found a module that is not well decoupled from the rest of the system.

Bug fixing is also a good time to assess the orthogonality of the system as a whole. When you come across a problem, assess how localized the fix is. Do you change just one module, or are the changes scattered throughout the entire system? When you make a change, does it fix everything, or do other problems mysteriously arise? This is a good opportunity to bring automation to bear. If you use a version control system (and you will after reading Topic 19, *Version Control*, on page 84), tag bug fixes when you check the code back in after testing. You can then run monthly reports analyzing trends in the number of source files affected by each bug fix.

Documentation

Perhaps surprisingly, orthogonality also applies to documentation. The axes are content and presentation. With truly orthogonal documentation, you should be able to change the appearance dramatically without changing the content. Word processors provide style sheets and macros that help. We personally prefer using a markup system such as Markdown: when writing we focus only on the content, and leave the presentation to whichever tool we use to render it.[5]

Living with Orthogonality

Orthogonality is closely related to the DRY principle on page 30. With DRY, you're looking to minimize duplication within a system, whereas with orthogonality you reduce the interdependency among the system's components. It may be a clumsy word, but if you use the principle of orthogonality, combined closely with the DRY principle, you'll find that the systems you develop are more flexible, more understandable, and easier to debug, test, and maintain.

If you're brought into a project where people are desperately struggling to make changes, and where every change seems to cause four other things to go wrong, remember the nightmare with the helicopter. The project probably is not orthogonally designed and coded. It's time to refactor.

And, if you're a helicopter pilot, don't eat the fish....

Related Sections Include

- Topic 3, *Software Entropy*, on page 6
- Topic 8, *The Essence of Good Design*, on page 28
- Topic 11, *Reversibility*, on page 47
- Topic 28, *Decoupling*, on page 130
- Topic 31, *Inheritance Tax*, on page 158

---

5. In fact, this book is written in Markdown, and typeset directly from the Markdown source.

- Topic 33, *Breaking Temporal Coupling*, on page 170
- Topic 34, *Shared State Is Incorrect State*, on page 174
- Topic 36, *Blackboards*, on page 187

Challenges

- Consider the difference between tools which have a graphical user interface and small but combinable command-line utilities used at shell prompts. Which set is more orthogonal, and why? Which is easier to use for exactly the purpose for which it was intended? Which set is easier to combine with other tools to meet new challenges? Which set is easier to learn?

- C++ supports multiple inheritance, and Java allows a class to implement multiple interfaces. Ruby has mixins. What impact does using these facilities have on orthogonality? Is there a difference in impact between using multiple inheritance and multiple interfaces? Is there a difference between using delegation and using inheritance?

Exercises

Exercise 1 (possible answer on page 293)

You're asked to read a file a line at a time. For each line, you have to split it into fields. Which of the following sets of pseudo class definitions is likely to be more orthogonal?

```
class Split1 {
    constructor(fileName)     # opens the file for reading
    def readNextLine()        # moves to the next line
    def getField(n)           # returns nth field in current line
}
```

or

```
class Split2 {
    constructor(line)         # splits a line
    def getField(n)           # returns nth field in current line
}
```

Exercise 2 (possible answer on page 293)

What are the differences in orthogonality between object-oriented and functional languages? Are these differences inherent in the languages themselves, or just in the way people use them?

11 Reversibility

Nothing is more dangerous than an idea if it's the only one you have.

> *Emil-Auguste Chartier (Alain), Propos sur la religion, 1938*

Engineers prefer simple, singular solutions to problems. Math tests that allow you to proclaim with great confidence that $x = 2$ are much more comfortable than fuzzy, warm essays about the myriad causes of the French Revolution. Management tends to agree with the engineers: singular, easy answers fit nicely on spreadsheets and project plans.

If only the real world would cooperate! Unfortunately, while x is 2 today, it may need to be 5 tomorrow, and 3 next week. Nothing is forever—and if you rely heavily on some fact, you can almost guarantee that it *will* change.

There is always more than one way to implement something, and there is usually more than one vendor available to provide a third-party product. If you go into a project hampered by the myopic notion that there is only *one* way to do it, you may be in for an unpleasant surprise. Many project teams have their eyes forcibly opened as the future unfolds:

> "But you said we'd use database XYZ! We are 85% done coding the project, we can't change now!" the programmer protested. "Sorry, but our company decided to standardize on database PDQ instead—for all projects. It's out of my hands. We'll just have to recode. All of you will be working weekends until further notice."

Changes don't have to be that Draconian, or even that immediate. But as time goes by, and your project progresses, you may find yourself stuck in an untenable position. With every critical decision, the project team commits to a smaller target—a narrower version of reality that has fewer options.

By the time many critical decisions have been made, the target becomes so small that if it moves, or the wind changes direction, or a butterfly in Tokyo flaps its wings, you miss.[6] And you may miss by a huge amount.

The problem is that critical decisions aren't easily reversible.

---

6. Take a nonlinear, or chaotic, system and apply a small change to one of its inputs. You may get a large and often unpredictable result. The clichéd butterfly flapping its wings in Tokyo could be the start of a chain of events that ends up generating a tornado in Texas. Does this sound like any projects you know?

Once you decide to use this vendor's database, or that architectural pattern, or a certain deployment model, you are committed to a course of action that cannot be undone, except at great expense.

Reversibility

Many of the topics in this book are geared to producing flexible, adaptable software. By sticking to their recommendations—especially the DRY principle on page 30, decoupling on page 130, and use of external configuration on page 166—we don't have to make as many critical, irreversible decisions. This is a good thing, because we don't always make the best decisions the first time around. We commit to a certain technology only to discover we can't hire enough people with the necessary skills. We lock in a certain third-party vendor just before they get bought out by their competitor. Requirements, users, and hardware change faster than we can get the software developed.

Suppose you decide, early in the project, to use a relational database from vendor A. Much later, during performance testing, you discover that the database is simply too slow, but that the document database from vendor B is faster. With most conventional projects, you'd be out of luck. Most of the time, calls to third-party products are entangled throughout the code. But if you *really* abstracted the idea of a database out—to the point where it simply provides persistence as a service—then you have the flexibility to change horses in midstream.

Similarly, suppose the project begins as a browser-based application, but then, late in the game, marketing decides that what they really want is a mobile app. How hard would that be for you? In an ideal world, it shouldn't impact you too much, at least on the server side. You'd be stripping out some HTML rendering and replacing it with an API.

The mistake lies in assuming that any decision is cast in stone—and in not preparing for the contingencies that might arise. Instead of carving decisions in stone, think of them more as being written in the sand at the beach. A big wave can come along and wipe them out at any time.

| Tip 18 | There Are No Final Decisions |

Flexible Architecture

While many people try to keep their *code* flexible, you also need to think about maintaining flexibility in the areas of architecture, deployment, and vendor integration.

We're writing this in 2019. Since the turn of the century we've seen the following "best practice" server-side architectures:

- Big hunk of iron
- Federations of big iron
- Load-balanced clusters of commodity hardware
- Cloud-based virtual machines running applications
- Cloud-based virtual machines running services
- Containerized versions of the above
- Cloud-supported serverless applications
- And, inevitably, an apparent move back to big hunks of iron for some tasks

Go ahead and add the very latest and greatest fads to this list, and then regard it with awe: it's a miracle that anything ever worked.

How can you plan for this kind of architectural volatility? You can't.

What you can do is make it easy to change. Hide third-party APIs behind your own abstraction layers. Break your code into components: even if you end up deploying them on a single massive server, this approach is a lot easier than taking a monolithic application and splitting it. (We have the scars to prove it.)

And, although this isn't particularly a reversibility issue, one final piece of advice.

> Tip 19   Forgo Following Fads

No one knows what the future may hold, especially not us! So enable your code to rock-n-roll: to "rock on" when it can, to roll with the punches when it must.

Related Sections Include

- Topic 8, *The Essence of Good Design*, on page 28
- Topic 10, *Orthogonality*, on page 39
- Topic 19, *Version Control*, on page 84
- Topic 28, *Decoupling*, on page 130
- Topic 45, *The Requirements Pit*, on page 244
- Topic 51, *Pragmatic Starter Kit*, on page 273

Challenges

- Time for a little quantum mechanics with Schrödinger's cat.

  Suppose you have a cat in a closed box, along with a radioactive particle. The particle has exactly a 50% chance of fissioning into two. If it does, the cat will be killed. If it doesn't, the cat will be okay. So, is the cat dead or alive? According to Schrödinger, the correct answer is *both* (at least while the box remains closed). Every time a subnuclear reaction takes place that has two possible outcomes, the universe is cloned. In one, the event occurred, in the other it didn't. The cat's alive in one universe, dead in another. Only when you open the box do you know which universe *you* are in.

  No wonder coding for the future is difficult.

  But think of code evolution along the same lines as a box full of Schrödinger's cats: every decision results in a different version of the future. How many possible futures can your code support? Which ones are more likely? How hard will it be to support them when the time comes?

  Dare you open the box?

---

12 ▶ Tracer Bullets

Ready, fire, aim...
> ➤ *Anon*

We often talk about hitting targets when we develop software. We're not actually firing anything at the shooting range, but it's still a useful and very visual metaphor. In particular, it's interesting to consider *how* to hit a target in a complex and shifting world.

The answer, of course, depends on the nature of the device you're aiming with. With many you only get one chance to aim, and then get to see if you hit the bullseye or not. But there's a better way.

You know all those movies, TV shows, and video games where people are shooting machine guns? In these scenes, you'll often see the path of bullets as bright streaks in the air. These streaks come from tracer bullets.

Tracer bullets are loaded at intervals alongside regular ammunition. When they're fired, their phosphorus ignites and leaves a pyrotechnic trail from the gun to whatever they hit. If the tracers are hitting the target, then so are the regular bullets. Soldiers use these tracer rounds to refine their aim: it's pragmatic, real-time feedback under actual conditions.

That same principle applies to projects, particularly when you're building something that hasn't been built before. We use the term *tracer bullet development* to visually illustrate the need for immediate feedback under actual conditions with a moving goal.

Like the gunners, you're trying to hit a target in the dark. Because your users have never seen a system like this before, their requirements may be vague. Because you may be using algorithms, techniques, languages, or libraries you aren't familiar with, you face a large number of unknowns. And because projects take time to complete, you can pretty much guarantee the environment you're working in will change before you're done.

The classic response is to specify the system to death. Produce reams of paper itemizing every requirement, tying down every unknown, and constraining the environment. Fire the gun using dead reckoning. One big calculation up front, then shoot and hope.

Pragmatic Programmers, however, tend to prefer using the software equivalent of tracer bullets.

Code That Glows in the Dark

Tracer bullets work because they operate in the same environment and under the same constraints as the real bullets. They get to the target fast, so the gunner gets immediate feedback. And from a practical standpoint they're a relatively cheap solution.

To get the same effect in code, we look for something that gets us from a requirement to some aspect of the final system quickly, visibly, and repeatably.

Look for the important requirements, the ones that define the system. Look for the areas where you have doubts, and where you see the biggest risks. Then prioritize your development so that these are the first areas you code.

Tip 20	Use Tracer Bullets to Find the Target

In fact, given the complexity of today's project setup, with swarms of external dependencies and tools, tracer bullets become even more important. For us, the very first tracer bullet is simply *create the project, add a "hello world!," and make sure it compiles and runs.* Then we look for areas of uncertainty in the overall application and add the skeleton needed to make it work.

Have a look at the following diagram. This system has five architectural layers. We have some concerns about how they'd integrate, so we look for a simple feature that lets us exercise them together. The diagonal line shows the path that feature takes through the code. To make it work, we just have to implement the solidly shaded areas in each layer: the stuff with the squiggles will be done later.

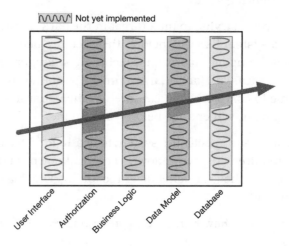

We once undertook a complex client-server database marketing project. Part of its requirement was the ability to specify and execute temporal queries. The servers were a range of relational and specialized databases. The client UI, written in random language A, used a set of libraries written in a different language to provide an interface to the servers. The user's query was stored on the server in a Lisp-like notation before being converted to optimized SQL just prior to execution. There were many unknowns and many different environments, and no one was too sure how the UI should behave.

This was a great opportunity to use tracer code. We developed the framework for the front end, libraries for representing the queries, and a structure for converting a stored query into a database-specific query. Then we put it all together and checked that it worked. For that initial build, all we could do was submit a query that listed all the rows in a table, but it proved that the UI could talk to the libraries, the libraries could serialize and unserialize a query, and the server could generate SQL from the result. Over the following months we gradually fleshed out this basic structure, adding new functionality by augmenting each component of the tracer code in parallel. When the UI added a new query type, the library grew and the SQL generation was made more sophisticated.

Tracer code is not disposable: you write it for keeps. It contains all the error checking, structuring, documentation, and self-checking that any piece of production code has. It simply is not fully functional. However, once you have achieved an end-to-end connection among the components of your system, you can check how close to the target you are, adjusting if necessary. Once you're on target, adding functionality is easy.

Tracer development is consistent with the idea that a project is never finished: there will always be changes required and functions to add. It is an incremental approach.

The conventional alternative is a kind of heavy engineering approach: code is divided into modules, which are coded in a vacuum. Modules are combined into subassemblies, which are then further combined, until one day you have a complete application. Only then can the application as a whole be presented to the user and tested.

The tracer code approach has many advantages:

Users get to see something working early
> If you have successfully communicated what you are doing (see Topic 52, *Delight Your Users*, on page 280), your users will know they are seeing something immature. They won't be disappointed by a lack of functionality; they'll be ecstatic to see some visible progress toward their system. They also get to contribute as the project progresses, increasing their buy-in. These same users will likely be the people who'll tell you how close to the target each iteration is.

Developers build a structure to work in
> The most daunting piece of paper is the one with nothing written on it. If you have worked out all the end-to-end interactions of your application, and have embodied them in code, then your team won't need to pull as much out of thin air. This makes everyone more productive, and encourages consistency.

You have an integration platform
> As the system is connected end-to-end, you have an environment to which you can add new pieces of code once they have been unit-tested. Rather than attempting a big-bang integration, you'll be integrating every day (often many times a day). The impact of each new change is more apparent, and the interactions are more limited, so debugging and testing are faster and more accurate.

You have something to demonstrate

Project sponsors and top brass have a tendency to want to see demos at the most inconvenient times. With tracer code, you'll always have something to show them.

You have a better feel for progress

In a tracer code development, developers tackle use cases one by one. When one is done, they move to the next. It is far easier to measure performance and to demonstrate progress to your user. Because each individual development is smaller, you avoid creating those monolithic blocks of code that are reported as 95% complete week after week.

Tracer Bullets Don't Always Hit Their Target

Tracer bullets show what you're hitting. This may not always be the target. You then adjust your aim until they're on target. That's the point.

It's the same with tracer code. You use the technique in situations where you're not 100% certain of where you're going. You shouldn't be surprised if your first couple of attempts miss: the user says "that's not what I meant," or data you need isn't available when you need it, or performance problems seem likely. So change what you've got to bring it nearer the target, and be thankful that you've used a lean development methodology; a small body of code has low inertia—it is easy and quick to change. You'll be able to gather feedback on your application and generate a new, more accurate version quickly and cheaply. And because every major application component is represented in your tracer code, your users can be confident that what they're seeing is based on reality, not just a paper specification.

Tracer Code versus Prototyping

You might think that this tracer code concept is nothing more than prototyping under an aggressive name. There is a difference. With a prototype, you're aiming to explore specific aspects of the final system. With a true prototype, you will throw away whatever you lashed together when trying out the concept, and recode it properly using the lessons you've learned.

For example, say you're producing an application that helps shippers determine how to pack odd-sized boxes into containers. Among other problems, the user interface needs to be intuitive and the algorithms you use to determine optimal packing are very complex.

You could prototype a user interface for your end users in a UI tool. You code only enough to make the interface responsive to user actions. Once they've agreed to the layout, you might throw it away and recode it, this time with the business logic behind it, using the target language. Similarly, you might want to prototype a number of algorithms that perform the actual packing. You might code functional tests in a high-level, forgiving language such as Python, and code low-level performance tests in something closer to the machine. In any case, once you'd made your decision, you'd start again and code the algorithms in their final environment, interfacing to the real world. This is *prototyping*, and it is very useful.

The tracer code approach addresses a different problem. You need to know how the application as a whole hangs together. You want to show your users how the interactions will work in practice, and you want to give your developers an architectural skeleton on which to hang code. In this case, you might construct a tracer consisting of a trivial implementation of the container packing algorithm (maybe something like first-come, first-served) and a simple but working user interface. Once you have all the components in the application plumbed together, you have a framework to show your users and your developers. Over time, you add to this framework with new functionality, completing stubbed routines. But the framework stays intact, and you know the system will continue to behave the way it did when your first tracer code was completed.

The distinction is important enough to warrant repeating. Prototyping generates disposable code. Tracer code is lean but complete, and forms part of the skeleton of the final system. Think of prototyping as the reconnaissance and intelligence gathering that takes place before a single tracer bullet is fired.

Related Sections Include

- Topic 13, *Prototypes and Post-it Notes*, on page 56
- Topic 27, *Don't Outrun Your Headlights*, on page 125
- Topic 40, *Refactoring*, on page 209
- Topic 49, *Pragmatic Teams*, on page 264
- Topic 50, *Coconuts Don't Cut It*, on page 270
- Topic 51, *Pragmatic Starter Kit*, on page 273
- Topic 52, *Delight Your Users*, on page 280

13   Prototypes and Post-it Notes

Many industries use prototypes to try out specific ideas; prototyping is much cheaper than full-scale production. Car makers, for example, may build many different prototypes of a new car design. Each one is designed to test a specific aspect of the car—the aerodynamics, styling, structural characteristics, and so on. Old school folks might use a clay model for wind tunnel testing, maybe a balsa wood and duct tape model will do for the art department, and so on. The less romantic will do their modeling on a computer screen or in virtual reality, reducing costs even further. In this way, risky or uncertain elements can be tried out without committing to building the real item.

We build software prototypes in the same fashion, and for the same reasons—to analyze and expose risk, and to offer chances for correction at a greatly reduced cost. Like the car makers, we can target a prototype to test one or more specific aspects of a project.

We tend to think of prototypes as code-based, but they don't always have to be. Like the car makers, we can build prototypes out of different materials. Post-it notes are great for prototyping dynamic things such as workflow and application logic. A user interface can be prototyped as a drawing on a whiteboard, as a nonfunctional mock-up drawn with a paint program, or with an interface builder.

Prototypes are designed to answer just a few questions, so they are much cheaper and faster to develop than applications that go into production. The code can ignore unimportant details—unimportant to you at the moment, but probably very important to the user later on. If you are prototyping a UI, for instance, you can get away with incorrect results or data. On the other hand, if you're just investigating computational or performance aspects, you can get away with a pretty poor UI, or perhaps even no UI at all.

But if you find yourself in an environment where you *cannot* give up the details, then you need to ask yourself if you are really building a prototype at all. Perhaps a tracer bullet style of development would be more appropriate in this case (see Topic 12, *Tracer Bullets*, on page 50).

Things to Prototype

What sorts of things might you choose to investigate with a prototype? Anything that carries risk. Anything that hasn't been tried before, or that is absolutely critical to the final system. Anything unproven, experimental, or doubtful. Anything you aren't comfortable with. You can prototype:

- Architecture
- New functionality in an existing system
- Structure or contents of external data
- Third-party tools or components
- Performance issues
- User interface design

Prototyping is a learning experience. Its value lies not in the code produced, but in the lessons learned. That's really the point of prototyping.

Tip 21	Prototype to Learn

How to Use Prototypes

When building a prototype, what details can you ignore?

Correctness
You may be able to use dummy data where appropriate.

Completeness
The prototype may function only in a very limited sense, perhaps with only one preselected piece of input data and one menu item.

Robustness
Error checking is likely to be incomplete or missing entirely. If you stray from the predefined path, the prototype may crash and burn in a glorious display of pyrotechnics. That's okay.

Style
Prototype code shouldn't have much in the way of comments or documentation (although you may produce reams of documentation as a result of your experience with the prototype).

Prototypes gloss over details, and focus in on specific aspects of the system being considered, so you may want to implement them using a high-level scripting language—higher than the rest of the project (maybe a language such as Python or Ruby), as these languages can get out of your way. You may choose to continue to develop in the language used for the prototype, or you can switch; after all, you're going to throw the prototype away anyway.

To prototype user interfaces, use a tool that lets you focus on the appearance and/or interactions without worrying about code or markup.

Scripting languages also work well as the "glue" to combine low-level pieces into new combinations. Using this approach, you can rapidly assemble existing components into new configurations to see how things work.

Prototyping Architecture

Many prototypes are constructed to model the entire system under consideration. As opposed to tracer bullets, none of the individual modules in the prototype system need to be particularly functional. In fact, you may not even need to code in order to prototype architecture—you can prototype on a whiteboard, with Post-it notes or index cards. What you are looking for is how the system hangs together as a whole, again deferring details. Here are some specific areas you may want to look for in the architectural prototype:

- Are the responsibilities of the major areas well defined and appropriate?
- Are the collaborations between major components well defined?
- Is coupling minimized?
- Can you identify potential sources of duplication?
- Are interface definitions and constraints acceptable?
- Does every module have an access path to the data it needs during execution? Does it have that access *when* it needs it?

This last item tends to generate the most surprises and the most valuable results from the prototyping experience.

How *Not* to Use Prototypes

Before you embark on any code-based prototyping, make sure that everyone understands that you are writing disposable code. Prototypes can be deceptively attractive to people who don't know that they are just prototypes. You must make it *very* clear that this code is disposable, incomplete, and unable to be completed.

It's easy to become misled by the apparent completeness of a demonstrated prototype, and project sponsors or management may insist on deploying the prototype (or its progeny) if you don't set the right expectations. Remind them that you can build a great prototype of a new car out of balsa wood and duct tape, but you wouldn't try to drive it in rush-hour traffic!

If you feel there is a strong possibility in your environment or culture that the purpose of prototype code may be misinterpreted, you may be better off with the tracer bullet approach. You'll end up with a solid framework on which to base future development.

Properly used prototypes can save you huge amounts of time, money, and pain by identifying and correcting potential problem spots early in the development cycle—the time when fixing mistakes is both cheap and easy.

Related Sections Include

- Topic 12, *Tracer Bullets*, on page 50
- Topic 14, *Domain Languages*, on page 59
- Topic 17, *Shell Games*, on page 78
- Topic 27, *Don't Outrun Your Headlights*, on page 125
- Topic 37, *Listen to Your Lizard Brain*, on page 192
- Topic 45, *The Requirements Pit*, on page 244
- Topic 52, *Delight Your Users*, on page 280

Exercises

Exercise 3 (possible answer on page 294)

Marketing would like to sit down and brainstorm a few web page designs with you. They are thinking of clickable image maps to take you to other pages, and so on. But they can't decide on a model for the image—maybe it's a car, or a phone, or a house. You have a list of target pages and content; they'd like to see a few prototypes. Oh, by the way, you have 15 minutes. What tools might you use?

---

14 Domain Languages

The limits of language are the limits of one's world.

➤ *Ludwig Wittgenstein*

Computer languages influence *how* you think about a problem, and how you think about communicating. Every language comes with a list of features: buzzwords such as static versus dynamic typing, early versus late binding, functional versus OO, inheritance models, mixins, macros—all of which may suggest or obscure certain solutions. Designing a solution with C++ in mind will produce different results than a solution based on Haskell-style thinking, and vice versa. Conversely, and we think more importantly, the language of the problem domain may also suggest a programming solution.

We always try to write code using the vocabulary of the application domain (see *Maintain a Glossary*, on page 251). In some cases, Pragmatic Programmers can go to the next level and actually program using the vocabulary, syntax, and semantics—the language—of the domain.

Tip 22	Program Close to the Problem Domain

Some Real-World Domain Languages

Let's look at a few examples where folks have done just that.

RSpec

RSpec[7] is a testing library for Ruby. It inspired versions for most other modern languages. A test in RSpec is intended to reflect the behavior you expect from your code.

```ruby
describe BowlingScore do
  it "totals 12 if you score 3 four times" do
    score = BowlingScore.new
    4.times { score.add_pins(3) }
    expect(score.total).to eq(12)
  end
end
```

Cucumber

Cucumber[8] is programming-language neutral way of specifying tests. You run the tests using a version of Cucumber appropriate to the language you're using. In order to support the natural-language like syntax, you also have to write specific matchers that recognize phrases and extract parameters for the tests.

```
Feature: Scoring

Background:
  Given an empty scorecard

Scenario: bowling a lot of 3s
  Given I throw a 3
  And I throw a 3
  And I throw a 3
  And I throw a 3
  Then the score should be 12
```

Cucumber tests were intended to be read by the customers of the software (although that happens fairly rarely in practice; the following aside considers why that might be).

---

7. https://rspec.info
8. https://cucumber.io/

> ## Why Don't Many Business Users Read Cucumber Features?
>
> One of the reasons that the classic *gather requirements, design, code, ship* approach doesn't work is that it is anchored by the concept that we know what the requirements are. But we rarely do. Your business users will have a vague idea of what they want to achieve, but they neither know nor care about the details. That's part of our value: we intuit intent and convert it to code.
>
> So when you force a business person to sign off on a requirements document, or get them to agree to a set of Cucumber features, you're doing the equivalent of getting them to check the spelling in an essay written in Sumerian. They'll make some random changes to save face and sign it off to get you out of their office.
>
> Give them code that runs, however, and they can play with it. That's where their real needs will surface.

Phoenix Routes

Many web frameworks have a routing facility, mapping incoming HTTP requests onto handler functions in the code. Here's an example from Phoenix.[9]

```
scope "/", HelloPhoenix do
  pipe_through :browser # Use the default browser stack

  get "/", PageController, :index
  resources "/users", UserController
end
```

This says that requests starting "/" will be run through a series of filters appropriate for browsers. A request to "/" itself will be handled by the index function in the PageController module. The UsersController implements the functions needed to manage a resource accessible via the url /users.

Ansible

Ansible[10] is a tool that configures software, typically on a bunch of remote servers. It does this by reading a specification that you provide, then doing whatever is needed on the servers to make them mirror that spec. The specification can be written in YAML,[11] a language that builds data structures from text descriptions:

---

9. https://phoenixframework.org/
10. https://www.ansible.com/
11. https://yaml.org/

```
---
- name: install nginx
  apt: name=nginx state=latest

- name: ensure nginx is running (and enable it at boot)
  service: name=nginx state=started enabled=yes

- name: write the nginx config file
  template: src=templates/nginx.conf.j2 dest=/etc/nginx/nginx.conf
  notify:
  - restart nginx
```

This example ensures that the latest version of nginx is installed on my servers, that it is started by default, and that it uses a configuration file that you've provided.

Characteristics of Domain Languages

Let's look at these examples more closely.

RSpec and the Phoenix router are written in their host languages (Ruby and Elixir). They employ some fairly devious code, including metaprogramming and macros, but ultimately they are compiled and run as regular code.

Cucumber tests and Ansible configurations are written in their own languages. A Cucumber test is converted into code to be run or into a datastructure, whereas Ansible specs are always converted into a data structure that is run by Ansible itself.

As a result, RSpec and the router code are embedded into the code you run: they are true extensions to your code's vocabulary. Cucumber and Ansible are *read* by code and converted into some form the code can use.

We call RSpec and the router examples of *internal* domain languages, while Cucumber and Ansible use *external* languages.

Trade-Offs Between Internal and External Languages

In general, an internal domain language can take advantage of the features of its host language: the domain language you create is more powerful, and that power comes for free. For example, you could use some Ruby code to create a bunch of RSpec tests automatically. In this case we can test scores where there are no spares or strikes:

```
describe BowlingScore do
  (0..4).each do |pins|
    (1..20).each do |throws|
      target = pins * throws

      it "totals #{target} if you score #{pins} #{throws} times" do
        score = BowlingScore.new
        throws.times { score.add_pins(pins) }
        expect(score.total).to eq(target)
      end
    end
  end
end
```

That's 100 tests you just wrote. Take the rest of the day off.

The downside of internal domain languages is that you're bound by the syntax and semantics of that language. Although some languages are remarkably flexible in this regards, you're still forced to compromise between the language you want and the language you can implement.

Ultimately, whatever you come up with must still be valid syntax in your target language. Languages with macros (such as Elixir, Clojure, and Crystal) gives you a little more flexibility, but ultimately syntax is syntax.

External languages have no such restrictions. As long as you can write a parser for the language, you're good to go. Sometimes you can use someone else's parser (as Ansible did by using YAML), but then you're back to making a compromise.

Writing a parser probably means adding new libraries and possibly tools to your application. And writing a good parser is not a trivial job. But, if you're feeling stout of heart, you could look at parser generators such as bison or ANTLR, and parsing frameworks such as the many PEG parsers out there.

Our suggestion is fairly simple: don't spend more effort than you save. Writing a domain language adds some cost to your project, and you'll need to be convinced that there are offsetting savings (potentially in the long term).

In general, use off-the-shelf external languages (such as YAML, JSON, or CSV) if you can. If not, look at internal languages. We'd recommend using external languages only in cases where your language will be written by the users of your application.

An Internal Domain Language on the Cheap

Finally, there's a cheat for creating internal domain languages if you don't mind the host language syntax leaking through. Don't do a bunch of metaprogramming. Instead, just write functions to do the work. In fact, this is pretty much what RSpec does:

```
describe BowlingScore do
  it "totals 12 if you score 3 four times" do
    score = BowlingScore.new
    4.times { score.add_pins(3) }
    expect(score.total).to eq(12)
  end
end
```

In this code, describe, it, expect, to, and eq are just Ruby methods. There's a little plumbing behind the scenes in terms of how objects are passed around, but it's all just code. We'll explore that a little in the exercises.

Related Sections Include

- Topic 8, *The Essence of Good Design*, on page 28
- Topic 13, *Prototypes and Post-it Notes*, on page 56
- Topic 32, *Configuration*, on page 166

Challenges

- Could some of the requirements of your current project be expressed in a domain-specific language? Would it be possible to write a compiler or translator that could generate most of the code required?

- If you decide to adopt mini-languages as a way of programming closer to the problem domain, you're accepting that some effort will be required to implement them. Can you see ways in which the framework you develop for one project can be reused in others?

Exercises

Exercise 4 (possible answer on page 294)

We want to implement a mini-language to control a simple turtle-graphics system. The language consists of single-letter commands, some followed by a single number. For example, the following input would draw a rectangle:

```
P 2  # select pen 2
D    # pen down
W 2  # draw west 2cm
N 1  # then north 1
E 2  # then east 2
S 1  # then back south
U    # pen up
```

Implement the code that parses this language. It should be designed so that it is simple to add new commands.

Exercise 5 (possible answer on page 295)

In the previous exercise we implemented a parser for the drawing language—it was an external domain language. Now implement it again as an internal language. Don't do anything clever: just write a function for each of the commands. You may have to change the names of the commands to lower case, and maybe to wrap them inside something to provide some context.

Exercise 6 (possible answer on page 295)

Design a BNF grammar to parse a time specification. All of the following examples should be accepted:

```
4pm, 7:38pm, 23:42, 3:16, 3:16am
```

Exercise 7 (possible answer on page 296)

Implement a parser for the BNF grammar in the previous exercise using a PEG parser generator in the language of your choice. The output should be an integer containing the number of minutes past midnight.

Exercise 8 (possible answer on page 297)

Implement the time parser using a scripting language and regular expressions.

---

15 Estimating

The Library of Congress in Washington, DC, currently has about 75 terabytes of digital information online. Quick! How long will it take to send all that information over a 1Gbps network? How much storage will you need for a million names and addresses? How long does it take to compress 100Mb of text? How many months will it take to deliver your project?

At one level, these are all meaningless questions—they are all missing information. And yet they can all be answered, as long as you are comfortable estimating. And, in the process of producing an estimate, you'll come to understand more about the world your programs inhabit.

By learning to estimate, and by developing this skill to the point where you have an intuitive feel for the magnitudes of things, you will be able to show an apparent magical ability to determine their feasibility. When someone says "we'll send the backup over a network connection to S3," you'll be able to know intuitively whether this is practical. When you're coding, you'll be able to know which subsystems need optimizing and which ones can be left alone.

Tip 23	Estimate to Avoid Surprises

As a bonus, at the end of this section we'll reveal the single correct answer to give whenever anyone asks you for an estimate.

How Accurate Is Accurate Enough?

To some extent, all answers are estimates. It's just that some are more accurate than others. So the first question you have to ask yourself when someone asks you for an estimate is the context in which your answer will be taken. Do they need high accuracy, or are they looking for a ballpark figure?

One of the interesting things about estimating is that the units you use make a difference in the interpretation of the result. If you say that something will take about 130 working days, then people will be expecting it to come in pretty close. However, if you say "Oh, about six months," then they know to look for it any time between five and seven months from now. Both numbers represent the same duration, but "130 days" probably implies a higher degree of accuracy than you feel. We recommend that you scale time estimates as follows:

Duration	Quote estimate in
1–15 days	Days
3–6 weeks	Weeks
8–20 weeks	Months
20+ weeks	Think hard before giving an estimate

So, if after doing all the necessary work, you decide that a project will take 125 working days (25 weeks), you might want to deliver an estimate of "about six months."

The same concepts apply to estimates of any quantity: choose the units of your answer to reflect the accuracy you intend to convey.

Where Do Estimates Come From?

All estimates are based on models of the problem. But before we get too deeply into the techniques of building models, we have to mention a basic estimating trick that always gives good answers: ask someone who's already done it. Before you get too committed to model building, cast around for someone who's been in a similar situation in the past. See how their problem got solved. It's unlikely you'll ever find an exact match, but you'd be surprised how many times you can successfully draw on others' experiences.

Understand What's Being Asked

The first part of any estimation exercise is building an understanding of what's being asked. As well as the accuracy issues discussed above, you need to have a grasp of the scope of the domain. Often this is implicit in the question, but you need to make it a habit to think about the scope before starting to guess. Often, the scope you choose will form part of the answer you give: "Assuming there are no traffic accidents and there's gas in the car, I should be there in 20 minutes."

Build a Model of the System

This is the fun part of estimating. From your understanding of the question being asked, build a rough-and-ready bare-bones mental model. If you're estimating response times, your model may involve a server and some kind of arriving traffic. For a project, the model may be the steps that your organization uses during development, along with a very rough picture of how the system might be implemented.

Model building can be both creative and useful in the long term. Often, the process of building the model leads to discoveries of underlying patterns and processes that weren't apparent on the surface. You may even want to reexamine the original question: "You asked for an estimate to do X. However, it looks like Y, a variant of X, could be done in about half the time, and you lose only one feature."

Building the model introduces inaccuracies into the estimating process. This is inevitable, and also beneficial. You are trading off model simplicity for accuracy. Doubling the effort on the model may give you only a slight increase in accuracy. Your experience will tell you when to stop refining.

Break the Model into Components

Once you have a model, you can decompose it into components. You'll need to discover the mathematical rules that describe how these components interact. Sometimes a component contributes a single value that is added into the result. Some components may supply multiplying factors, while others may be more complicated (such as those that simulate the arrival of traffic at a node).

You'll find that each component will typically have parameters that affect how it contributes to the overall model. At this stage, simply identify each parameter.

Give Each Parameter a Value

Once you have the parameters broken out, you can go through and assign each one a value. You expect to introduce some errors in this step. The trick is to work out which parameters have the most impact on the result, and concentrate on getting them about right. Typically, parameters whose values are added into a result are less significant than those that are multiplied or divided. Doubling a line speed may double the amount of data received in an hour, while adding a 5ms transit delay will have no noticeable effect.

You should have a justifiable way of calculating these critical parameters. For the queuing example, you might want to measure the actual transaction arrival rate of the existing system, or find a similar system to measure. Similarly, you could measure the current time taken to serve a request, or come up with an estimate using the techniques described in this section. In fact, you'll often find yourself basing an estimate on other subestimates. This is where your largest errors will creep in.

Calculate the Answers

Only in the simplest of cases will an estimate have a single answer. You might be happy to say "I can walk five cross-town blocks in 15 minutes." However, as the systems get more complex, you'll want to hedge your answers. Run multiple calculations, varying the values of the critical parameters, until you work out which ones really drive the model. A spreadsheet can be a big help. Then couch your answer in terms of these parameters. "The response time is roughly three quarters of a second if the system has SSDs and 32GB of memory, and one second with 16GB memory." (Notice how "three quarters of a second" conveys a different feeling of accuracy than 750ms.)

During the calculation phase, you get answers that seem strange. Don't be too quick to dismiss them. If your arithmetic is correct, your understanding of the problem or your model is probably wrong. This is valuable information.

Keep Track of Your Estimating Prowess

We think it's a great idea to record your estimates so you can see how close you were. If an overall estimate involved calculating subestimates, keep track of these as well. Often you'll find your estimates are pretty good—in fact, after a while, you'll come to expect this.

When an estimate turns out wrong, don't just shrug and walk away—find out why. Maybe you chose some parameters that didn't match the reality of the problem. Maybe your model was wrong. Whatever the reason, take some time to uncover what happened. If you do, your next estimate will be better.

Estimating Project Schedules

Normally you'll be asked to estimate how long something will take. If that "something" is complex, the estimate can be very difficult to produce. In this section, we'll look at two techniques for reducing that uncertainty.

Painting the Missile

"How long will it take to paint the house?"

"Well, if everything goes right, and this paint has the coverage they claim, it might be as few as 10 hours. But that's unlikely: I'd guess a more realistic figure is closer to 18 hours. And, of course, if the weather turns bad, that could push it out to 30 or more."

That's how people estimate in the real world. Not with a single number (unless you force them to give you one) but with a range of scenarios.

When the U.S. Navy needed to plan the Polaris submarine project, they adopted this style of estimating with a methodology they called the *Program Evaluation Review Technique*, or PERT.

Every PERT task has an *optimistic*, a *most likely*, and a *pessimistic estimate*. The tasks are arranged into a dependency network, and then you use some simple statistics to identify likely best and worst times for the overall project.

Using a range of values like this is a great way to avoid one of the most common causes of estimation error: padding a number because you're unsure. Instead, the statistics behind PERT spreads the uncertainty out for you, giving you better estimations of the whole project.

However, we're not big fans of this. People tend to produce wall-sized charts of all the tasks in a project, and implicitly believe that, just because they used a *formula*, they have an accurate estimate. The chances are they don't, because they have never done this before.

Eating the Elephant

We find that often the only way to determine the timetable for a project is by gaining experience on that same project. This needn't be a paradox if you practice incremental development, repeating the following steps with very thin slices of functionality:

- Check requirements
- Analyze risk (and prioritize riskiest items earlier)
- Design, implement, integrate
- Validate with the users

Initially, you may have only a vague idea of how many iterations will be required, or how long they may be. Some methods require you to nail this down as part of the initial plan; however, for all but the most trivial of projects this is a mistake. Unless you are doing an application similar to a previous one, with the same team and the same technology, you'd just be guessing.

So you complete the coding and testing of the initial functionality and mark this as the end of the first iteration. Based on that experience, you can refine your initial guess on the number of iterations and what can be included in each. The refinement gets better and better each time, and confidence in the schedule grows along with it. This kind of estimating is often done during the team's review at the end of each iterative cycle.

That's also how the old joke says to eat an elephant: one bite at a time.

> Tip 24   **Iterate the Schedule with the Code**

This may not be popular with management, who typically want a single, hard-and-fast number before the project even starts. You'll have to help them understand that the team, their productivity, and the environment will determine the schedule. By formalizing this, and refining the schedule as part of each iteration, you'll be giving them the most accurate scheduling estimates you can.

What to Say When Asked for an Estimate

You say *"I'll get back to you."*

You almost always get better results if you slow the process down and spend some time going through the steps we describe in this section. Estimates given at the coffee machine will (like the coffee) come back to haunt you.

Related Sections Include

- Topic 7, *Communicate!*, on page 19
- Topic 39, *Algorithm Speed*, on page 203

Challenges

- Start keeping a log of your estimates. For each, track how accurate you turned out to be. If your error was greater than 50%, try to find out where your estimate went wrong.

Exercises

Exercise 9 (possible answer on page 297)

You are asked "Which has a higher bandwidth: a 1Gbps net connection or a person walking between two computers with a full 1TB of storage device in their pocket?" What constraints will you put on your answer to ensure that the scope of your response is correct? (For example, you might say that the time taken to access the storage device is ignored.)

Exercise 10 (possible answer on page 298)

So, which has the higher bandwidth?

## CHAPTER 3

The Basic Tools

Every maker starts their journey with a basic set of good-quality tools. A woodworker might need rules, gauges, a couple of saws, some good planes, fine chisels, drills and braces, mallets, and clamps. These tools will be lovingly chosen, will be built to last, will perform specific jobs with little overlap with other tools, and, perhaps most importantly, will feel right in the budding woodworker's hands.

Then begins a process of learning and adaptation. Each tool will have its own personality and quirks, and will need its own special handling. Each must be sharpened in a unique way, or held just so. Over time, each will wear according to use, until the grip looks like a mold of the woodworker's hands and the cutting surface aligns perfectly with the angle at which the tool is held. At this point, the tools become conduits from the maker's brain to the finished product—they have become extensions of their hands. Over time, the woodworker will add new tools, such as biscuit cutters, laser-guided miter saws, dovetail jigs—all wonderful pieces of technology. But you can bet that they'll be happiest with one of those original tools in hand, feeling the plane sing as it slides through the wood.

Tools amplify your talent. The better your tools, and the better you know how to use them, the more productive you can be. Start with a basic set of generally applicable tools. As you gain experience, and as you come across special requirements, you'll add to this basic set. Like the maker, expect to add to your toolbox regularly. Always be on the lookout for better ways of doing things. If you come across a situation where you feel your current tools can't cut it, make a note to look for something different or more powerful that would have helped. Let need drive your acquisitions.

Many new programmers make the mistake of adopting a single power tool, such as a particular integrated development environment (IDE), and never leave its cozy interface. This really is a mistake. You need to be comfortable beyond the limits imposed by an IDE. The only way to do this is to keep the basic tool set sharp and ready to use.

In this chapter we'll talk about investing in your own basic toolbox. As with any good discussion on tools, we'll start (in *The Power of Plain Text*) by looking at your raw materials, the stuff you'll be shaping. From there we'll move to the workbench, or in our case the computer. How can you use your computer to get the most out of the tools you use? We'll discuss this in *Shell Games*. Now that we have material and a bench to work on, we'll turn to the tool you'll probably use more than any other, your editor. In *Power Editing*, we'll suggest ways of making you more efficient.

To ensure that we never lose any of our precious work, we should always use a *Version Control* system—even for personal things such as recipes or notes. And, since Murphy was really an optimist after all, you can't be a great programmer until you become highly skilled at *Debugging*.

You'll need some glue to bind much of the magic together. We discuss some possibilities in *Text Manipulation*.

Finally, the palest ink is still better than the best memory. Keep track of your thoughts and your history, as we describe in *Engineering Daybooks*.

Spend time learning to use these tools, and at some point you'll be surprised to discover your fingers moving over the keyboard, manipulating text without conscious thought. The tools will have become extensions of your hands.

 ## The Power of Plain Text

As Pragmatic Programmers, our base material isn't wood or iron, it's knowledge. We gather requirements as knowledge, and then express that knowledge in our designs, implementations, tests, and documents. And we believe that the best format for storing knowledge persistently is *plain text*. With plain text, we give ourselves the ability to manipulate knowledge, both manually and programmatically, using virtually every tool at our disposal.

The problem with most binary formats is that the context necessary to understand the data is separate from the data itself. You are artificially divorcing the data from its meaning. The data may as well be encrypted; it is absolutely meaningless without the application logic to parse it. With plain text, however, you can achieve a self-describing data stream that is independent of the application that created it.

What Is Plain Text?

Plain text is made up of printable characters in a form that conveys information. It can be as simple as a shopping list:

```
* milk
* lettuce
* coffee
```

or as complex as the source of this book (yes, it's in plain text, much to the chagrin of the publisher, who wanted us to use a word processor).

The information part is important. The following is not useful plain text:

```
hlj;uijn bfjxrrctvh jkni'pio6p7gu;vh bjxrdi5rgvhj
```

Neither is this:

```
Field19=467abe
```

The reader has no idea what the significance of 467abe may be. We like our plain text to be *understandable* to humans.

| Tip 25 | Keep Knowledge in Plain Text |

The Power of Text

Plain text doesn't mean that the text is unstructured; HTML, JSON, YAML, and so on are all plain text. So are the majority of the fundamental protocols on the net, such as HTTP, SMTP, IMAP, and so on. And that's for some good reasons:

- Insurance against obsolescence
- Leverage existing tools
- Easier testing

Insurance Against Obsolescence

Human-readable forms of data, and self-describing data, will outlive all other forms of data and the applications that created them. Period. As long as the data survives, you will have a chance to be able to use it—potentially long after the original application that wrote it is defunct.

You can parse such a file with only partial knowledge of its format; with most binary files, you must know all the details of the entire format in order to parse it successfully.

Consider a data file from some legacy system that you are given.[1] You know little about the original application; all that's important to you is that it maintained a list of clients' Social Security numbers, which you need to find and extract. Among the data, you see

```
<FIELD10>123-45-6789</FIELD10>
...
<FIELD10>567-89-0123</FIELD10>
...
<FIELD10>901-23-4567</FIELD10>
```

Recognizing the format of a Social Security number, you can quickly write a small program to extract that data—even if you have no information on anything else in the file.

But imagine if the file had been formatted this way instead:

```
AC27123456789B11P
...
XY43567890123QTYL
...
6T2190123456788AM
```

You may not have recognized the significance of the numbers quite as easily. This is the difference between *human readable* and *human understandable*.

While we're at it, FIELD10 doesn't help much either. Something like

```
<SOCIAL-SECURITY-NO>123-45-6789</SOCIAL-SECURITY-NO>
```

makes the exercise a no-brainer—and ensures that the data will outlive any project that created it.

Leverage

Virtually every tool in the computing universe, from version control systems to editors to command-line tools, can operate on plain text.

For instance, suppose you have a production deployment of a large application with a complex site-specific configuration file. If this file is in plain text, you could place it under a version control system (see Topic 19, *Version Control*, on page 84), so that you automatically keep a history of all changes. File comparison tools such as diff and fc allow you to see at a glance what changes

---

1. All software becomes legacy software as soon as it's written.

The Unix Philosophy

Unix is famous for being designed around the philosophy of small, sharp tools, each intended to do one thing well. This philosophy is enabled by using a common underlying format—the line-oriented, plain-text file. Databases used for system administration (users and passwords, networking configuration, and so on) are all kept as plain-text files. (Some systems also maintain a binary form of certain databases as a performance optimization. The plain-text version is kept as an interface to the binary version.)

When a system crashes, you may be faced with only a minimal environment to restore it (you may not be able to access graphics drivers, for instance). Situations such as this can really make you appreciate the simplicity of plain text.

Plain text is also easier to search. If you can't remember which configuration file manages your system backups, a quick `grep -r backup /etc` should tell you.

have been made, while `sum` allows you to generate a checksum to monitor the file for accidental (or malicious) modification.

Easier Testing

If you use plain text to create synthetic data to drive system tests, then it is a simple matter to add, update, or modify the test data *without having to create any special tools to do so.* Similarly, plain-text output from regression tests can be trivially analyzed with shell commands or a simple script.

Lowest Common Denominator

Even in the future of blockchain-based intelligent agents that travel the wild and dangerous internet autonomously, negotiating data interchange among themselves, the ubiquitous text file will still be there. In fact, in heterogeneous environments the advantages of plain text can outweigh all of the drawbacks. You need to ensure that all parties can communicate using a common standard. Plain text is that standard.

Related Sections Include

- Topic 17, *Shell Games*, on page 78
- Topic 21, *Text Manipulation*, on page 97
- Topic 32, *Configuration*, on page 166

Challenges

- Design a small address book database (name, phone number, and so on) using a straightforward binary representation in your language of choice. Do this before reading the rest of this challenge.

    – Translate that format into a plain-text format using XML or JSON.

    – For each version, add a new, variable-length field called *directions* in which you might enter directions to each person's house.

    What issues come up regarding versioning and extensibility? Which form was easier to modify? What about converting existing data?

Shell Games

Every woodworker needs a good, solid, reliable workbench, somewhere to hold work pieces at a convenient height while they're being shaped. The workbench becomes the center of the woodshop, the maker returning to it time and time again as a piece takes shape.

For a programmer manipulating files of text, that workbench is the command shell. From the shell prompt, you can invoke your full repertoire of tools, using pipes to combine them in ways never dreamt of by their original developers. From the shell, you can launch applications, debuggers, browsers, editors, and utilities. You can search for files, query the status of the system, and filter output. And by programming the shell, you can build complex macro commands for activities you perform often.

For programmers raised on GUI interfaces and integrated development environments (IDEs), this might seem an extreme position. After all, can't you do everything equally well by pointing and clicking?

The simple answer is "no." GUI interfaces are wonderful, and they can be faster and more convenient for some simple operations. Moving files, reading and writing email, and building and deploying your project are all things that you might want to do in a graphical environment. But if you do all your work using GUIs, you are missing out on the full capabilities of your environment. You won't be able to automate common tasks, or use the full power of the tools available to you. And you won't be able to combine your tools to create customized *macro tools*. A benefit of GUIs is WYSIWYG—what you see is what you get. The disadvantage is WYSIAYG—what you see is *all* you get.

GUI environments are normally limited to the capabilities that their designers intended. If you need to go beyond the model the designer provided, you are usually out of luck—and more often than not, you *do* need to go beyond the model. Pragmatic Programmers don't just cut code, or develop object models, or write documentation, or automate the build process—we do *all* of these things. The scope of any one tool is usually limited to the tasks that the tool is expected to perform. For instance, suppose you need to integrate a code preprocessor (to implement design-by-contract, or multi-processing pragmas, or some such) into your IDE. Unless the designer of the IDE explicitly provided hooks for this capability, you can't do it.

> ### Tip 26   Use the Power of Command Shells

Gain familiarity with the shell, and you'll find your productivity soaring. Need to create a list of all the unique package names explicitly imported by your Java code? The following stores it in a file called "list":

sh/packages.sh
```
grep '^import ' *.java |
  sed -e's/.*import  *//' -e's/;.*$//' |
  sort -u >list
```

If you haven't spent much time exploring the capabilities of the command shell on the systems you use, this might appear daunting. However, invest some energy in becoming familiar with your shell and things will soon start falling into place. Play around with your command shell, and you'll be surprised at how much more productive it makes you.

A Shell of Your Own

In the same way that a woodworker will customize their workspace, a developer should customize their shell. This typically also involves changing the configuration of the terminal program you use.

Common changes include:

- *Setting color themes.* Many, many hours can be spent trying out *every single* theme that's available online for your particular shell.

- *Configuring a prompt.* The prompt that tells you the shell is ready for you to type a command can be configured to display just about any information you might want (and a bunch of stuff you'd never want). Personal preferences are everything here: we tend to like simple prompts, with a shortened current directory name and version control status along with the time.

- *Aliases and shell functions.* Simplify your workflow by turning commands you use a lot into simple aliases. Maybe you regularly update your Linux box, but can never remember whether you update and upgrade, or upgrade and update. Create an alias:

```
alias apt-up='sudo apt-get update && sudo apt-get upgrade'
```

Maybe you've accidentally deleted files with the rm command just one time too often. Write an alias so that it will always prompt in future:

```
alias rm ='rm -iv'
```

- *Command completion.* Most shells will complete the names of commands and files: type the first few characters, hit tab, and it'll fill in what it can. But you can take this a lot further, configuring the shell to recognize the command you're entering and offer context-specific completions. Some even customize the completion depending on the current directory.

You'll spend a lot of time living in one of these shells. Be like a hermit crab and make it your own home.

Related Sections Include

- Topic 13, *Prototypes and Post-it Notes*, on page 56
- Topic 16, *The Power of Plain Text*, on page 74
- Topic 21, *Text Manipulation*, on page 97
- Topic 30, *Transforming Programming*, on page 147
- Topic 51, *Pragmatic Starter Kit*, on page 273

Challenges

- Are there things that you're currently doing manually in a GUI? Do you ever pass instructions to colleagues that involve a number of individual "click this button," "select this item" steps? Could these be automated?

- Whenever you move to a new environment, make a point of finding out what shells are available. See if you can bring your current shell with you.

- Investigate alternatives to your current shell. If you come across a problem your shell can't address, see if an alternative shell would cope better.

Power Editing

We've talked before about tools being an extension of your hand. Well, this applies to editors more than to any other software tool. You need to be able to manipulate text as effortlessly as possible, because text is the basic raw material of programming.

In the first edition of this book we recommended using a single editor for everything: code, documentation, memos, system administration, and so on. We've softened that position a little. We're happy for you to use as many editors as you want. We'd just like you to be working toward fluency in each.

> **Tip 27** Achieve Editor Fluency

Why is this a big deal? Are we saying you'll save lots of time? Actually yes: over the course of a year, you might actually gain an additional week if you make your editing just 4% more efficient and you edit for 20 hours a week.

But that's not the real benefit. No, the major gain is that by becoming fluent, you no longer have to think about the mechanics of editing. The distance between thinking something and having it appear in an editor buffer drop way down. Your thoughts will flow, and your programming will benefit. (If you've ever taught someone to drive, then you'll understand the difference between someone who has to think about every action they take and a more experienced driver who controls the car instinctively.)

What Does "Fluent" Mean?

What counts as being fluent? Here's the challenge list:

- When editing text, move and make selections by character, word, line, and paragraph.
- When editing code, move by various syntactic units (matching delimiters, functions, modules, ...).
- Reindent code following changes.
- Comment and uncomment blocks of code with a single command.
- Undo and redo changes.
- Split the editor window into multiple panels, and navigate between them.

- Navigate to a particular line number.

- Sort selected lines.

- Search for both strings and regular expressions, and repeat previous searches.

- Temporarily create multiple cursors based on a selection or on a pattern match, and edit the text at each in parallel.

- Display compilation errors in the current project.

- Run the current project's tests.

Can you do all this without using a mouse/trackpad?

You might say that your current editor can't do some of these things. Maybe it's time to switch?

Moving Toward Fluency

We doubt there are more than a handful of people who know *all* the commands in any particular powerful editor. We don't expect you to, either. Instead, we suggest a more pragmatic approach: learn the commands that make your life easier.

The recipe for this is fairly simple.

First, look at yourself while you're editing. Every time you find yourself doing something repetitive, get into the habit of thinking "there must be a better way." Then find it.

Once you've discovered a new, useful feature, you now need to get it installed into your muscle memory, so you can use it without thinking. The only way we know to do that is through repetition. Consciously look for opportunities to use your new superpower, ideally many times a day. After a week or so, you'll find you use it without thinking.

Growing Your Editor

Most of the powerful code editors are built around a basic core that is then augmented through extensions. Many are supplied with the editor, and others can be added later.

When you bump into some apparent limitation of the editor you're using, search around for an extension that will do the job. The chances are that you are not alone in needing that capability, and if you're lucky someone else will have published their solution.

Take this a step further. Dig into your editor's extension language. Work out how to use it to automate some of the repetitive things you do. Often you'll just need a line or two of code.

Sometimes you might take it further still, and you'll find yourself writing a full-blown extension. If so, publish it: if you had a need for it, other people will, too.

Related Sections Include

- Topic 7, *Communicate!*, on page 19

Challenges

- No more autorepeat.

  Everyone does it: you need to delete the last word you typed, so you press down on backspace and wait for autorepeat to kick in. In fact, we bet that your brain has done this so much that you can judge pretty much exactly when to release the key.

  So turn off autorepeat, and instead learn the key sequences to move, select, and delete by characters, words, lines, and blocks.

- This one is going to hurt.

  Lose the mouse/trackpad. For one whole week, edit using just the keyboard. You'll discover a bunch of stuff that you can't do without pointing and clicking, so now's the time to learn. Keep notes (we recommend going old-school and using pencil and paper) of the key sequences you learn.

  You'll take a productivity hit for a few days. But, as you learn to do stuff without moving your hands away from the home position, you'll find that your editing becomes faster and more fluent than it ever was in the past.

- Look for integrations. While writing this chapter, Dave wondered if he could preview the final layout (a PDF file) in an editor buffer. One download later, the layout is sitting alongside the original text, all in the editor. Keep a list of things you'd like to bring into your editor, then look for them.

- Somewhat more ambitiously, if you can't find a plugin or extension that does what you want, write one. Andy is fond of making custom, local file-based Wiki plugins for his favorite editors. If you can't find it, build it!

Version Control

Progress, far from consisting in change, depends on retentiveness.
Those who cannot remember the past are condemned to repeat it.

> ➤ George Santayana, *Life of Reason*

One of the important things we look for in a user interface is the undo key—a single button that forgives us our mistakes. It's even better if the environment supports multiple levels of undo and redo, so you can go back and recover from something that happened a couple of minutes ago.

But what if the mistake happened last week, and you've turned your computer on and off ten times since then? Well, that's one of the many benefits of using a version control system (VCS): it's a giant undo key—a project-wide time machine that can return you to those halcyon days of last week, when the code actually compiled and ran.

For many folks, that's the limit of their VCS usage. Those folks are missing out on a whole bigger world of collaboration, deployment pipelines, issue tracking, and general team interaction.

So let's take a look at VCS, first as a repository of changes, and then as a central meeting place for your team and their code.

> ### Shared Directories Are *NOT* Version Control
>
> We still come across the occasional team who share their project source files across a network: either internally or using some kind of cloud storage.
>
> This is not viable.
>
> Teams that do this are constantly messing up each other's work, losing changes, breaking builds, and getting into fist fights in the car park. It's like writing concurrent code with shared data and no synchronization mechanism. Use version control.
>
> But there's more! Some folks *do* use version control, and keep their main repository on a network or cloud drive. They reason that this is the best of both worlds: their files are accessible anywhere and (in the case of cloud storage) it's backed up off-site.
>
> Turns out that this is even worse, and you risk losing everything. The version control software uses a set of interacting files and directories. If two instances simultaneously make changes, the overall state can become corrupted, and there's no telling how much damage will be done. And no one likes seeing developers cry.

It Starts at the Source

Version control systems keep track of every change you make in your source code and documentation. With a properly configured source code control system, *you can always go back to a previous version of your software.*

But a version control system does far more than undo mistakes. A good VCS will let you track changes, answering questions such as: Who made changes in this line of code? What's the difference between the current version and last week's? How many lines of code did we change in this release? Which files get changed most often? This kind of information is invaluable for bug-tracking, audit, performance, and quality purposes.

A VCS will also let you identify releases of your software. Once identified, you will always be able to go back and regenerate the release, independent of changes that may have occurred later.

Version control systems may keep the files they maintain in a central repository—a great candidate for archiving.

Finally, version control systems allow two or more users to be working concurrently on the same set of files, even making concurrent changes in the same file. The system then manages the merging of these changes when the files are sent back to the repository. Although seemingly risky, such systems work well in practice on projects of all sizes.

> Tip 28   **Always Use Version Control**

Always. Even if you are a single-person team on a one-week project. Even if it's a "throw-away" prototype. Even if the stuff you're working on isn't source code. Make sure that *everything* is under version control: documentation, phone number lists, memos to vendors, makefiles, build and release procedures, that little shell script that tidies up log files—everything. We routinely use version control on just about everything we type (including the text of this book). Even if we're not working on a project, our day-to-day work is secured in a repository.

Branching Out

Version control systems don't just keep a single history of your project. One of their most powerful and useful features is the way they let you isolate islands of development into things called *branches*. You can create a branch at any point in your project's history, and any work you do in that branch will be isolated from all other branches. At some time in the future you can *merge* the branch you're working on back into another branch, so the target branch now contains the changes you made in your branch. Multiple people can even be working on a branch: in a way, branches are like little clone projects.

One benefit of branches is the isolation they give you. If you develop feature A in one branch, and a teammate works on feature B in another, you're not going to interfere with each other.

A second benefit, which may be surprising, is that branches are often at the heart of a team's project workflow.

And this is where things get a little confusing. Version control branches and test organization have something in common: they both have thousands of people out there telling you how you should do it. And that advice is largely meaningless, because what they're really saying is "this is what worked for me."

So use version control in your project, and if you bump into workflow issues, search for possible solutions. And remember to review and adjust what you're doing as you gain experience.

A Thought Experiment

Spill an entire cup of tea (English breakfast, with a little milk) onto your laptop keyboard. Take the machine to the smart-person bar, and have them tut and frown. Buy a new computer. Take it home.

How long would it take to get that machine back to the same state it was in (with all the SSH keys, editor configuration, shell setup, installed applications, and so on) at the point where you first lifted that fateful cup? This was an issue one of us faced recently.

Just about everything that defined the configuration and usage of the original machine was stored in version control, including:

- All the user preferences and dotfiles
- The editor configuration
- The list of software installed using Homebrew
- The Ansible script used to configure apps
- All current projects

The machine was restored by the end of the afternoon.

Version Control as a Project Hub

Although version control is incredibly useful on personal projects, it really comes into its own when working with a team. And much of this value comes from how you host your repository.

Now, many version control systems don't need any hosting. They are completely decentralized, with each developer cooperating on a peer-to-peer basis. But even with these systems, it's worth looking into having a central repository, because once you do, you can take advantage of a ton of integrations to make the project flow easier.

Many of the repository systems are open source, so you can install and run them in your company. But that's not really your line of business, so we'd recommend most people host with a third party. Look for features such as:

- Good security and access control
- Intuitive UI
- The ability to do everything from the command line, too (because you may need to automate it)
- Automated builds and tests
- Good support for branch merging (sometimes called pull requests)
- Issue management (ideally integrated into commits and merges, so you can keep metrics)
- Good reporting (a Kanban board-like display of pending issues and tasks can be very useful)
- Good team communications: emails or other notifications on changes, a wiki, and so on

Many teams have their VCS configured so that a push to a particular branch will automatically build the system, run the tests, and if successful deploy the new code into production.

Sound scary? Not when you realize you're using version control. You can always roll it back.

Related Sections Include

- Topic 11, *Reversibility*, on page 47
- Topic 49, *Pragmatic Teams*, on page 264
- Topic 51, *Pragmatic Starter Kit*, on page 273

Challenges

- Knowing you can roll back to any previous state using the VCS is one thing, but can you actually do it? Do you know the commands to do it properly? Learn them now, not when disaster strikes and you're under pressure.

- Spend some time thinking about recovering your own laptop environment in case of a disaster. What would you need to recover? Many of the things you need are just text files. If they're not in a VCS (hosted off your laptop), find a way to add them. Then think about the other stuff: installed applications, system configuration, and so on. How can you express all that stuff in text files so it, too, can be saved?

  An interesting experiment, once you've made some progress, is to find an old computer you no longer use and see if your new system can be used to set it up.

- Consciously explore the features of your current VCS and hosting provider that you're not using. If your team isn't using feature branches, experiment with introducing them. The same with pull/merge requests. Continuous integration. Build pipelines. Even continuous deployment. Look into the team communication tools, too: wikis, Kanban boards, and the like.

  You don't have to use any of it. But you do need to know what it does so you can make that decision.

- Use version control for nonproject things, too.

 # Debugging

It is a painful thing
To look at your own trouble and know
That you yourself and no one else has made it

> ➤ Sophocles, Ajax

The word *bug* has been used to describe an "object of terror" ever since the fourteenth century. Rear Admiral Dr. Grace Hopper, the inventor of COBOL, is credited with observing the first *computer bug*—literally, a moth caught in a relay in an early computer system. When asked to explain why the machine wasn't behaving as intended, a technician reported that there was "a bug in the system," and dutifully taped it—wings and all—into the log book.

Regrettably, we still have bugs in the system, albeit not the flying kind. But the fourteenth century meaning—a bogeyman—is perhaps even more applicable now than it was then. Software defects manifest themselves in a variety of ways, from misunderstood requirements to coding errors. Unfortunately, modern computer systems are still limited to doing what you *tell* them to do, not necessarily what you *want* them to do.

No one writes perfect software, so it's a given that debugging will take up a major portion of your day. Let's look at some of the issues involved in debugging and some general strategies for finding elusive bugs.

Psychology of Debugging

Debugging is a sensitive, emotional subject for many developers. Instead of attacking it as a puzzle to be solved, you may encounter denial, finger pointing, lame excuses, or just plain apathy.

Embrace the fact that debugging is just *problem solving*, and attack it as such.

Having found someone else's bug, you can spend time and energy laying blame on the filthy culprit who created it. In some workplaces this is part of the culture, and may be cathartic. However, in the technical arena, you want to concentrate on fixing the *problem*, not the blame.

> **Tip 29**   Fix the Problem, Not the Blame

It doesn't really matter whether the bug is your fault or someone else's. It is still your problem.

A Debugging Mindset

The easiest person to deceive is one's self.
> ➤ *Edward Bulwer-Lytton, The Disowned*

Before you start debugging, it's important to adopt the right mindset. You need to turn off many of the defenses you use each day to protect your ego, tune out any project pressures you may be under, and get yourself comfortable. Above all, remember the first rule of debugging:

> **Tip 30**   Don't Panic

It's easy to get into a panic, especially if you are facing a deadline, or have a nervous boss or client breathing down your neck while you are trying to find the cause of the bug. But it is very important to step back a pace, and actually *think* about what could be causing the symptoms that you believe indicate a bug.

If your first reaction on witnessing a bug or seeing a bug report is "that's impossible," you are plainly wrong. Don't waste a single neuron on the train of thought that begins "but that can't happen" because quite clearly it *can*, and has.

Beware of myopia when debugging. Resist the urge to fix just the symptoms you see: it is more likely that the actual fault may be several steps removed from what you are observing, and may involve a number of other related things. Always try to discover the root cause of a problem, not just this particular appearance of it.

Where to Start

Before you *start* to look at the bug, make sure that you are working on code that built cleanly—without warnings. We routinely set compiler warning levels as high as possible. It doesn't make sense to waste time trying to find a problem that the computer could find for you! We need to concentrate on the harder problems at hand.

When trying to solve any problem, you need to gather all the relevant data. Unfortunately, bug reporting isn't an exact science. It's easy to be misled by coincidences, and you can't afford to waste time debugging coincidences. You first need to be accurate in your observations.

Accuracy in bug reports is further diminished when they come through a third party—you may actually need to *watch* the user who reported the bug in action to get a sufficient level of detail.

Andy once worked on a large graphics application. Nearing release, the testers reported that the application crashed every time they painted a stroke with a particular brush. The programmer responsible argued that there was nothing wrong with it; he had tried painting with it, and it worked just fine. This dialog went back and forth for several days, with tempers rapidly rising.

Finally, we got them together in the same room. The tester selected the brush tool and painted a stroke from the upper right corner to the lower left corner. The application exploded. "Oh," said the programmer, in a small voice, who then sheepishly admitted that he had made test strokes only from the lower left to the upper right, which did not expose the bug.

There are two points to this story:

- You may need to interview the user who reported the bug in order to gather more data than you were initially given.

- Artificial tests (such as the programmer's single brush stroke from bottom to top) don't exercise enough of an application. You must brutally test both boundary conditions and realistic end-user usage patterns. You need to do this systematically (see *Ruthless and Continuous Testing*, on page 275).

Debugging Strategies

Once *you* think you know what is going on, it's time to find out what the *program* thinks is going on.

Reproducing Bugs

No, our bugs aren't really multiplying (although some of them are probably old enough to do it legally). We're talking about a different kind of reproduction.

The best way to start fixing a bug is to make it reproducible. After all, if you can't reproduce it, how will you know if it is ever fixed?

But we want more than a bug that can be reproduced by following some long series of steps; we want a bug that can be reproduced with a *single command*. It's a lot harder to fix a bug if you have to go through 15 steps to get to the point where the bug shows up.

So here's the most important rule of debugging:

> Tip 31   **Failing Test Before Fixing Code**

Sometimes by forcing yourself to isolate the circumstances that display the bug, you'll even gain an insight on how to fix it. The act of writing the test informs the solution.

Coder in a Strange Land

All this talk about isolating the bug is fine, when faced with 50,000 lines of code and a ticking clock, what's a poor coder to do?

First, look at the problem. Is it a crash? It's always surprising when we teach courses that involve programming how many developers see an exception pop up in red and immediately tab across to the code.

| Tip 32 | Read the Damn Error Message |

'nuf said.

Bad Results

What if it's not a crash? What if it's just a bad result?

Get in there with a debugger and use your failing test to trigger the problem.

Before anything else, make sure that you're also seeing the incorrect value in the debugger. We've both wasted hours trying to track down a bug only to discover that this particular run of the code worked fine.

Sometimes the problem is obvious: interest_rate is 4.5 and should be 0.045. More often you have to look deeper to find out why the value is wrong in the first place. Make sure you know how to move up and down the call stack and examine the local stack environment.

We find it often helps to keep pen and paper nearby so we can jot down notes. In particular we often come across a clue and chase it down, only to find it didn't pan out. If we didn't jot down where we were when we started the chase, we could lose a lot of time getting back there.

Sometimes you're looking at a stack trace that seems to scroll on forever. In this case, there's often a quicker way to find the problem than examining each and every stack frame: use a *binary chop*. But before we discuss that, let's look at two other common bug scenarios.

Sensitivity to Input Values

You've been there. Your program works fine with all the test data, and survives its first week in production with honor. Then it suddenly crashes when fed a particular dataset.

You can try looking at the place it crashes and work backwards. But sometimes it's easier to start with the data. Get a copy of the dataset and feed it through a locally running copy of the app, making sure it still crashes. Then binary chop the data until you isolate exactly which input values are leading to the crash.

Regressions Across Releases

You're on a good team, and you release your software into production. At some point a bug pops up in code that worked OK a week ago. Wouldn't it be nice if you could identify the specific change that introduced it? Guess what? Binary chop time.

The Binary Chop

Every CS undergraduate has been forced to code a binary chop (sometimes called a binary search). The idea is simple. You're looking for a particular value in a sorted array. You could just look at each value in turn, but you'd end up looking at roughly half the entries on average until you either found the value you wanted, or you found a value greater than it, which would mean the value's not in the array.

But it's faster to use a *divide and conquer* approach. Choose a value in the middle of the array. If it's the one you're looking for, stop. Otherwise you can chop the array in two. If the value you find is greater than the target then you know it must be in the first half of the array, otherwise it's in the second half. Repeat the procedure in the appropriate subarray, and in no time you'll have a result. (As we'll see when we talk about *Big-O Notation*, on page 204, a linear search is $O(n)$, and a binary chop is $O(\log n)$).

So, the binary chop is way, way faster on any decent sized problem. Let's see how to apply it to debugging.

When you're facing a massive stacktrace and you're trying to find out exactly which function mangled the value in error, you do a chop by choosing a stack frame somewhere in the middle and seeing if the error is manifest there. If it is, then you know to focus on the frames before, otherwise the problem is in the frames after. Chop again. Even if you have 64 frames in the stacktrace, this approach will give you an answer after at most six attempts.

If you find bugs that appear on certain datasets, you might be able to do the same thing. Split the dataset into two, and see if the problem occurs if you feed one or the other through the app. Keep dividing the data until you get a minimum set of values that exhibit the problem.

If your team has introduced a bug during a set of releases, you can use the same type of technique. Create a test that causes the current release to fail. Then choose a half-way release between now and the last known working version. Run the test again, and decide how to narrow your search. Being able to do this is just one of the many benefits of having good version control in your projects. Indeed, many version control systems will take this further and will automate the process, picking releases for you depending on the result of the test.

Logging and/or Tracing

Debuggers generally focus on the state of the program *now*. Sometimes you need more—you need to watch the state of a program or a data structure over time. Seeing a stack trace can only tell you how you got here directly. It typically can't tell you what you were doing prior to this call chain, especially in event-based systems.[2]

Tracing statements are those little diagnostic messages you print to the screen or to a file that say things such as "got here" and "value of x = 2." It's a primitive technique compared with IDE-style debuggers, but it is peculiarly effective at diagnosing several classes of errors that debuggers can't. Tracing is invaluable in any system where time itself is a factor: concurrent processes, real-time systems, and event-based applications.

You can use tracing statements to drill down into the code. That is, you can add tracing statements as you descend the call tree.

Trace messages should be in a regular, consistent format as you may want to parse them automatically. For instance, if you needed to track down a resource leak (such as unbalanced file opens/closes), you could trace each open and each close in a log file. By processing the log file with text processing tools or shell commands, you can easily identify where the offending open was occurring.

Rubber Ducking

A very simple but particularly useful technique for finding the cause of a problem is simply to explain it to someone else. The other person should look over your shoulder at the screen, and nod his or her head constantly (like a rubber duck bobbing up and down in a bathtub). They do not need to say a word; the simple act of explaining, step by step, what the code is supposed to do often causes the problem to leap off the screen and announce itself.[3]

It sounds simple, but in explaining the problem to another person you must explicitly state things that you may take for granted when going through the

---

2. Although the Elm language does have a time-traveling debugger.
3. Why "rubber ducking"? While an undergraduate at Imperial College in London, Dave did a lot of work with a research assistant named Greg Pugh, one of the best developers Dave has known. For several months Greg carried around a small yellow rubber duck, which he'd place on his terminal while coding. It was a while before Dave had the courage to ask....

code yourself. By having to verbalize some of these assumptions, you may suddenly gain new insight into the problem. And if you don't have a person, a rubber duck, or teddy bear, or potted plant will do.[4]

Process of Elimination

In most projects, the code you are debugging may be a mixture of application code written by you and others on your project team, third-party products (database, connectivity, web framework, specialized communications or algorithms, and so on) and the platform environment (operating system, system libraries, and compilers).

It is possible that a bug exists in the OS, the compiler, or a third-party product—but this should not be your first thought. It is much more likely that the bug exists in the application code under development. It is generally more profitable to assume that the application code is incorrectly calling into a library than to assume that the library itself is broken. Even if the problem *does* lie with a third party, you'll still have to eliminate your code before submitting the bug report.

We worked on a project where a senior engineer was convinced that the select system call was broken on a Unix system. No amount of persuasion or logic could change his mind (the fact that every other networking application on the box worked fine was irrelevant). He spent weeks writing workarounds, which, for some odd reason, didn't seem to fix the problem. When finally forced to sit down and read the documentation on select, he discovered the problem and corrected it in a matter of minutes. We now use the phrase "select is broken" as a gentle reminder whenever one of us starts blaming the system for a fault that is likely to be our own.

> Tip 33   "select" Isn't Broken

Remember, if you see hoof prints, think horses—not zebras. The OS is probably not broken. And select is probably just fine.

If you "changed only one thing" and the system stopped working, that one thing was likely to be responsible, directly or indirectly, no matter how far-fetched it seems. Sometimes the thing that changed is outside of your control: new versions of the OS, compiler, database, or other third-party software can wreak havoc with previously correct code. New bugs might show up. Bugs

---

4. Earlier versions of the book talked about talking to your *pot plant*. It was a typo. Honest.

for which you had a workaround get fixed, breaking the workaround. APIs change, functionality changes; in short, it's a whole new ball game, and you must retest the system under these new conditions. So keep a close eye on the schedule when considering an upgrade; you may want to wait until *after* the next release.

The Element of Surprise

When you find yourself surprised by a bug (perhaps even muttering "that's impossible" under your breath where we can't hear you), you must reevaluate truths you hold dear. In that discount calculation algorithm—the one you knew was bulletproof and couldn't possibly be the cause of this bug—did you test *all* the boundary conditions? That other piece of code you've been using for years—it couldn't possibly still have a bug in it. Could it?

Of course it can. The amount of surprise you feel when something goes wrong is proportional to the amount of trust and faith you have in the code being run. That's why, when faced with a "surprising" failure, you must accept that one or more of your assumptions is wrong. Don't gloss over a routine or piece of code involved in the bug because you "know" it works. Prove it. Prove it in *this* context, with *this* data, with *these* boundary conditions.

Tip 34	Don't Assume It—Prove It

When you come across a surprise bug, beyond merely fixing it, you need to determine why this failure wasn't caught earlier. Consider whether you need to amend the unit or other tests so that they would have caught it.

Also, if the bug is the result of bad data that was propagated through a couple of levels before causing the explosion, see if better parameter checking in those routines would have isolated it earlier (see the discussions on crashing early and assertions on page 113 and on page 115, respectively).

While you're at it, are there any other places in the code that may be susceptible to this same bug? Now is the time to find and fix them. Make sure that *whatever* happened, you'll know if it happens again.

If it took a long time to fix this bug, ask yourself why. Is there anything you can do to make fixing this bug easier the next time around? Perhaps you could build in better testing hooks, or write a log file analyzer.

Finally, if the bug is the result of someone's wrong assumption, discuss the problem with the whole team: if one person misunderstands, then it's possible many people do.

Do all this, and hopefully you won't be surprised next time.

Debugging Checklist

- Is the problem being reported a direct result of the underlying bug, or merely a symptom?

- Is the bug *really* in the framework you're using? Is it in the OS? Or is it in your code?

- If you explained this problem in detail to a coworker, what would you say?

- If the suspect code passes its unit tests, are the tests complete enough? What happens if you run the tests with *this* data?

- Do the conditions that caused this bug exist anywhere else in the system? Are there other bugs still in the larval stage, just waiting to hatch?

Related Sections Include

- Topic 24, *Dead Programs Tell No Lies*, on page 112

Challenges

- Debugging is challenge enough.

---

21 Text Manipulation

Pragmatic Programmers manipulate text the same way woodworkers shape wood. In previous sections we discussed some specific tools—shells, editors, debuggers—that we use. These are similar to a woodworker's chisels, saws, and planes—tools specialized to do one or two jobs well. However, every now and then we need to perform some transformation not readily handled by the basic tool set. We need a general-purpose text manipulation tool.

Text manipulation languages are to programming what routers[5] are to wood-working. They are noisy, messy, and somewhat brute force. Make mistakes

---

5. Here *router* means the tool that spins cutting blades very, very fast, not a device for interconnecting networks.

with them, and entire pieces can be ruined. Some people swear they have no place in the toolbox. But in the right hands, both routers and text manipulation languages can be incredibly powerful and versatile. You can quickly trim something into shape, make joints, and carve. Used properly, these tools have surprising finesse and subtlety. But they take time to master.

Fortunately, there are a number of great text manipulation languages. Unix developers (and we include macOS users here) often like to use the power of their command shells, augmented with tools such as awk and sed. People who prefer a more structured tool may prefer languages such as Python or Ruby.

These languages are important enabling technologies. Using them, you can quickly hack up utilities and prototype ideas—jobs that might take five or ten times as long using conventional languages. And that multiplying factor is crucially important to the kind of experimenting that we do. Spending 30 minutes trying out a crazy idea is a whole lot better than spending five hours. Spending a day automating important components of a project is acceptable; spending a week might not be. In their book *The Practice of Programming* *[KP99]*, Kernighan and Pike built the same program in five different languages. The Perl version was the shortest (17 lines, compared with C's 150). With Perl you can manipulate text, interact with programs, talk over networks, drive web pages, perform arbitrary precision arithmetic, and write programs that look like Snoopy swearing.

Tip 35	Learn a Text Manipulation Language

To show the wide-ranging applicability of text manipulation languages, here's a sample of some stuff we've done with Ruby and Python just related to the creation of this book:

Building the Book
   The build system for the Pragmatic Bookshelf is written in Ruby. Authors, editors, layout people, and support folks use Rake tasks to coordinate the building of PDFs and ebooks.

Code inclusion and highlighting
   We think it is important that any code presented in a book should have been tested first. Most of the code in this book has been. However, using the DRY principle (see Topic 9, *DRY—The Evils of Duplication*, on page 30) we didn't want to copy and paste lines of code from the tested programs into the book. That would mean we'd be duplicating code, virtually guaranteeing that we'd forget to update an example when the corresponding

program was changed. For some examples, we also didn't want to bore you with all the framework code needed to make our example compile and run. We turned to Ruby. A relatively simple script is invoked when we format the book—it extracts a named segment of a source file, does syntax highlighting, and converts the result into the typesetting language we use.

Website update

We have a simple script that does a partial book build, extracts the table of contents, then uploads it to the book's page on our website. We also have a script that extracts sections of a book and uploads them as samples.

Including equations

There's a Python script that converts LaTeX math markup into nicely formatted text.

Index generation

Most indexes are created as separate documents (which makes maintaining them difficult if a document changes). Ours are marked up in the text itself, and a Ruby script collates and formats the entries.

And so on. In a very real way, the Pragmatic Bookshelf is built around text manipulation. And if you follow our advice to keep things in plain text, then using these languages to manipulate that text will bring a whole host of benefits.

Related Sections Include

- Topic 16, *The Power of Plain Text*, on page 74
- Topic 17, *Shell Games*, on page 78

Exercises

Exercise 11

You're rewriting an application that used to use YAML as a configuration language. Your company has now standardized on JSON, so you have a bunch of .yaml files that need to be turned into .json. Write a script that takes a directory and converts each .yaml file into a corresponding .json file (so database.yaml becomes database.json, and the contents are valid JSON).

Exercise 12

Your team initially chose to use camelCase names for variables, but then changed their collective mind and switched to snake_case. Write a script that scans all the source files for camelCase names and reports on them.

Exercise 13

Following on from the previous exercise, add the ability to change those variable names automatically in one or more files. Remember to keep a backup of the originals in case something goes horribly, horribly wrong.

 # Engineering Daybooks

Dave once worked for a small computer manufacturer, which meant working alongside electronic and sometimes mechanical engineers.

Many of them walked around with a paper notebook, normally with a pen stuffed down the spine. Every now and then when we were talking, they'd pop the notebook open and scribble something.

Eventually Dave asked the obvious question. It turned out that they'd been trained to keep an engineering *daybook*, a kind of journal in which they recorded what they did, things they'd learned, sketches of ideas, readings from meters: basically anything to do with their work. When the notebook became full, they'd write the date range on the spine, then stick it on the shelf next to previous daybooks. There may have been a gentle competition going on for whose set of books took the most shelf space.

We use daybooks to take notes in meetings, to jot down what we're working on, to note variable values when debugging, to leave reminders where we put things, to record wild ideas, and sometimes just to doodle.[6]

The daybook has three main benefits:

- It is more reliable than memory. People might ask "What was the name of that company you called last week about the power supply problem?" and you can flip back a page or so and give them the name and number.

---

6. There is some evidence that doodling helps focus and improves cognitive skills, for example, see *What does doodling do?* [And10].

- It gives you a place to store ideas that aren't immediately relevant to the task at hand. That way you can continue to concentrate on what you are doing, knowing that the great idea won't be forgotten.

- It acts as a kind of rubber duck (described on page 94). When you stop to write something down, your brain may switch gears, almost as if talking to someone—a great chance to reflect. You may start to make a note and then suddenly realize that what you'd just done, the topic of the note, is just plain wrong.

There's an added benefit, too. Every now and then you can look back at what you were doing oh-so-many-years-ago and think about the people, the projects, and the awful clothes and hairstyles.

So, try keeping an engineering daybook. Use paper, not a file or a wiki: there's something special about the act of writing compared to typing. Give it a month, and see if you're getting any benefits.

If nothing else, it'll make writing your memoir easier when you're rich and famous.

Related Sections Include

- Topic 6, *Your Knowledge Portfolio*, on page 13
- Topic 37, *Listen to Your Lizard Brain*, on page 192

## CHAPTER 4

Pragmatic Paranoia

| Tip 36 | You Can't Write Perfect Software |

Did that hurt? It shouldn't. Accept it as an axiom of life. Embrace it. Celebrate it. Because perfect software doesn't exist. No one in the brief history of computing has ever written a piece of perfect software. It's unlikely that you'll be the first. And unless you accept this as a fact, you'll end up wasting time and energy chasing an impossible dream.

So, given this depressing reality, how does a Pragmatic Programmer turn it into an advantage? That's the topic of this chapter.

Everyone knows that they personally are the only good driver on Earth. The rest of the world is out there to get them, blowing through stop signs, weaving between lanes, not indicating turns, texting on the phone, and just generally not living up to our standards. So we drive defensively. We look out for trouble before it happens, anticipate the unexpected, and never put ourselves into a position from which we can't extricate ourselves.

The analogy with coding is pretty obvious. We are constantly interfacing with other people's code—code that might not live up to our high standards—and dealing with inputs that may or may not be valid. So we are taught to code defensively. If there's any doubt, we validate all information we're given. We use assertions to detect bad data, and distrust data from potential attackers or trolls. We check for consistency, put constraints on database columns, and generally feel pretty good about ourselves.

But Pragmatic Programmers take this a step further. *They don't trust themselves, either.* Knowing that no one writes perfect code, including themselves, Pragmatic Programmers build in defenses against their own mistakes. We describe the first defensive measure in *Design by Contract*: clients and suppliers must agree on rights and responsibilities.

In *Dead Programs Tell No Lies*, we want to ensure that we do no damage while we're working the bugs out. So we try to check things often and terminate the program if things go awry.

Assertive Programming describes an easy method of checking along the way—write code that actively verifies your assumptions.

As your programs get more dynamic, you'll find yourself juggling system resources—memory, files, devices, and the like. In *How to Balance Resources*, we'll suggest ways of ensuring that you don't drop any of the balls.

And most importantly, we stick to small steps always, as described in *Don't Outrun Your Headlights*, so we don't fall off the edge of the cliff.

In a world of imperfect systems, ridiculous time scales, laughable tools, and impossible requirements, let's play it safe. As Woody Allen said, "When everybody actually *is* out to get you, paranoia is just good thinking."

23 Design by Contract

Nothing astonishes men so much as common sense and plain dealing.
> ➤ *Ralph Waldo Emerson, Essays*

Dealing with computer systems is hard. Dealing with people is even harder. But as a species, we've had longer to figure out issues of human interactions. Some of the solutions we've come up with during the last few millennia can be applied to writing software as well. One of the best solutions for ensuring plain dealing is the *contract*.

A contract defines your rights and responsibilities, as well as those of the other party. In addition, there is an agreement concerning repercussions if either party fails to abide by the contract.

Maybe you have an employment contract that specifies the hours you'll work and the rules of conduct you must follow. In return, the company pays you a salary and other perks. Each party meets its obligations and everyone benefits.

It's an idea used the world over—both formally and informally—to help humans interact. Can we use the same concept to help software modules interact? The answer is "yes."

DBC

Bertrand Meyer (*Object-Oriented Software Construction* [Mey97]) developed the concept of *Design by Contract* for the language Eiffel.[1] It is a simple yet powerful technique that focuses on documenting (and agreeing to) the rights and responsibilities of software modules to ensure program correctness. What is a correct program? One that does no more and no less than it claims to do. Documenting and verifying that claim is the heart of *Design by Contract* (DBC, for short).

Every function and method in a software system *does something*. Before it starts that *something*, the function may have some expectation of the state of the world, and it may be able to make a statement about the state of the world when it concludes. Meyer describes these expectations and claims as follows:

Preconditions
What must be true in order for the routine to be called; the routine's requirements. A routine should never get called when its preconditions would be violated. It is the caller's responsibility to pass good data (see the box on page 110).

Postconditions
What the routine is guaranteed to do; the state of the world when the routine is done. The fact that the routine has a postcondition implies that it *will* conclude: infinite loops aren't allowed.

Class invariants
A class ensures that this condition is always true from the perspective of a caller. During internal processing of a routine, the invariant may not hold, but by the time the routine exits and control returns to the caller, the invariant must be true. (Note that a class cannot give unrestricted write-access to any data member that participates in the invariant.)

The contract between a routine and any potential caller can thus be read as

If all the routine's preconditions are met by the caller, the routine shall guarantee that all postconditions and invariants will be true when it completes.

If either party fails to live up to the terms of the contract, then a remedy (which was previously agreed to) is invoked—maybe an exception is raised, or the program terminates. Whatever happens, make no mistake that failure to live up to the contract is a bug. It is not something that should ever happen,

---

1. Based in part on earlier work by Dijkstra, Floyd, Hoare, Wirth, and others.

which is why preconditions should not be used to perform things such as user-input validation.

Some languages have better support for these concepts than others. Clojure, for example, supports pre- and post-conditions as well as the more comprehensive instrumentation provided by *specs*. Here's an example of a banking function to make a deposit using simple pre- and post-conditions:

```clojure
(defn accept-deposit [account-id amount]
   { :pre [   (> amount 0.00)
             (account-open? account-id) ]
    :post [ (contains? (account-transactions account-id) %) ] }
   "Accept a deposit and return the new transaction id"
   ;; Some other processing goes here...
   ;; Return the newly created transaction:
   (create-transaction account-id :deposit amount))
```

There are two preconditions for the accept-deposit function. The first is that the amount is greater than zero, and the second is that the account is open and valid, as determined by some function named account-open?. There is also a postcondition: the function guarantees that the new transaction (the return value of this function, represented here by '%') can be found among the transactions for this account.

If you call accept-deposit with a positive amount for the deposit and a valid account, it will proceed to create a transaction of the appropriate type and do whatever other processing it does. However, if there's a bug in the program and you somehow passed in a negative amount for the deposit, you'll get a runtime exception:

```
Exception in thread "main"...
Caused by: java.lang.AssertionError: Assert failed: (> amount 0.0)
```

Similarly, this function requires that the specified account is open and valid. If it's not, you'll see that exception instead:

```
Exception in thread "main"...
Caused by: java.lang.AssertionError: Assert failed: (account-open? account-id)
```

Other languages have features that, while not DBC-specific, can still be used to good effect. For example, Elixir uses *guard clauses* to dispatch function calls against several available bodies:

```
defmodule Deposits do
  def accept_deposit(account_id, amount) when (amount > 100000) do
    # Call the manager!
  end
  def accept_deposit(account_id, amount) when (amount > 10000) do
    # Extra Federal requirements for reporting
    # Some processing...
  end
  def accept_deposit(account_id, amount) when (amount > 0) do
    # Some processing...
  end
end
```

In this case, calling accept_deposit with a large enough amount may trigger additional steps and processing. Try to call it with an amount less than or equal to zero, however, and you'll get an exception informing you that you can't:

```
** (FunctionClauseError) no function clause matching in Deposits.accept_deposit/2
```

This is a better approach than simply checking your inputs; in this case, you simply *can not* call this function if your arguments are out of range.

| Tip 37 | Design with Contracts |

In *Orthogonality*, we recommended writing "shy" code. Here, the emphasis is on "lazy" code: be strict in what you will accept before you begin, and promise as little as possible in return. Remember, if your contract indicates that you'll accept anything and promise the world in return, then you've got a lot of code to write!

In any programming language, whether it's functional, object-oriented, or procedural, DBC forces you to *think*.

Class Invariants and Functional Languages

It's a naming thing. Eiffel is an object-oriented language, so Meyer named this idea "class invariant." But, really, it's more general than that. What this idea really refers to is *state*. In an object-oriented language, the state is associated with instances of classes. But other languages have state, too.

In a functional language, you typically pass state to functions and receive updated state as a result. The concepts of invariants is just as useful in these circumstances.

DBC and Test-Driven Development

Is Design by Contract needed in a world where developers practice unit testing, test-driven development (TDD), property-based testing, or defensive programming?

The short answer is "yes."

DBC and testing are different approaches to the broader topic of program correctness. They both have value and both have uses in different situations. DBC offers several advantages over specific testing approaches:

- DBC doesn't require any setup or mocking

- DBC defines the parameters for success or failure in *all* cases, whereas testing can only target one specific case at a time

- TDD and other testing happens only at "test time" within the build cycle. But DBC and assertions are forever: during design, development, deployment, and maintenance

- TDD does not focus on checking internal invariants within the code under test, it's more black-box style to check the public interface

- DBC is more efficient (and DRY-er) than defensive programming, where *everyone* has to validate data in case no one else does.

TDD is a great technique, but as with many techniques, it might invite you to concentrate on the "happy path," and not the real world full of bad data, bad actors, bad versions, and bad specifications.

Implementing DBC

Simply enumerating what the input domain range is, what the boundary conditions are, and what the routine promises to deliver—or, more importantly, what it *doesn't* promise to deliver—before you write the code is a huge leap forward in writing better software. By not stating these things, you are back to *programming by coincidence* (see the discussion on page 197), which is where many projects start, finish, and fail.

In languages that do not support DBC in the code, this might be as far as you can go—and that's not too bad. DBC is, after all, a *design* technique. Even without automatic checking, you can put the contract in the code as comments or in the unit tests and still get a very real benefit.

Assertions

While documenting these assumptions is a great start, you can get much greater benefit by having the compiler check your contract for you. You can partially emulate this in some languages by using *assertions:* runtime checks of logical conditions (see Topic 25, *Assertive Programming*, on page 115). Why only partially? Can't you use assertions to do everything DBC can do?

Unfortunately, the answer is no. To begin with, in object-oriented languages there probably is no support for propagating assertions down an inheritance hierarchy. This means that if you override a base class method that has a contract, the assertions that implement that contract will not be called correctly (unless you duplicate them manually in the new code). You must remember to call the class invariant (and all base class invariants) manually before you exit every method. The basic problem is that the contract is not automatically enforced.

In other environments, the exceptions generated from DBC-style assertions might be turned off globally or ignored in the code.

Also, there is no built-in concept of "old" values; that is, values as they existed at the entry to a method. If you're using assertions to enforce contracts, you must add code to the precondition to save any information you'll want to use in the postcondition, if the language will even allow that. In the Eiffel language, where DBC was born, you can just use old *expression*.

Finally, conventional runtime systems and libraries are not designed to support contracts, so these calls are not checked. This is a big loss, because it is often at the boundary between your code and the libraries it uses that the most problems are detected (see Topic 24, *Dead Programs Tell No Lies*, on page 112 for a more detailed discussion).

DBC and Crashing Early

DBC fits in nicely with our concept of crashing early (see Topic 24, *Dead Programs Tell No Lies*, on page 112). By using an assert or DBC mechanism to validate the preconditions, postconditions, and invariants, you can crash early and report more accurate information about the problem.

For example, suppose you have a method that calculates square roots. It needs a DBC precondition that restricts the domain to positive numbers. In languages that support DBC, if you pass sqrt a negative parameter, you'll get an informative error such as sqrt_arg_must_be_positive, along with a stack trace.

This is better than the alternative in other languages such as Java, C, and C++ where passing a negative number to sqrt returns the special value NaN (Not a Number). It may be some time later in the program that you attempt to do some math on NaN, with surprising results.

Who's Responsible?

Who is responsible for checking the precondition, the caller or the routine being called? When implemented as part of the language, the answer is neither: the precondition is tested behind the scenes after the caller invokes the routine but before the routine itself is entered. Thus if there is any explicit checking of parameters to be done, it must be performed by the *caller*, because the routine itself will never see parameters that violate its precondition. (For languages without built-in support, you would need to bracket the *called* routine with a preamble and/or postamble that checks these assertions.)

Consider a program that reads a number from the console, calculates its square root (by calling sqrt), and prints the result. The sqrt function has a precondition—its argument must not be negative. If the user enters a negative number at the console, it is up to the calling code to ensure that it never gets passed to sqrt. This calling code has many options: it could terminate, it could issue a warning and read another number, or it could make the number positive and append an *i* to the result returned by sqrt. Whatever its choice, this is definitely not sqrt's problem.

By expressing the domain of the square root function in the precondition of the sqrt routine, you shift the burden of correctness to the caller—where it belongs. You can then design the sqrt routine secure in the knowledge that its input will be in range.

It's much easier to find and diagnose the problem by crashing early, at the site of the problem.

Semantic Invariants

You can use *semantic invariants* to express inviolate requirements, a kind of "philosophical contract."

We once wrote a debit card transaction switch. A major requirement was that the user of a debit card should never have the same transaction applied to their account twice. In other words, no matter what sort of failure mode might happen, the error should be on the side of *not* processing a transaction rather than processing a duplicate transaction.

This simple law, driven directly from the requirements, proved to be very helpful in sorting out complex error recovery scenarios, and guided the detailed design and implementation in many areas.

Be sure not to confuse requirements that are fixed, inviolate laws with those that are merely policies that might change with a new management regime. That's why we use the term *semantic* invariants—it must be central to the very *meaning* of a thing, and not subject to the whims of policy (which is what more dynamic business rules are for).

When you find a requirement that qualifies, make sure it becomes a well-known part of whatever documentation you are producing—whether it is a bulleted list in the requirements document that gets signed in triplicate or just a big note on the common whiteboard that everyone sees. Try to state it clearly and unambiguously. For example, in the debit card example, we might write

> Err in favor of the consumer.

This is a clear, concise, unambiguous statement that's applicable in many different areas of the system. It is our contract with all users of the system, our guarantee of behavior.

Dynamic Contracts and Agents

Until now, we have talked about contracts as fixed, immutable specifications. But in the landscape of autonomous agents, this doesn't need to be the case. By the definition of "autonomous," agents are free to *reject* requests that they do not want to honor. They are free to renegotiate the contract—"I can't provide that, but if you give me this, then I might provide something else."

Certainly any system that relies on agent technology has a *critical* dependence on contractual arrangements—even if they are dynamically generated.

Imagine: with enough components and agents that can negotiate their own contracts among themselves to achieve a goal, we might just solve the software productivity crisis by letting software solve it for us.

But if we can't use contracts by hand, we won't be able to use them automatically. So next time you design a piece of software, design its contract as well.

Related Sections Include

- Topic 24, *Dead Programs Tell No Lies*, on page 112
- Topic 25, *Assertive Programming*, on page 115
- Topic 38, *Programming by Coincidence*, on page 197
- Topic 42, *Property-Based Testing*, on page 224
- Topic 43, *Stay Safe Out There*, on page 231
- Topic 45, *The Requirements Pit*, on page 244

Challenges

- Points to ponder: If DBC is so powerful, why isn't it used more widely? Is it hard to come up with the contract? Does it make you think about issues you'd rather ignore for now? Does it force you to *THINK!*? Clearly, this is a dangerous tool!

Exercises

Exercise 14 (possible answer on page 298)

Design an interface to a kitchen blender. It will eventually be a web-based, IoT-enabled blender, but for now we just need the interface to control it. It has ten speed settings (0 means off). You can't operate it empty, and you can change the speed only one unit at a time (that is, from 0 to 1, and from 1 to 2, not from 0 to 2).

Here are the methods. Add appropriate pre- and postconditions and an invariant.

```
int getSpeed()
void setSpeed(int x)
boolean isFull()
void fill()
void empty()
```

Exercise 15 (possible answer on page 299)

How many numbers are in the series 0, 5, 10, 15, ..., 100?

Dead Programs Tell No Lies

Have you noticed that sometimes other people can detect that things aren't well with you before you're aware of the problem yourself? It's the same with other people's code. If something is starting to go awry with one of our programs, sometimes it is a library or framework routine that catches it first. Maybe we've passed in a nil value, or an empty list. Maybe there's a missing key in that hash, or the value we thought contained a hash really contains a list instead. Maybe there was a network error or filesystem error that we didn't catch, and we've got empty or corrupted data. A logic error a couple of million instructions ago means that the selector for a case statement is no longer the expected 1, 2, or 3. We'll hit the default case unexpectedly. That's also one reason why each and every case/switch statement needs to have a default clause: we want to know when the "impossible" has happened.

It's easy to fall into the "it can't happen" mentality. Most of us have written code that didn't check that a file closed successfully, or that a trace statement got written as we expected. And all things being equal, it's likely that we didn't need to—the code in question wouldn't fail under any normal conditions. But we're coding defensively. We're making sure that the data is what we think it is, that the code in production is the code we think it is. We're checking that the correct versions of dependencies were actually loaded.

All errors give you information. You could convince yourself that the error can't happen, and choose to ignore it. Instead, Pragmatic Programmers tell themselves that if there is an error, something very, very bad has happened. Don't forget to Read the Damn Error Message (see *Coder in a Strange Land,* on page 91).

Catch and Release Is for Fish

Some developers feel that is it good style to catch or rescue all exceptions, re-raising them after writing some kind of message. Their code is full of things like this (where a bare raise statement reraises the current exception):

```
try do
    add_score_to_board(score);
rescue InvalidScore
    Logger.error("Can't add invalid score. Exiting");
    raise
rescue BoardServerDown
    Logger.error("Can't add score: board is down. Exiting");
    raise
rescue StaleTransaction
    Logger.error("Can't add score: stale transaction. Exiting");
    raise
end
```

Here's how Pragmatic Programmers would write this:

```
add_score_to_board(score);
```

We prefer it for two reasons. First, the application code isn't eclipsed by the error handling. Second, and perhaps more important, the code is less coupled. In the verbose example, we have to list every exception the add_score_to_board method could raise. If the writer of that method adds another exception, our code is subtly out of date. In the more pragmatic second version, the new exception is automatically propagated.

Tip 38	Crash Early

Crash, Don't Trash

One of the benefits of detecting problems as soon as you can is that you can crash earlier, and crashing is often the best thing you can do. The alternative may be to continue, writing corrupted data to some vital database or commanding the washing machine into its twentieth consecutive spin cycle.

The Erlang and Elixir languages embrace this philosophy. Joe Armstrong, inventor of Erlang and author of *Programming Erlang: Software for a Concurrent World [Arm07]*, is often quoted as saying, "Defensive programming is a waste of time. Let it crash!" In these environments, programs are designed to fail, but that failure is managed with *supervisors*. A supervisor is responsible for running code and knows what to do in case the code fails, which could include cleaning up after it, restarting it, and so on. What happens when the supervisor itself fails? Its own supervisor manages that event, leading to a design composed of *supervisor trees*. The technique is very effective and helps to account for the use of these languages in high-availability, fault-tolerant systems.

In other environments, it may be inappropriate simply to exit a running program. You may have claimed resources that might not get released, or you may need to write log messages, tidy up open transactions, or interact with other processes.

However, the basic principle stays the same—when your code discovers that something that was supposed to be impossible just happened, your program is no longer viable. Anything it does from this point forward becomes suspect, so terminate it as soon as possible.

A dead program normally does a lot less damage than a crippled one.

Related Sections Include

- Topic 20, *Debugging*, on page 88
- Topic 23, *Design by Contract*, on page 104
- Topic 25, *Assertive Programming*, on page 115
- Topic 26, *How to Balance Resources*, on page 118
- Topic 43, *Stay Safe Out There*, on page 231

25 Assertive Programming

There is a luxury in self-reproach. When we blame ourselves we feel no one else has a right to blame us.

➤ Oscar Wilde, *The Picture of Dorian Gray*

It seems that there's a mantra that every programmer must memorize early in his or her career. It is a fundamental tenet of computing, a core belief that we learn to apply to requirements, designs, code, comments, just about everything we do. It goes

This can never happen...

"This application will never be used abroad, so why internationalize it?" "count can't be negative." "Logging can't fail."

Let's not practice this kind of self-deception, particularly when coding.

Tip 39	Use Assertions to Prevent the Impossible

Whenever you find yourself thinking "but of course that could never happen," add code to check it. The easiest way to do this is with assertions. In many language implementations, you'll find some form of assert that checks a Boolean condition.[2] These checks can be invaluable. If a parameter or a result should never be null, then check for it explicitly:

```
assert (result != null);
```

In the Java implementation, you can (and should) add a descriptive string:

```
assert result != null && result.size() > 0 : "Empty result from XYZ";
```

Assertions are also useful checks on an algorithm's operation. Maybe you've written a clever sort algorithm, named my_sort. Check that it works:

```
books = my_sort(find("scifi"))
assert(is_sorted?(books))
```

Don't use assertions in place of real error handling. Assertions check for things that should never happen: you don't want to be writing code such as the following:

---

2. In C and C++ these are usually implemented as macros. In Java, assertions are disabled by default. Invoke the Java VM with the -enableassertions flag to enable them, and leave them enabled.

```
puts("Enter 'Y' or 'N': ")
ans = gets[0] # Grab first character of response
assert((ch == 'Y') || (ch == 'N'))    # Very bad idea!
```

And just because most assert implementations will terminate the process when an assertion fails, there's no reason why versions you write should. If you need to free resources, catch the assertion's exception or trap the exit, and run your own error handler. Just make sure the code you execute in those dying milliseconds doesn't rely on the information that triggered the assertion failure in the first place.

Assertions and Side Effects

It's embarrassing when the code we add to detect errors actually ends up creating new errors. This can happen with assertions if evaluating the condition has side effects. For example, it would be a bad idea to code something such as

```
while (iter.hasMoreElements()) {
  assert(iter.nextElement() != null);
  Object obj = iter.nextElement();
  // ....
}
```

The .nextElement() call in the assertion has the side effect of moving the iterator past the element being fetched, and so the loop will process only half the elements in the collection. It would be better to write

```
while (iter.hasMoreElements()) {
  Object obj = iter.nextElement();
  assert(obj != null);
  // ....
}
```

This problem is a kind of Heisenbug[3]—debugging that changes the behavior of the system being debugged.

(We also believe that nowadays, when most languages have decent support for iterating functions over collections, this kind of explicit loop is unnecessary and bad form.)

Leave Assertions Turned On

There is a common misunderstanding about assertions. It goes something like this:

---

3.   http://www.eps.mcgill.ca/jargon/jargon.html#heisenbug

Assertions add some overhead to code. Because they check for things that should never happen, they'll get triggered only by a bug in the code. Once the code has been tested and shipped, they are no longer needed, and should be turned off to make the code run faster. Assertions are a debugging facility.

There are two patently wrong assumptions here. First, they assume that testing finds all the bugs. In reality, for any complex program you are unlikely to test even a minuscule percentage of the permutations your code will be put through. Second, the optimists are forgetting that your program runs in a dangerous world. During testing, rats probably won't gnaw through a communications cable, someone playing a game won't exhaust memory, and log files won't fill the storage partition. These things might happen when your program runs in a production environment. Your first line of defense is checking for any possible error, and your second is using assertions to try to detect those you've missed.

Turning off assertions when you deliver a program to production is like crossing a high wire without a net because you once made it across in practice. There's dramatic value, but it's hard to get life insurance.

Even if you *do* have performance issues, turn off only those assertions that really hit you. The sort example above may be a critical part of your application, and may need to be fast. Adding the check means another pass through the data, which might be unacceptable. Make that particular check optional, but leave the rest in.

Use Assertions in Production, Win Big Money

A former neighbor of Andy's headed up a small startup company that made network devices. One of their secrets to success was the decision to leave assertions in place in production releases. These assertions were well crafted to report all the pertinent data leading to the failure, and presented via a nice-looking UI to the end user. This level of feedback, from real users under actual conditions, allowed the developers to plug the holes and fix these obscure, hard-to-reproduce bugs, resulting in remarkably stable, bullet-proof software.

This small, unknown company had such a solid product, it was soon acquired for hundreds of millions of dollars.

Just sayin'.

Exercise 16 (possible answer on page 299)

A quick reality check. Which of these "impossible" things can happen?

- A month with fewer than 28 days
- Error code from a system call: can't access the current directory
- In C++: a = 2; b = 3; but (a + b) does not equal 5
- A triangle with an interior angle sum $\neq 180°$
- A minute that doesn't have 60 seconds
- (a + 1) <= a

Related Sections Include

- Topic 23, *Design by Contract*, on page 104
- Topic 24, *Dead Programs Tell No Lies*, on page 112
- Topic 42, *Property-Based Testing*, on page 224
- Topic 43, *Stay Safe Out There*, on page 231

---

26 ▶ How to Balance Resources

To light a candle is to cast a shadow...

> ➤ Ursula K. Le Guin, A Wizard of Earthsea

We all manage resources whenever we code: memory, transactions, threads, network connections, files, timers—all kinds of things with limited availability. Most of the time, resource usage follows a predictable pattern: you allocate the resource, use it, and then deallocate it.

However, many developers have no consistent plan for dealing with resource allocation and deallocation. So let us suggest a simple tip:

> **Tip 40**   Finish What You Start

This tip is easy to apply in most circumstances. It simply means that the function or object that allocates a resource should be responsible for deallocating it. Let's see how it applies by looking at an example of some bad code—part of a Ruby program that opens a file, reads customer information from it, updates a field, and writes the result back. We've eliminated error handling to make the example clearer:

```
def read_customer
  @customer_file = File.open(@name + ".rec", "r+")
  @balance       = BigDecimal(@customer_file.gets)
end

def write_customer
  @customer_file.rewind
  @customer_file.puts @balance.to_s
  @customer_file.close
end

def update_customer(transaction_amount)
  read_customer
  @balance = @balance.add(transaction_amount,2)
  write_customer
end
```

At first sight, the routine update_customer looks reasonable. It seems to implement the logic we require—reading a record, updating the balance, and writing the record back out. However, this tidiness hides a major problem. The routines read_customer and write_customer are tightly coupled[4]—they share the instance variable customer_file. read_customer opens the file and stores the file reference in customer_file, and then write_customer uses that stored reference to close the file when it finishes. This shared variable doesn't even appear in the update_customer routine.

Why is this bad? Let's consider the unfortunate maintenance programmer who is told that the specification has changed—the balance should be updated only if the new value is not negative. They go into the source and change update_customer:

```
def update_customer(transaction_amount)
  read_customer
  if (transaction_amount >= 0.00)
    @balance = @balance.add(transaction_amount,2)
    write_customer
  end
end
```

All seems fine during testing. However, when the code goes into production, it collapses after several hours, complaining of *too many open files*. It turns out that write_customer is not getting called in some circumstances. When that happens, the file is not getting closed.

A very *bad* solution to this problem would be to deal with the special case in update_customer:.

---

4. For a discussion of the dangers of coupled code, see Topic 28, *Decoupling*, on page 130.

```
def update_customer(transaction_amount)
  read_customer
  if (transaction_amount >= 0.00)
    @balance += BigDecimal(transaction_amount, 2)
    write_customer
  else
    @customer_file.close # Bad idea!
  end
end
```

This will fix the problem—the file will now get closed regardless of the new balance—but the fix now means that *three* routines are coupled through the shared variable customer_file, and keeping track of when the file is open or not is going to start to get messy. We're falling into a trap, and things are going to start going downhill rapidly if we continue on this course. This is not balanced!

The *finish what you start* tip tells us that, ideally, the routine that allocates a resource should also free it. We can apply it here by refactoring the code slightly:

```
def read_customer(file)
  @balance=BigDecimal(file.gets)
end
```

```
def write_customer(file)
  file.rewind
  file.puts @balance.to_s
end
```

```
def update_customer(transaction_amount)
  file=File.open(@name + ".rec", "r+")       # >--
  read_customer(file)                        # |
  @balance = @balance.add(transaction_amount,2) # |
  file.close                                 # <--
end
```

Instead of holding on to the file reference, we've changed the code to pass it as a parameter.[5] Now all the responsibility for the file is in the update_customer routine. It opens the file and (finishing what it starts) closes it before returning. The routine balances the use of the file: the open and close are in the same place, and it is apparent that for every open there will be a corresponding close. The refactoring also removes an ugly shared variable.

There's another small but important improvement we can make. In many modern languages, you can scope the lifetime of a resource to an enclosed

---

5. See the tip on page 153.

block of some sort. In Ruby, there's a variation of the file open that passes in
the open file reference to a block, shown here between the do and the end:

```
def update_customer(transaction_amount)
  File.open(@name + ".rec", "r+") do |file|         # >--
    read_customer(file)                             #   |
    @balance = @balance.add(transaction_amount,2)   #   |
    write_customer(file)                            #   |
  end                                               # <--
end
```

In this case, at the end of the block the file variable goes out of scope and the
external file is closed. Period. No need to remember to close the file and release
the source, it is guaranteed to happen for you.

When in doubt, it always pays to reduce scope.

| Tip 41 | Act Locally |

Nest Allocations

The basic pattern for resource allocation can be extended for routines that
need more than one resource at a time. There are just two more suggestions:

- Deallocate resources in the opposite order to that in which you allocate
  them. That way you won't orphan resources if one resource contains references to another.

- When allocating the same set of resources in different places in your code,
  always allocate them in the same order. This will reduce the possibility
  of deadlock. (If process A claims resource1 and is about to claim resource2,
  while process B has claimed resource2 and is trying to get resource1, the two
  processes will wait forever.)

It doesn't matter what kind of resources we're using—transactions, network
connections, memory, files, threads, windows—the basic pattern applies:
whoever allocates a resource should be responsible for deallocating it. However, in some languages we can develop the concept further.

> ## Balancing Over Time
>
> In this topic we're mostly looking at ephemeral resources used by your running process. But you might want to consider what other messes you might be leaving behind.
>
> For instance, how are your logging files handled? You are creating data and using up storage space. Is there something in place to rotate the logs and clean them up? How about for your unofficial debug files you're dropping? If you're adding logging records in a database, is there a similar process in place to expire them? For anything that you create that takes up a finite resource, consider how to balance it.
>
> What else are you leaving behind?

Objects and Exceptions

The equilibrium between allocations and deallocations is reminiscent of an object-oriented class's constructor and destructor. The class represents a resource, the constructor gives you a particular object of that resource type, and the destructor removes it from your scope.

If you are programming in an object-oriented language, you may find it useful to encapsulate resources in classes. Each time you need a particular resource type, you instantiate an object of that class. When the object goes out of scope, or is reclaimed by the garbage collector, the object's destructor then deallocates the wrapped resource.

This approach has particular benefits when you're working with languages where exceptions can interfere with resource deallocation.

Balancing and Exceptions

Languages that support exceptions can make resource deallocation tricky. If an exception is thrown, how do you guarantee that everything allocated prior to the exception is tidied up? The answer depends to some extent on the language support. You generally have two choices:

1. Use variable scope (for example, stack variables in C++ or Rust)
2. Use a finally clause in a try...catch block

With usual scoping rules in languages such as C++ or Rust, the variable's memory will be reclaimed when the variable goes out of scope via a return, block exit, or exception. But you can also hook in to the variable's destructor to cleanup any external resources. In this example, the Rust variable named accounts will automatically close the associated file when it goes out of scope:

```
{
  let mut accounts = File::open("mydata.txt")?; // >--
  // use 'accounts'                              //    |
  ...                                            //    |
}                                                // <--
// 'accounts' is now out of scope, and the file is
// automatically closed
```

The other option, if the language supports it, is the finally clause. A finally clause will ensure that the specified code will run whether or not an exception was raised in the try...catch block:

```
try
    // some dodgy stuff
catch
    // exception was raised
finally
    // clean up in either case
```

However, there is a catch.

An Exception Antipattern

We commonly see folks writing something like this:

```
begin
    thing = allocate_resource()
    process(thing)
finally
    deallocate(thing)
end
```

Can you see what's wrong?

What happens if the resource allocation fails and raises an exception? The finally clause will catch it, and try to deallocate a *thing* that was never allocated.

The correct pattern for handling resource deallocation in an environment with exceptions is

```
thing = allocate_resource()
begin
    process(thing)
finally
    deallocate(thing)
end
```

When You Can't Balance Resources

There are times when the basic resource allocation pattern just isn't appropriate. Commonly this is found in programs that use dynamic data structures. One routine will allocate an area of memory and link it into some larger structure, where it may stay for some time.

The trick here is to establish a semantic invariant for memory allocation. You need to decide who is responsible for data in an aggregate data structure. What happens when you deallocate the top-level structure? You have three main options:

- The top-level structure is also responsible for freeing any substructures that it contains. These structures then recursively delete data they contain, and so on.

- The top-level structure is simply deallocated. Any structures that it pointed to (that are not referenced elsewhere) are orphaned.

- The top-level structure refuses to deallocate itself if it contains any substructures.

The choice here depends on the circumstances of each individual data structure. However, you need to make it explicit for each, and implement your decision consistently. Implementing any of these options in a procedural language such as C can be a problem: data structures themselves are not active. Our preference in these circumstances is to write a module for each major structure that provides standard allocation and deallocation facilities for that structure. (This module can also provide facilities such as debug printing, serialization, deserialization, and traversal hooks.)

Checking the Balance

Because Pragmatic Programmers trust no one, including ourselves, we feel that it is always a good idea to build code that actually checks that resources are indeed freed appropriately. For most applications, this normally means producing wrappers for each type of resource, and using these wrappers to keep track of all allocations and deallocations. At certain points in your code, the program logic will dictate that the resources will be in a certain state: use the wrappers to check this. For example, a long-running program that services requests will probably have a single point at the top of its main processing loop where it waits for the next request to arrive. This is a good place to ensure that resource usage has not increased since the last execution of the loop.

At a lower, but no less useful level, you can invest in tools that (among other things) check your running programs for memory leaks.

Related Sections Include

- Topic 24, *Dead Programs Tell No Lies*, on page 112
- Topic 30, *Transforming Programming*, on page 147
- Topic 33, *Breaking Temporal Coupling*, on page 170

Challenges

- Although there are no guaranteed ways of ensuring that you always free resources, certain design techniques, when applied consistently, will help. In the text we discussed how establishing a semantic invariant for major data structures could direct memory deallocation decisions. Consider how Topic 23, *Design by Contract*, on page 104, could help refine this idea.

Exercise 17 (possible answer on page 299)

Some C and C++ developers make a point of setting a pointer to NULL after they deallocate the memory it references. Why is this a good idea?

Exercise 18 (possible answer on page 299)

Some Java developers make a point of setting an object variable to NULL after they have finished using the object. Why is this a good idea?

---

27 Don't Outrun Your Headlights

It's tough to make predictions, especially about the future.
> ➤ *Lawrence "Yogi" Berra, after a Danish Proverb*

It's late at night, dark, pouring rain. The two-seater whips around the tight curves of the twisty little mountain roads, barely holding the corners. A hairpin comes up and the car misses it, crashing though the skimpy guardrail and soaring to a fiery crash in the valley below. State troopers arrive on the scene, and the senior officer sadly shakes their head. "Must have outrun their headlights."

Had the speeding two-seater been going faster than the speed of light? No, that speed limit is firmly fixed. What the officer referred to was the driver's ability to stop or steer in time in response to the headlight's illumination.

Headlights have a certain limited range, known as the *throw distance*. Past that point, the light spread is too diffuse to be effective. In addition, headlights only project in a straight line, and won't illuminate anything off-axis, such as curves, hills, or dips in the road. According to the National Highway Traffic Safety Administration, the average distance illuminated by low-beam headlights is about 160 feet. Unfortunately, stopping distance at 40mph is 189 feet, and at 70mph a whopping 464 feet.[6] So indeed, it's actually pretty easy to outrun your headlights.

In software development, our "headlights" are similarly limited. We can't see too far ahead into the future, and the further off-axis you look, the darker it gets. So Pragmatic Programmers have a firm rule:

Tip 42	Take Small Steps—Always

Always take small, deliberate steps, checking for feedback and adjusting before proceeding. Consider that the rate of feedback is your speed limit. You never take on a step or a task that's "too big."

What do we mean exactly by feedback? Anything that independently confirms or disproves your action. For example:

- Results in a REPL provide feedback on your understanding of APIs and algorithms
- Unit tests provide feedback on your last code change
- User demo and conversation provide feedback on features and usability

What's a task that's too big? Any task that requires "fortune telling." Just as the car headlights have limited throw, we can only see into the future perhaps one or two steps, maybe a few hours or days at most. Beyond that, you can quickly get past *educated guess* and into *wild speculation*. You might find yourself slipping into fortune telling when you have to:

- Estimate completion dates months in the future
- Plan a design for future maintenance or extendability
- Guess user's future needs
- Guess future tech availability

But, we hear you cry, aren't we supposed to design for future maintenance? Yes, but only to a point: only as far ahead as you can see. The more you have to predict what the future will look like, the more risk you incur that you'll be wrong. Instead of wasting effort designing for an uncertain future, you can always fall back on designing your code to be replaceable. Make it easy to

---

6. Per the NHTSA, Stopping Distance = Reaction Distance + Braking Distance, assuming an average reaction time of 1.5s and deceleration of 17.02ft/s².

throw out your code and replace it with something better suited. Making code replaceable will also help with cohesion, coupling, and DRY, leading to a better design overall.

Even though you may feel confident of the future, there's always the chance of a black swan around the corner.

Black Swans

In his book, *The Black Swan: The Impact of the Highly Improbable [Tal10]*, Nassim Nicholas Taleb posits that all significant events in history have come from high-profile, hard-to-predict, and rare events that are beyond the realm of normal expectations. These outliers, while statistically rare, have disproportionate effects. In addition, our own cognitive biases tend to blind us to changes creeping up on the edges of our work (see *Stone Soup and Boiled Frogs*).

Around the time of the first edition of *The Pragmatic Programmer*, debate raged in computer magazines and online forums over the burning question: "Who would win the desktop GUI wars, Motif or OpenLook?"[7] It was the wrong question. Odds are you've probably never heard of these technologies as neither "won" and the browser-centric web quickly dominated the landscape.

Tip 43	Avoid Fortune-Telling

Much of the time, tomorrow looks a lot like today. But don't count on it.

Related Sections Include

- Topic 12, *Tracer Bullets*, on page 50
- Topic 13, *Prototypes and Post-it Notes*, on page 56
- Topic 40, *Refactoring*, on page 209
- Topic 41, *Test to Code*, on page 214
- Topic 48, *The Essence of Agility*, on page 259
- Topic 50, *Coconuts Don't Cut It*, on page 270

---

7. Motif and OpenLook were GUI standards for X-Windows based Unix workstations.

## CHAPTER 5

Bend, or Break

Life doesn't stand still. Neither can the code that we write. In order to keep up with today's near-frantic pace of change, we need to make every effort to write code that's as loose—as flexible—as possible. Otherwise we may find our code quickly becoming outdated, or too brittle to fix, and may ultimately be left behind in the mad dash toward the future.

Back in *Reversibility* we talked about the perils of irreversible decisions. In this chapter, we'll tell you how to make *reversible* decisions, so your code can stay flexible and adaptable in the face of an uncertain world.

First we look at *coupling*—the dependencies between bits of code. *Decoupling* shows how to keep separate concepts separate, decreasing coupling.

Next, we'll look at different techniques you can use when *Juggling the Real World*. We'll examine four different strategies to help manage and react to events—a critical aspect of modern software applications.

Traditional procedural and object-oriented code might be too tightly coupled for your purposes. In *Transforming Programming*, we'll take advantage of the more flexible and clearer style offered by function pipelines, even if your language doesn't support them directly.

Common object-oriented style can tempt you with another trap. Don't fall for it, or you'll end up paying a hefty *Inheritance Tax*. We'll explore better alternatives to keep your code flexible and easier to change.

And of course a good way to stay flexible is to write *less* code. Changing code leaves you open to the possibility of introducing new bugs. *Configuration* will explain how to move details out of the code completely, where they can be changed more safely and easily.

All these techniques will help you write code that bends and doesn't break.

28 ▶ Decoupling

When we try to pick out anything by itself, we find it hitched to everything else in the Universe.

> ➤ John Muir, My First Summer in the Sierra

In Topic 8, *The Essence of Good Design,* on page 28 we claim that using good design principles will make the code you write easy to change. Coupling is the enemy of change, because it links together things that must change in parallel. This makes change more difficult: either you spend time tracking down all the parts that need changing, or you spend time wondering why things broke when you changed "just one thing" and not the other things to which it was coupled.

When you are designing something you want to be rigid, a bridge or a tower perhaps, you couple the components together:

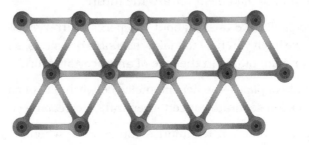

The links work together to make the structure rigid.

Compare that with something like this:

Here there's no structural rigidity: individual links can change and others just accommodate it.

When you're designing bridges, you want them to hold their shape; you need them to be rigid. But when you're designing software that you'll want to change, you want exactly the opposite: you want it to be flexible. And to be flexible, individual components should be coupled to as few other components as possible.

And, to make matters worse, coupling is transitive: if A is coupled to B and C, and B is coupled to M and N, and C to X and Y, then A is actually coupled to B, C, M, N, X, and Y.

This means there's a simple principle you should follow:

> **Tip 44**   Decoupled Code Is Easier to Change

Given that we don't normally code using steel beams and rivets, just what does it mean to decouple code? In this section we'll talk about:

- Train wrecks—chains of method calls
- Globalization—the dangers of static things
- Inheritance—why subclassing is dangerous

To some extent this list is artificial: coupling can occur just about any time two pieces of code share something, so as you read what follows keep an eye out for the underlying patterns so you can apply them to *your* code. And keep a lookout for some of the symptoms of coupling:

- Wacky dependencies between unrelated modules or libraries.

- "Simple" changes to one module that propagate through unrelated modules in the system or break stuff elsewhere in the system.

- Developers who are afraid to change code because they aren't sure what might be affected.

- Meetings where everyone has to attend because no one is sure who will be affected by a change.

Train Wrecks

We've all seen (and probably written) code like this:

```
public void applyDiscount(customer, order_id, discount) {
  totals = customer
           .orders
           .find(order_id)
           .getTotals();
  totals.grandTotal = totals.grandTotal - discount;
  totals.discount   = discount;
}
```

We're getting a reference to some orders from a customer object, using that to find a particular order, and then getting the set of totals for the order.

Using those totals, we subtract the discount from the order grand total and also update them with that discount.

This chunk of code is traversing five levels of abstraction, from customer to total amounts. Ultimately our top-level code has to know that a customer object exposes orders, that the orders have a find method that takes an order id and returns an order, and that the order object has a totals object which has getters and setters for grand totals and discounts. That's a lot of implicit knowledge. But worse, that's a lot of things that *cannot change in the future* if this code is to continue to work. All the cars in a train are coupled together, as are all the methods and attributes in a train wreck.

Let's imagine that the business decides that no order can have a discount of more than 40%. Where would we put the code that enforces that rule?

You might say it belongs in the applyDiscount function we just wrote. That's certainly part of the answer. But with the code the way it is now, you can't know that this is the *whole* answer. Any piece of code, anywhere, could set fields in the totals object, and if the maintainer of that code didn't get the memo, it wouldn't be checking against the new policy.

One way to look at this is to think about responsibilities. Surely the totals object should be responsible for managing the totals. And yet it isn't: it's really just a container for a bunch of fields that anyone can query and update.

The fix for that is to apply something we call:

> **Tip 45**   Tell, Don't Ask

This principle says that you shouldn't make decisions based on the internal state of an object and then update that object. Doing so totally destroys the benefits of encapsulation and, in doing so, spreads the knowledge of the implementation throughout the code. So the first fix for our train wreck is to delegate the discounting to the total object:

```
public void applyDiscount(customer, order_id, discount) {
  customer
    .orders
    .find(order_id)
    .getTotals()
    .applyDiscount(discount);
}
```

We have the same kind of *tell-don't-ask* (TDA) issue with the customer object and its orders: we shouldn't fetch its list of orders and search them. We should instead get the order we want directly from the customer:

```
public void applyDiscount(customer, order_id, discount) {
  customer
    .findOrder(order_id)
    .getTotals()
    .applyDiscount(discount);
}
```

The same thing applies to our order object and its totals. Why should the outside world have to know that the implementation of an order uses a separate object to store its totals?

```
public void applyDiscount(customer, order_id, discount) {
  customer
    .findOrder(order_id)
    .applyDiscount(discount);
}
```

And this is where we'd probably stop.

At this point you might be thinking that TDA would make us add an applyDiscountToOrder(order_id) method to customers. And, if followed slavishly, it would.

But TDA is not a law of nature; it's just a pattern to help us recognize problems. In this case, we're comfortable exposing the fact that a customer has orders, and that we can find one of those orders by asking the customer object for it. This is a pragmatic decision.

In every application there are certain top-level concepts that are universal. In this application, those concepts include *customers* and *orders*. It makes no sense to hide orders totally inside customer objects: they have an existence of their own. So we have no problem creating APIs that expose order objects.

The Law of Demeter

People often talk about something called the *Law of Demeter*, or LoD, in relation to coupling. The LoD is a set of guidelines[1] written in the late '80s by Ian Holland. He created them to help developers on the Demeter Project keep their functions cleaner and decoupled.

---

1. So it's not really a law. It's more like The Jolly Good Idea of Demeter.

The LoD says that a method defined in a class *C* should only call:

- Other instance methods in C
- Its parameters
- Methods in objects that it creates, both on the stack and in the heap
- Global variables

In the first edition of this book we spent some time describing the LoD. In the intervening 20 years the bloom has faded on that particular rose. We now don't like the "global variable" clause (for reasons we'll go into in the next section). We also discovered that it's difficult to use this in practice: it's a little like having to parse a legal document whenever you call a method.

However, the principle is still sound. We just recommend a somewhat simpler way of expressing almost the same thing:

Tip 46	Don't Chain Method Calls

Try not to have more than one "." when you access something. And *access something* also covers cases where you use intermediate variables, as in the following code:

```
# This is pretty poor style
amount = customer.orders.last().totals().amount;

# and so is this…
orders = customer.orders;
last    = orders.last();
totals  = last.totals();
amount  = totals.amount;
```

There's a big exception to the one-dot rule: the rule doesn't apply if the things you're chaining are really, really unlikely to change. In practice, anything in your application should be considered likely to change. Anything in a third-party library should be considered volatile, particularly if the maintainers of that library are known to change APIs between releases. Libraries that come with the language, however, are probably pretty stable, and so we'd be happy with code such as:

```
people
.sort_by {|person| person.age }
.first(10)
.map {| person | person.name }
```

That Ruby code worked when we wrote the first edition, 20 years ago, and will likely still work when we enter the home for old programmers (any day now...).

Chains and Pipelines

In Topic 30, *Transforming Programming*, on page 147 we talk about composing functions into pipelines. These pipelines transform data, passing it from one function to the next. This is not the same as a train wreck of method calls, as we are not relying on hidden implementation details.

That's not to say that pipelines don't introduce some coupling: they do. The format of the data returned by one function in a pipeline must be compatible with the format accepted by the next.

Our experience is that this form of coupling is far less a barrier to changing the code than the form introduced by train wrecks.

The Evils of Globalization

Globally accessible data is an insidious source of coupling between application components. Each piece of global data acts as if every method in your application suddenly gained an additional parameter: after all, that global data is available inside *every* method.

Globals couple code for many reasons. The most obvious is that a change to the implementation of the global potentially affects all the code in the system. In practice, of course, the impact is fairly limited; the problem really comes down to knowing that you've found every place you need to change.

Global data also creates coupling when it comes to teasing your code apart.

Much has been made of the benefits of code reuse. Our experience has been that reuse should probably not be a primary concern when creating code, but the thinking that goes into making code reusable should be part of your coding routine. When you make code reusable, you give it clean interfaces, decoupling it from the rest of your code. This allows you to extract a method or module without dragging everything else along with it. And if your code uses global data, then it becomes difficult to split it out from the rest.

You'll see this problem when you're writing unit tests for code that uses global data. You'll find yourself writing a bunch of setup code to create a global environment just to allow your test to run.

Tip 47	Avoid Global Data

Global Data Includes Singletons

In the previous section we were careful to talk about *global data* and not *global variables*. That's because people often tell us "Look! No global variables. I wrapped it all as instance data in a singleton object or global module."

Try again, Skippy. If all you have is a singleton with a bunch of exported instance variables, then it's still just global data. It just has a longer name.

So then folks take this singleton and hide all the data behind methods. Instead of coding Config.log_level they now say Config.log_level() or Config.getLogLevel(). This is better, because it means that your global data has a bit of intelligence behind it. If you decide to change the representation of log levels, you can maintain compatibility by mapping between the new and old in the Config API. But you still have only the one set of configuration data.

Global Data Includes External Resources

Any mutable external resource is global data. If your application uses a database, datastore, file system, service API, and so on, it risks falling into the globalization trap. Again, the solution is to make sure you always wrap these resources behind code that you control.

Tip 48	If It's Important Enough to Be Global, Wrap It in an API

Inheritance Adds Coupling

The misuse of subclassing, where a class inherits state and behavior from another class, is so important that we discuss it in its own section, Topic 31, *Inheritance Tax*, on page 158.

Again, It's All About Change

Coupled code is hard to change: alterations in one place can have secondary effects elsewhere in the code, and often in hard-to-find places that only come to light a month later in production.

Keeping your code shy: having it only deal with things it directly knows about, will help keep your applications decoupled, and that will make them more amenable to change.

Related Sections Include

- Topic 8, *The Essence of Good Design*, on page 28
- Topic 9, *DRY—The Evils of Duplication*, on page 30
- Topic 10, *Orthogonality*, on page 39
- Topic 11, *Reversibility*, on page 47
- Topic 29, *Juggling the Real World*, on page 137
- Topic 30, *Transforming Programming*, on page 147
- Topic 31, *Inheritance Tax*, on page 158
- Topic 32, *Configuration*, on page 166
- Topic 33, *Breaking Temporal Coupling*, on page 170
- Topic 34, *Shared State Is Incorrect State*, on page 174
- Topic 35, *Actors and Processes*, on page 181
- Topic 36, *Blackboards*, on page 187
- We discuss *Tell, Don't Ask* in our 2003 Software Construction article *The Art of Enbugging.*[2]

---

29 Juggling the Real World

Things don't just happen; they are made to happen.

> ➤ John F. Kennedy

In the old days, when your authors still had their boyish good looks, computers were not particularly flexible. We'd typically organize the way we interacted with them based on their limitations.

Today, we expect more: computers have to integrate into *our* world, not the other way around. And our world is messy: things are constantly happening, stuff gets moved around, we change our minds, ... And the applications we write somehow have to work out what to do.

This section is all about writing these responsive applications.

We'll start off with the concept of an *event*.

Events

An *event* represents the availability of information. It might come from the outside world: a user clicking a button, or a stock quote update. It might be internal: the result of a calculation is ready, a search finishes. It can even be something as trivial as fetching the next element in a list.

---

2. https://media.pragprog.com/articles/jan_03_enbug.pdf

Whatever the source, if we write applications that respond to events, and adjust what they do based on those events, those applications will work better in the real world. Their users will find them to be more interactive, and the applications themselves will make better use of resources.

But how can we write these kinds of applications? Without some kind of strategy, we'll quickly find ourselves confused, and our applications will be a mess of tightly coupled code.

Let's look at four strategies that help.

1. Finite State Machines
2. The Observer Pattern
3. Publish/Subscribe
4. Reactive Programming and Streams

Finite State Machines

Dave finds that he writes code using a Finite State Machine (FSM) just about every week. Quite often, the FSM implementation will be just a couple of lines of code, but those few lines help untangle a whole lot of potential mess.

Using an FSM is trivially easy, and yet many developers shy away from them. There seems to be a belief that they are difficult, or that they only apply if you're working with hardware, or that you need to use some hard-to-understand library. None of these are true.

The Anatomy of a Pragmatic FSM

A state machine is basically just a specification of how to handle events. It consists of a set of states, one of which is the *current state*. For each state, we list the events that are significant to that state. For each of those events, we define the new current state of the system.

For example, we may be receiving multipart messages from a websocket. The first message is a header. This is followed by any number of data messages, followed by a trailing message. This could be represented as an FSM like this:

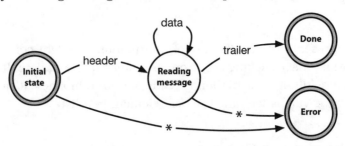

We start in the "Initial state." If we receive a header message, we *transition* to the "Reading message" state. If we receive anything else while we're in the initial state (the line labeled with an asterisk) we transition to the "Error" state and we're done.

While we're in the "Reading message" state, we can accept either data messages, in which case we continue reading in the same state, or we can accept a trailer message, which transitions us to the "Done" state. Anything else causes a transition to the error state.

The neat thing about FSMs is that we can express them purely as data. Here's a table representing our message parser:

State	Events			
	Header	Data	Trailer	Other
Initial	Reading	Error	Error	Error
Reading	Error	Reading	Done	Error

The rows in the table represent the states. To find out what to do when an event occurs, look up the row for the current state, scan along for the column representing the event, the contents of that cell are the new state.

The code that handles it is equally simple:

```ruby
event/simple_fsm.rb
TRANSITIONS = {
    initial: {header: :reading},
    reading: {data: :reading, trailer: :done},
}

state = :initial

while state != :done && state != :error
    msg = get_next_message()
    state = TRANSITIONS[state][msg.msg_type] || :error
end
```

The code that implements the transitions between states is on line 10. It indexes the transition table using the current state, and then indexes the transitions for that state using the message type. If there is no matching new state, it sets the state to :error.

Adding Actions

A pure FSM, such as the one we were just looking at, is an event stream parser. Its only output is the final state. We can beef it up by adding actions that are triggered on certain transitions.

For example, we might need to extract all of the strings in a source file. A string is text between quotes, but a backslash in a string escapes the next character, so "Ignore \"quotes\"" is a single string. Here's an FSM that does this:

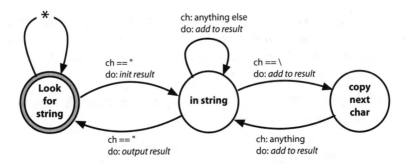

This time, each transition has two labels. The top one is the event that triggers it, and the bottom one is the action to take as we move between states.

We'll express this in a table, as we did last time. However, in this case each entry in the table is a two-element list containing the next state and the name of an action:

```
event/strings_fsm.rb
TRANSITIONS = {

  # current          new state           action to take
  #------------------------------------------------------------
  look_for_string: {
    '"'     => [ :in_string,       :start_new_string ],
    :default => [ :look_for_string, :ignore ],
  },

  in_string: {
    '"'      => [ :look_for_string, :finish_current_string ],
    '\\'     => [ :copy_next_char,  :add_current_to_string ],
    :default => [ :in_string,       :add_current_to_string ],
  },

  copy_next_char: {
    :default => [ :in_string,       :add_current_to_string ],
  },
}
```

We've also added the ability to specify a default transition, taken if the event doesn't match any of the other transitions for this state.

Now let's look at the code:

```
event/strings_fsm.rb
state = :look_for_string
result = []

while ch = STDIN.getc
  state, action = TRANSITIONS[state][ch] || TRANSITIONS[state][:default]
  case action
  when :ignore
  when :start_new_string
    result = []
  when :add_current_to_string
    result << ch
  when :finish_current_string
    puts result.join
  end
end
```

This is similar to the previous example, in that we loop through the events (the characters in the input), triggering transitions. But it does more than the previous code. The result of each transition is both a new state and the name of an action. We use the action name to select the code to run before we go back around the loop.

This code is very basic, but it gets the job done. There are many other variants: the transition table could use anonymous functions or function pointers for the actions, you could wrap the code that implements the state machine in a separate class, with its own state, and so on.

There's nothing to say that you have to process all the state transitions at the same time. If you're going through the steps to sign up a user on your app, there's likely to be a number of transitions as they enter their details, validate their email, agree to the 107 different legislated warnings that online apps must now give, and so on. Keeping the state in external storage, and using it to drive a state machine, is a great way to handle these kind of workflow requirements.

State Machines Are a Start

State machines are underused by developers, and we'd like to encourage you to look for opportunities to apply them. But they don't solve all the problems associated with events. So let's move on to some other ways of looking at the problems of juggling events.

The Observer Pattern

In the *observer pattern* we have a source of events, called the *observable* and a list of clients, the *observers*, who are interested in those events.

An observer registers its interest with the observable, typically by passing a reference to a function to be called. Subsequently, when the event occurs, the observable iterates down its list of observers and calls the function that each passed it. The event is given as a parameter to that call.

Here's a simple example in Ruby. The Terminator module is used to terminate the application. Before it does so, however, it notifies all its observers that the application is going to exit.[3] They might use this notification to tidy up temporary resources, commit data, and so on:

```ruby
event/observer.rb
module Terminator
  CALLBACKS = []

  def self.register(callback)
    CALLBACKS << callback
  end

  def self.exit(exit_status)
    CALLBACKS.each { |callback| callback.(exit_status) }
    exit!(exit_status)
  end
end

Terminator.register(-> (status) { puts "callback 1 sees #{status}" })
Terminator.register(-> (status) { puts "callback 2 sees #{status}" })

Terminator.exit(99)
```

```
$ ruby event/observer.rb
callback 1 sees 99
callback 2 sees 99
```

There's not much code involved in creating an observable: you push a function reference onto a list, and then call those functions when the event occurs. This is a good example of when *not* to use a library.

The observer/observable pattern has been used for decades, and it has served us well. It is particularly prevalent in user interface systems, where the callbacks are used to inform the application that some interaction has occurred.

But the observer pattern has a problem: because each of the observers has to register with the observable, it introduces coupling. In addition, because

---

3. Yes, we know that Ruby already has this capability with its at_exit function.

in the typical implementation the callbacks are handled inline by the observable, synchronously, it can introduce performance bottlenecks.

This is solved by the next strategy, Publish/Subscribe.

Publish/Subscribe

Publish/Subscribe (pubsub) generalizes the observer pattern, at the same time solving the problems of coupling and performance.

In the pubsub model, we have *publishers* and *subscribers*. These are connected via channels. The channels are implemented in a separate body of code: sometimes a library, sometimes a process, and sometimes a distributed infrastructure. All this implementation detail is hidden from your code.

Every channel has a name. Subscribers register interest in one or more of these named channels, and publishers write events to them. Unlike the observer pattern, the communication between the publisher and subscriber is handled outside your code, and is potentially asynchronous.

Although you could implement a very basic pubsub system yourself, you probably don't want to. Most cloud service providers have pubsub offerings, allowing you to connect applications around the world. Every popular language will have at least one pubsub library.

Pubsub is a good technology for decoupling the handling of asynchronous events. It allows code to be added and replaced, potentially while the application is running, without altering existing code. The downside is that it can be hard to see what is going on in a system that uses pubsub heavily: you can't look at a publisher and immediately see which subscribers are involved with a particular message.

Compared to the observer pattern, pubsub is a great example of reducing coupling by abstracting up through a shared interface (the channel). However, it is still basically just a message passing system. Creating systems that respond to combinations of events will need more than this, so let's look at ways we can add a time dimension to event processing.

Reactive Programming, Streams, and Events

If you've ever used a spreadsheet, then you'll be familiar with *reactive programming*. If a cell contains a formula which refers to a second cell, then updating that second cell causes the first to update as well. The values *react* as the values they use change.

There are many frameworks that can help with this kind of data-level reactivity: in the realm of the browser React and Vue.js are current favorites (but, this being JavaScript, this information will be out-of-date before this book is even printed).

It's clear that events can also be used to trigger reactions in code, but it isn't necessarily easy to plumb them in. That's where *streams* come in.

Streams let us treat events as if they were a collection of data. It's as if we had a list of events, which got longer when new events arrive. The beauty of that is that we can treat streams just like any other collection: we can manipulate, combine, filter, and do all the other data-ish things we know so well. We can even combine event streams and regular collections. And streams can be asynchronous, which means your code gets the opportunity to respond to events as they arrive.

The current *de facto* baseline for reactive event handling is defined on the site http://reactivex.io, which defines a language-agnostic set of principles and documents some common implementations. Here we'll use the RxJs library for JavaScript.

Our first example takes two streams and zips them together: the result is a new stream where each element contains one item from the first input stream and one item from the other. In this case, the first stream is simply a list of five animal names. The second stream is more interesting: it's an interval timer which generates an event every 500ms. Because the streams are zipped together, a result is only generated when data is available on both, and so our result stream only emits a value every half second:

```
event/rx0/index.js
import * as Observable from 'rxjs'
import { logValues }    from "../rxcommon/logger.js"

let animals  = Observable.of("ant", "bee", "cat", "dog", "elk")
let ticker   = Observable.interval(500)

let combined = Observable.zip(animals, ticker)

combined.subscribe(next => logValues(JSON.stringify(next)))
```

This code uses a simple logging function[4] which adds items to a list in the browser window. Each item is timestamped with the time in milliseconds since the program started to run. Here's what it shows for our code:

---

4. https://media.pragprog.com/titles/tpp20/code/event/rxcommon/logger.js

```
502 ms
   ["ant",0]
```
```
1002 ms
   ["bee",1]
```
```
1502 ms
   ["cat",2]
```
```
2002 ms
   ["dog",3]
```
```
2502 ms
   ["elk",4]
```

Notice the timestamps: we're getting one event from the stream every 500ms. Each event contains a serial number (created by the interval observable) and the name of the next animal from the list. Watching it live in a browser, the log lines appear at every half second.

Event streams are normally populated as events occur, which implies that the observables that populate them can run in parallel. Here's an example that fetches information about users from a remote site. For this we'll use https://reqres.in, a public site that provides an open REST interface. As part of its API, we can fetch data on a particular (fake) user by performing a GET request to users/«id». Our code fetches the users with the IDs 3, 2, and 1:

event/rx1/index.js

```javascript
import * as Observable from 'rxjs'
import { mergeMap }    from 'rxjs/operators'
import { ajax }        from 'rxjs/ajax'
import { logValues }   from "../rxcommon/logger.js"

let users = Observable.of(3, 2, 1)

let result = users.pipe(
  mergeMap((user) => ajax.getJSON(`https://reqres.in/api/users/${user}`))
)

result.subscribe(
  resp => logValues(JSON.stringify(resp.data)),
  err  => console.error(JSON.stringify(err))
)
```

The internal details of the code are not too important. What's exciting is the result, shown in the following screenshot:

```
82 ms
  {"id":2,"first_name":"Janet","last_name":"Weaver","avatar":"https

132 ms
  {"id":1,"first_name":"George","last_name":"Bluth","avatar":"https

133 ms
  {"id":3,"first_name":"Emma","last_name":"Wong","avatar":"https://
```

Look at the timestamps: the three requests, or three separate streams, were processed in parallel, The first to come back, for id 2, took 82ms, and the next two came back 50 and 51ms later.

Streams of Events Are Asynchronous Collections

In the previous example, our list of user IDs (in the observable users) was static. But it doesn't have to be. Perhaps we want to collect this information when people log in to our site. All we have to do is to generate an observable event containing their user ID when their session is created, and use that observable instead of the static one. We'd then be fetching details about the users as we received these IDs, and presumably storing them somewhere.

This is a very powerful abstraction: we no longer need to think about time as being something we have to manage. Event streams unify synchronous and asynchronous processing behind a common, convenient API.

Events Are Ubiquitous

Events are everywhere. Some are obvious: a button click, a timer expiring. Other are less so: someone logging in, a line in a file matching a pattern. But whatever their source, code that's crafted around events can be more responsive and better decoupled than its more linear counterpart.

Related Sections Include

- Topic 28, *Decoupling*, on page 130
- Topic 36, *Blackboards*, on page 187

Exercises

Exercise 19 (possible answer on page 300)

In the FSM section we mentioned that you could move the generic state machine implementation into its own class. That class would probably be initialized by passing in a table of transitions and an initial state.

Try implementing the string extractor that way.

Exercise 20 (possible answer on page 300)

Which of these technologies (perhaps in combination) would be a good fit for the following situations:

- If you receive three *network interface down* events within five minutes, notify the operations staff.

- If it is after sunset, and there is motion detected at the bottom of the stairs followed by motion detected at the top of the stairs, turn on the upstairs lights.

- You want to notify various reporting systems that an order was completed.

- In order to determine whether a customer qualifies for a car loan, the application needs to send requests to three backend services and wait for the responses.

---

30 Transforming Programming

If you can't describe what you are doing as a process, you don't know what you're doing.

➤ W. Edwards Deming, (attr)

All programs transform data, converting an input into an output. And yet when we think about design, we rarely think about creating transformations. Instead we worry about classes and modules, data structures and algorithms, languages and frameworks.

We think that this focus on code often misses the point: we need to get back to thinking of programs as being something that transforms inputs into outputs. When we do, many of the details we previously worried about just evaporate. The structure becomes clearer, the error handling more consistent, and the coupling drops way down.

To start our investigation, let's take the time machine back to the 1970s and ask a Unix programmer to write us a program that lists the five longest files in a directory tree, where longest means "having the largest number of lines."

You might expect them to reach for an editor and start typing in C. But they wouldn't, because they are thinking about this in terms of what we have (a directory tree) and what we want (a list of files). Then they'd go to a terminal and type something like:

```
$ find . -type f | xargs wc -l | sort -n | tail -5
```

This is a series of transformations:

find . -type f

> Write a list of all the files (-type f) in or below the current directory (.) to standard output.

xargs wc -l

> Read lines from standard input and arrange for them all to be passed as arguments to the command wc -l. The wc program with the -l option counts the number of lines in each of its arguments and writes each result as "count filename" to standard output.

sort -n

> Sort standard input assuming each line starts with a number (-n), writing the result to standard output.

tail -5

> Read standard input and write just the last five lines to standard output.

Run this in our book's directory and we get

```
 470 ./test_to_build.pml
 487 ./dbc.pml
 719 ./domain_languages.pml
 727 ./dry.pml
9561 total
```

That last line is the total number of lines in all the files (not just those shown), because that's what wc does. We can strip it off by requesting one more line from tail, and then ignoring the last line:

```
$ find . -type f | xargs wc -l | sort -n | tail -6 | head -5
    470 ./debug.pml
    470 ./test_to_build.pml
    487 ./dbc.pml
    719 ./domain_languages.pml
    727 ./dry.pml
```

Let's look at this in terms of the data that flows between the individual steps. Our original requirement, "top 5 files in terms of lines," becomes a series of transformations (also show in the figure on page 149).

directory name
→ list of files
→ list with line numbers
→ sorted list
→ highest five + total
→ highest five

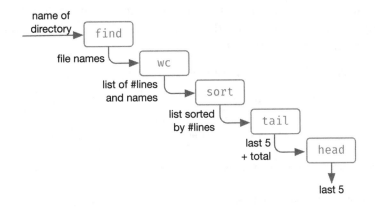

Figure 1—The find pipeline as a series of transformations

It's almost like an industrial assembly line: feed raw data in one end and the finished product (information) comes out the other.

And we like to think about all code this way.

> **Tip 49**   Programming Is About Code, But Programs Are About Data

Finding Transformations

Sometimes the easiest way to find the transformations is to start with the requirement and determine its inputs and outputs. Now you've defined the function representing the overall program. You can then find steps that lead you from input to output. This is a *top-down* approach.

For example, you want to create a website for folks playing word games that finds all the words that can be made from a set of letters. Your input here is a set of letters, and your output is a list of three-letter words, four-letter words, and so on:

"Ivyin"   is transformed to →   3 => ivy, lin, nil, yin
4 => inly, liny, viny
5 => vinyl

(Yes, they are all words, at least according to the macOS dictionary.)

The trick behind the overall application is simple: we have a dictionary which groups words by a *signature*, chosen so that all words containing the same letters will have the same signature. The simplest signature function is just the sorted list of letters in the word. We can then look up an input string by generating a signature for it, and then seeing which words (if any) in the dictionary have that same signature.

Thus the *anagram finder* breaks down into four separate transformations:

Step	Transformation	Sample data
Step 0:	Initial input	"ylvin"
Step 1:	All combinations of three or more letters	vin, viy, vil, vny, vnl, vyl, iny, inl, iyl, nyl, viny, vinl, viyl, vnyl, inyl, vinyl
Step 2:	Signatures of the combinations	inv, ivy, ilv, nvy, lnv, lvy, iny, iln, ily, lny, invy, ilnv, ilvy, lnvy, ilny, ilnvy
Step 3:	List of all dictionary words which match any of the signatures	ivy, yin, nil, lin, viny, liny, inly, vinyl
Step 4:	Words grouped by length	3 => ivy, lin, nil, yin 4 => inly, liny, viny 5 => vinyl

Transformations All the Way Down

Let's start by looking at step 1, which takes a word and creates a list of all combinations of three or more letters. This step can itself be expressed as a list of transformations:

Step	Transformation	Sample data
Step 1.0:	Initial input	"vinyl"
Step 1.1:	Convert to characters	v, i, n, y, l
Step 1.2:	Get all subsets	[], [v], [i], … [v,i], [v,n], [v,y], … [v,i,n], [v,i,y], … [v,n,y,l], [i,n,y,l], [v,i,n,y,l]
Step 1.3:	Only those longer than three characters	[v,i,n], [v,i,y], … [i,n,y,l], [v,i,n,y,l]
Step 1.4:	Convert back to strings	[vin,viy, … inyl,vinyl]

We've now reached the point where we can easily implement each transformation in code (using Elixir in this case):

```
function-pipelines/anagrams/lib/anagrams.ex
defp all_subsets_longer_than_three_characters(word) do
  word
  |> String.codepoints()
  |> Comb.subsets()
  |> Stream.filter(fn subset -> length(subset) >= 3 end)
  |> Stream.map(&List.to_string(&1))
end
```

What's with the |> Operator?

Elixir, along with many other functional languages, has a pipeline operator, sometimes called a *forward pipe* or just a *pipe*.[5] All it does is take the value on its left and insert it as the first parameter of the function on its right, so

```
"vinyl" |> String.codepoints |> Comb.subsets()
```

is the same as writing

```
Comb.subsets(String.codepoints("vinyl"))
```

(Other languages may inject this piped value as the *last* parameter of the next function—it largely depends on the style of the built-in libraries.)

You might think that this is just syntactic sugar. But in a very real way the pipeline operator is a revolutionary opportunity to think differently. Using a pipeline means that you're automatically thinking in terms of transforming data; each time you see |> you're actually seeing a place where data is flowing between one transformation and the next.

Many languages have something similar: Elm, F#, and Swift have |>, Clojure has -> and ->> (which work a little differently), R has %>%. Haskell both has pipe operators and makes it easy to declare new ones. As we write this, there's talk of adding |> to JavaScript.

If your current language supports something similar, you're in luck. If it doesn't, see *Language X Doesn't Have Pipelines*, on page 153.

Anyway, back to the code.

Keep on Transforming...

Now look at *Step 2* of the main program, where we convert the subsets into signatures. Again, it's a simple transformation—a list of subsets becomes a list of signatures:

Step	Transformation	Sample data
Step 2.0:	initial input	vin, viy, ... inyl, vinyl
Step 2.1:	convert to signatures	inv, ivy ... ilny, inlvy

The Elixir code in the following listing is just as simple:

---

5. It seems that the first use of the characters |> as a pipe dates to 1994, in a discussion about the language Isobelle/ML, archived at https://blogs.msdn.microsoft.com/dsyme/2011/05/17/archeological-semiotics-the-birth-of-the-pipeline-symbol-1994/

function-pipelines/anagrams/lib/anagrams.ex
```elixir
defp as_unique_signatures(subsets) do
  subsets
  |> Stream.map(&Dictionary.signature_of/1)
end
```

Now we transform that list of signatures: each signature gets mapped to the list of known words with the same signature, or nil if there are no such words. We then have to remove the nils and flatten the nested lists into a single level:

function-pipelines/anagrams/lib/anagrams.ex
```elixir
defp find_in_dictionary(signatures) do
  signatures
  |> Stream.map(&Dictionary.lookup_by_signature/1)
  |> Stream.reject(&is_nil/1)
  |> Stream.concat(&(&1))
end
```

Step 4, grouping the words by length, is another simple transformation, converting our list into a map where the keys are the lengths, and the values are all words with that length:

function-pipelines/anagrams/lib/anagrams.ex
```elixir
defp group_by_length(words) do
  words
  |> Enum.sort()
  |> Enum.group_by(&String.length/1)
end
```

Putting It All Together

We've written each of the individual transformations. Now it's time to string them all together into our main function:

function-pipelines/anagrams/lib/anagrams.ex
```elixir
  def anagrams_in(word) do
    word
    |> all_subsets_longer_than_three_characters()
    |> as_unique_signatures()
    |> find_in_dictionary()
    |> group_by_length()
end
```

Does it work? Let's try it:

```elixir
iex(1)> Anagrams.anagrams_in "lyvin"
%{
  3 => ["ivy", "lin", "nil", "yin"],
  4 => ["inly", "liny", "viny"],
  5 => ["vinyl"]
}
```

Language X Doesn't Have Pipelines

Pipelines have been around for a long time, but only in niche languages. They've only moved into the mainstream recently, and many popular languages still don't support the concept.

The good news is that thinking in transformations doesn't require a particular language syntax: it's more a philosophy of design. You still construct your code as transformations, but you write them as a series of assignments:

```
const content = File.read(file_name);
const lines   = find_matching_lines(content, pattern)
const result  = truncate_lines(lines)
```

It's a little more tedious, but it gets the job done.

Why Is This So Great?

Let's look at the body of the main function again:

```
word
|> all_subsets_longer_than_three_characters()
|> as_unique_signatures()
|> find_in_dictionary()
|> group_by_length()
```

It's simply a chain of the transformations needed to meet our requirement, each taking input from the previous transformation and passing output to the next. That comes about as close to literate code as you can get.

But there's something deeper, too. If your background is object-oriented programming, then your reflexes demand that you hide data, encapsulating it inside objects. These objects then chatter back and forth, changing each other's state. This introduces a lot of coupling, and it is a big reason that OO systems can be hard to change.

Tip 50	Don't Hoard State; Pass It Around

In the transformational model, we turn that on its head. Instead of little pools of data spread all over the system, think of data as a mighty river, a *flow*. Data becomes a peer to functionality: a pipeline is a sequence of code → data → code → data.... The data is no longer tied to a particular group of functions, as it is in a class definition. Instead it is free to represent the unfolding progress of our application as it transforms its inputs into its outputs. This means that we can greatly reduce coupling: a function can be used (and reused) anywhere its parameters match the output of some other function.

Yes, there is still a degree of coupling, but in our experience it's more manageable than the OO-style of command and control. And, if you're using a language with type checking, you'll get compile-time warnings when you try to connect two incompatible things.

What About Error Handling?

So far our transforms have worked in a world where nothing goes wrong. How can we use them in the real world, though? If we can only build linear chains, how can we add all that conditional logic that we need for error checking?

There are many ways of doing this, but they all rely on a basic convention: we never pass raw values between transformations. Instead, we wrap them in a data structure (or type) which also tells us if the contained value is valid. In Haskell, for example, this wrapper is called Maybe. In F# and Scala it's Option.

How you use this concept is language specific. In general, though, there are two basic ways of writing the code: you can handle checking for errors inside your transformations or outside them.

Elixir, which we've used so far, doesn't have this support built in. For our purposes this is a good thing, as we get to show an implementation from the ground up. Something similar should work in most other languages.

First, Choose a Representation

We need a representation for our wrapper (the data structure that carries around a value or an error indication). You can use structures for this, but Elixir already has a pretty strong convention: functions tend to return a tuple containing either {:ok, value} or {:error, reason}. For example, File.open returns either :ok and an IO process or :error and a reason code:

```
iex(1)> File.open("/etc/passwd")
{:ok, #PID<0.109.0>}
iex(2)> File.open("/etc/wombat")
{:error, :enoent}
```

We'll use the :ok/:error tuple as our wrapper when passing things through a pipeline.

Then Handle It Inside Each Transformation

Let's write a function that returns all the lines in a file that contain a given string, truncated to the first 20 characters. We want to write it as a transformation, so the input will be a file name and a string to match, and the output will be either an :ok tuple with a list of lines or an :error tuple with some kind of reason. The top-level function should look something like this:

```
function-pipelines/anagrams/lib/grep.ex
def find_all(file_name, pattern) do
  File.read(file_name)
  |> find_matching_lines(pattern)
  |> truncate_lines()
end
```

There's no explicit error checking here, but if any step in the pipeline returns an error tuple then the pipeline will return that error without executing the functions that follow.[6] We do this using Elixir's pattern matching:

```
function-pipelines/anagrams/lib/grep.ex
defp find_matching_lines({:ok, content}, pattern) do
  content
  |> String.split(~r/\n/)
  |> Enum.filter(&String.match?(&1, pattern))
  |> ok_unless_empty()
end

defp find_matching_lines(error, _), do: error

# ----------

defp truncate_lines({ :ok, lines }) do
  lines
  |> Enum.map(&String.slice(&1, 0, 20))
  |> ok()
end

defp truncate_lines(error), do: error

# ----------

defp ok_unless_empty([]),      do: error("nothing found")
defp ok_unless_empty(result), do: ok(result)

defp ok(result),      do: { :ok,      result }
defp error(reason), do: { :error, reason }
```

Have a look at the function find_matching_lines. If its first parameter is an :ok tuple, it uses the content in that tuple to find lines matching the pattern. However, if the first parameter is *not* an :ok tuple, the second version of the function runs, which just returns that parameter. This way the function simply forwards an error down the pipeline. The same thing applies to truncate_lines.

We can play with this at the console:

```
iex> Grep.find_all "/etc/passwd", ~r/www/
{:ok, ["_www:*:70:70:World W", "_wwwproxy:*:252:252:"]}
```

---

6. We've taken a liberty here. Technically we do execute the following functions. We just don't execute the code in them.

```
iex> Grep.find_all "/etc/passwd", ~r/wombat/
{:error, "nothing found"}
iex> Grep.find_all "/etc/koala", ~r/www/
{:error, :enoent}
```

You can see that an error anywhere in the pipeline immediately becomes the value of the pipeline.

Or Handle It in the Pipeline

You might be looking at the find_matching_lines and truncate_lines functions thinking that we've moved the burden of error handling into the transformations. You'd be right. In a language which uses pattern matching in function calls, such as Elixir, the effect is lessened, but it's still ugly.

It would be nice if Elixir had a version of the pipeline operator |> that knew about the :ok/:error tuples and which short-circuited execution when an error occurred.[7] But the fact that it doesn't allows us to add something similar, and in a way that is applicable to a number of other languages.

The problem we face is that when an error occurs we don't want to run code further down the pipeline, and that we don't want that code to know that this is happening. This means that we need to defer running pipeline functions until we know that previous steps in the pipeline were successful. To do this, we'll need to change them from function *calls* into function *values* that can be called later. Here's one implementation:

```
function-pipelines/anagrams/lib/grep1.ex
defmodule Grep1 do

  def and_then({ :ok, value }, func), do: func.(value)
  def and_then(anything_else, _func), do: anything_else

  def find_all(file_name, pattern) do
    File.read(file_name)
    |> and_then(&find_matching_lines(&1, pattern))
    |> and_then(&truncate_lines(&1))
  end

  defp find_matching_lines(content, pattern) do
    content
    |> String.split(~r/\n/)
    |> Enum.filter(&String.match?(&1, pattern))
    |> ok_unless_empty()
  end
end
```

---

7. In fact you could add such an operator to Elixir using its macro facility; an example of this is the Monad library in hex. You could also use Elixir's with construct, but then you lose much of the sense of writing transformations that you get with pipelines.

```
defp truncate_lines(lines) do
  lines
  |> Enum.map(&String.slice(&1, 0, 20))
  |> ok()
end

defp ok_unless_empty([]),      do: error("nothing found")
defp ok_unless_empty(result), do: ok(result)

defp ok(result),     do: { :ok, result }
defp error(reason), do: { :error, reason }
end
```

The and_then function is an example of a *bind* function: it takes a value wrapped in something, then applies a function to that value, returning a new wrapped value. Using the and_then function in the pipeline takes a little extra punctuation because Elixir needs to be told to convert function calls into function values, but that extra effort is offset by the fact that the transforming functions become simple: each just takes a value (and any extra parameters) and returns {:ok, new_value} or {:error, reason}.

Transformations Transform Programming

Thinking of code as a series of (nested) transformations can be a liberating approach to programming. It takes a while to get used to, but once you've developed the habit you'll find your code becomes cleaner, your functions shorter, and your designs flatter.

Give it a try.

Related Sections Include

- Topic 8, *The Essence of Good Design*, on page 28
- Topic 17, *Shell Games*, on page 78
- Topic 26, *How to Balance Resources*, on page 118
- Topic 28, *Decoupling*, on page 130
- Topic 35, *Actors and Processes*, on page 181

Exercises

Exercise 21 (possible answer on page 301)

Can you express the following requirements as a top-level transformation? That is, for each, identify the input and the output.

1. Shipping and sales tax are added to an order
2. Your application loads configuration information from a named file
3. Someone logs in to a web application

Exercise 22 (possible answer on page 301)

You've identified the need to validate and convert an input field from a string into an integer between 18 and 150. The overall transformation is described by

```
field contents as string
    → [validate & convert]
        → {:ok, value} | {:error, reason}
```

Write the individual transformations that make up *validate & convert*.

Exercise 23 (possible answer on page 301)

In *Language X Doesn't Have Pipelines*, on page 153 we wrote:

```
const content = File.read(file_name);
const lines   = find_matching_lines(content, pattern)
const result  = truncate_lines(lines)
```

Many people write OO code by chaining together method calls, and might be tempted to write this as something like:

```
const result = content_of(file_name)
              .find_matching_lines(pattern)
              .truncate_lines()
```

What's the difference between these two pieces of code? Which do you think we prefer?

---

31 ▶ Inheritance Tax

You wanted a banana but what you got was a gorilla holding the banana and the entire jungle.

➤ *Joe Armstrong*

Do you program in an object-oriented language? Do you use inheritance?

If so, stop! It probably isn't what you want to do.

Let's see why.

Some Background

Inheritance first appeared in Simula 67 in 1969. It was an elegant solution to the problem of queuing multiple types of events on the same list. The Simula approach was to use something called *prefix classes*. You could write something like this:

```
link CLASS car;
    ... implementation of car

link CLASS bicycle;
    ... implementation of bicycle
```

The link is a prefix class that adds the functionality of linked lists. This lets you add both cars and bicycles to the list of things waiting at (say) a traffic light. In current terminology, link would be a parent class.

The mental model used by Simula programmers was that the instance data and implementation of class link was prepended to the implementation of classes car and bicycle. The link part was almost viewed as being a *container* that carried around cars and bicycles. This gave them a form of polymorphism: cars and bicycles both implemented the link interface because they both contained the link code.

After Simula came Smalltalk. Alan Kay, one of the creators of Smalltalk, describes in a 2019 Quora answer[8] *why* Smalltalk has inheritance:

> So when I designed Smalltalk-72—and it was a lark for fun while thinking about Smalltalk-71—I thought it would be fun to use its Lisp-like dynamics to do experiments with "differential programming" (meaning: various ways to accomplish "this is like that except").

This is subclassing purely for behavior.

These two styles of inheritance (which actually had a fair amount in common) developed over the following decades. The Simula approach, which suggested inheritance was a way of combining types, continued in languages such as C++ and Java. The Smalltalk school, where inheritance was a dynamic organization of behaviors, was seen in languages such as Ruby and JavaScript.

So, now we're faced with a generation of OO developers who use inheritance for one of two reasons: they don't like typing, or they like types.

Those who don't like typing save their fingers by using inheritance to add common functionality from a base class into child classes: class User and class Product are both subclasses of ActiveRecord::Base.

Those who like types use inheritance to express the relationship between classes: a Car is-a-kind-of Vehicle.

Unfortunately both kinds of inheritance have problems.

---

8. https://www.quora.com/What-does-Alan-Kay-think-about-inheritance-in-object-oriented-programming

Problems Using Inheritance to Share Code

Inheritance *is* coupling. Not only is the child class coupled to the parent, the parent's parent, and so on, but the code that *uses* the child is also coupled to all the ancestors. Here's an example:

```
class Vehicle
  def initialize
    @speed = 0
  end
  def stop
    @speed = 0
  end
  def move_at(speed)
    @speed = speed
  end
end

class Car < Vehicle
  def info
    "I'm car driving at #{@speed}"
  end
end

# top-level code
my_ride = Car.new
my_ride.move_at(30)
```

When the top-level calls my_car.move_at, the method being invoked is in Vehicle, the parent of Car.

Now the developer in charge of Vehicle changes the API, so move_at becomes set_velocity, and the instance variable @speed becomes @velocity.

An API change is expected to break clients of Vehicle class. But the top-level is not: as far as it is concerned it is using a Car. What the Car class does in terms of implementation is not the concern of the top-level code, but it still breaks.

Similarly the name of an instance variable is purely an internal implementation detail, but when Vehicle changes it also (silently) breaks Car.

So much coupling.

Problems Using Inheritance to Build Types

Some folks view inheritance as a way of defining new types. Their favorite design diagram shows class hierarchies. They view problems the way Victorian gentleman scientists viewed nature, as something to be broken down into categories.

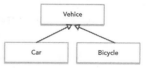

Unfortunately, these diagrams soon grow into wall-covering monstrosities, layer-upon-layer added in order to express the smallest nuance of differentiation between classes. This added complexity can make the application more brittle, as changes can ripple up and down many layers.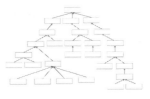

Even worse, though, is the multiple inheritance issue. A Car may be a kind of Vehicle, but it can also be a kind of Asset, InsuredItem, LoanCollateral and so on. Modeling this correctly would need multiple inheritance.

C++ gave multiple inheritance a bad name in the 1990s because of some questionable disambiguation semantics. As a result, many current OO languages don't offer it. So, even if you're happy with complex type trees, you won't be able to model your domain accurately anyway.

Tip 51	Don't Pay Inheritance Tax

The Alternatives Are Better

Let us suggest three techniques that mean you should never need to use inheritance again:

- Interfaces and protocols
- Delegation
- Mixins and traits

Interfaces and Protocols

Most OO languages allow you to specify that a class implements one or more sets of behaviors. You could say, for example, that a Car class implements the Drivable behavior and the Locatable behavior. The syntax used for doing this varies: in Java, it might look like this:

```
public class Car implements Drivable, Locatable {

  // Code for class Car. This code must include
  // the functionality of both Drivable
  // and Locatable

}
```

Drivable and Locatable are what Java calls *interfaces*; other languages call them *protocols*, and some call them *traits* (although this is not what we'll be calling a trait later).

Interfaces are defined like this:

```
public interface Drivable {
  double getSpeed();
  void    stop();
}

public interface Locatable() {
  Coordinate getLocation();
  boolean    locationIsValid();
}
```

These declarations create no code: they simply say that any class that implements Drivable must implement the two methods getSpeed and stop, and a class that's Locatable must implement getLocation and locationIsValid. This means that our previous class definition of Car will only be valid if it includes all four of these methods.

What makes interfaces and protocols so powerful is that we can use them as types, and any class that implements the appropriate interface will be compatible with that type. If Car and Phone both implement Locatable, we could store both in a list of locatable items:

```
List<Locatable> items = new ArrayList<>();

items.add(new Car(...));
items.add(new Phone(...));
items.add(new Car(...));
// ...
```

We can then process that list, safe in the knowledge that every item has getLocation and locationIsValid:

```
void printLocation(Locatable item) {
  if (item.locationIsValid() {
    print(item.getLocation().asString());
}

// ...

items.forEach(printLocation);
```

| Tip 52 | Prefer Interfaces to Express Polymorphism |

Interfaces and protocols give us polymorphism without inheritance.

Delegation

Inheritance encourages developers to create classes whose objects have large numbers of methods. If a parent class has 20 methods, and the subclass wants to make use of just two of them, its objects will still have the other 18 just lying around and callable. The class has lost control of its interface. This is a common problem—many persistence and UI frameworks insist that application components subclass some supplied base class:

```
class Account < PersistenceBaseClass
end
```

The Account class now carries all of the persistence class's API around with it. Instead, imagine an alternative using delegation, as in the following example:

```
class Account
  def initialize(. . .)
    @repo = Persister.for(self)
  end

  def save
    @repo.save()
  end
end
```

We now expose *none* of the framework API to the clients of our Account class: that decoupling is now broken. But there's more. Now that we're no longer constrained by the API of the framework we're using, we're free to create the API we need. Yes, we could do that before, but we always ran the risk that the interface *we* wrote can be bypassed, and the persistence API used instead. Now we control everything.

Tip 53	Delegate to Services: Has-A Trumps Is-A

In fact, we can take this a step further. Why should an Account have to know how to persist itself? Isn't its job to know and enforce the account business rules?

```
class Account
  # nothing but account stuff
end

class AccountRecord
  # wraps an account with the ability
  # to be fetched and stored
end
```

Now we're really decoupled, but it has come at a cost. We're having to write more code, and typically some of it will be boilerplate: it's likely that all our record classes will need a find method, for example.

Fortunately, that's what mixins and traits do for us.

Mixins, Traits, Categories, Protocol Extensions, …

As an industry, we love to give things names. Quite often we'll give the same thing many names. More is better, right?

That's what we're dealing with when we look at mixins. The basic idea is simple: we want to be able to extend classes and objects with new functionality without using inheritance. So we create a set of these functions, give that set a name, and then somehow extend a class or object with them. At that point, you've created a new class or object that combines the capabilities of the original and all its mixins. In most cases, you'll be able to make this extension even if you don't have access to the source code of the class you're extending.

Now the implementation and name of this feature varies between languages. We'll tend to call them *mixins* here, but we really want you to think of this as a language-agnostic feature. The important thing is the capability that all these implementations have: merging functionality between *existing things* and *new things*.

As an example, let's go back to our AccountRecord example. As we left it, an AccountRecord needed to know about both accounts and about our persistence framework. It also needed to delegate all the methods in the persistence layer that it wanted to expose to the outside world.

Mixins give us an alternative. First, we could write a mixin that implements (for example) two of three of the standard finder methods. We could then add them into AccountRecord as a mixin. And, as we write new classes for persisted things, we can add the mixin to them, too:

```
mixin CommonFinders {
  def find(id) { ... }
  def findAll() { ... }
end

class AccountRecord extends BasicRecord with CommonFinders
class OrderRecord   extends BasicRecord with CommonFinders
```

We can take this a lot further. For example, we all know our business objects need validation code to prevent bad data from infiltrating our calculations. But exactly what do we mean by *validation*?

If we take an account, for example, there are probably many different layers of validation that could be applied:

- Validating that a hashed password matches one entered by the user
- Validating form data entered by the user when an account is created

- Validating form data entered by an admin person updating the user details
- Validating data added to the account by other system components
- Validating data for consistency before it is persisted

A common (and we believe less-than-ideal) approach is to bundle all the validations into a single class (the business object/persistence object) and then add flags to control which fire in which circumstances.

We think a better way is to use mixins to create specialized classes for appropriate situations:

```
class AccountForCustomer extends Account
    with AccountValidations,AccountCustomerValidations

class AccountForAdmin extends Account
    with AccountValidations,AccountAdminValidations
```

Here, both derived classes include validations common to all account objects. The customer variant also includes validations appropriate for the customer-facing APIs, while the admin variant contained (the presumably less restrictive) admin validations.

Now, by passing instances of AccountForCustomer or AccountForAdmin back and forth, our code *automatically* ensures the correct validation is applied.

Tip 54	Use Mixins to Share Functionality

Inheritance Is Rarely the Answer

We've had a quick look at three alternatives to traditional class inheritance:

- Interfaces and protocols
- Delegation
- Mixins and traits

Each of these methods may be better for you in different circumstances, depending on whether your goal is sharing type information, adding functionality, or sharing methods. As with anything in programming, aim to use the technique that best expresses your intent.

And try not to drag the whole jungle along for the ride.

Related Sections Include

- Topic 8, *The Essence of Good Design*, on page 28
- Topic 10, *Orthogonality*, on page 39
- Topic 28, *Decoupling*, on page 130

Challenges

- The next time you find yourself subclassing, take a minute to examine the options. Can you achieve what you want with interfaces, delegation, and/or mixins? Can you reduce coupling by doing so?

---

32 ▶ Configuration

Let all your things have their places; let each part of your business have its time.

> ➤ *Benjamin Franklin, Thirteen Virtues, autobiography*

When code relies on values that may change after the application has gone live, keep those values external to the app. When your application will run in different environments, and potentially for different customers, keep the environment- and customer-specific values outside the app. In this way, you're parameterizing your application; the code adapts to the places it runs.

> **Tip 55**   Parameterize Your App Using External Configuration

Common things you will probably want to put in configuration data include:

- Credentials for external services (database, third party APIs, and so on)
- Logging levels and destinations
- Port, IP address, machine, and cluster names the app uses
- Environment-specific validation parameters
- Externally set parameters, such as tax rates
- Site-specific formatting details
- License keys

Basically, look for anything that you know will have to change that you can express outside your main body of code, and slap it into some configuration bucket.

Static Configuration

Many frameworks, and quite a few custom applications, keep configuration in either flat files or database tables. If the information is in flat files, the trend is to use some off-the-shelf plain-text format. Currently YAML and JSON are popular for this. Sometimes applications written in scripting languages use special purpose source-code files, dedicated to containing just configuration. If the information is structured, and is likely to be changed by the customer (sales tax rates, for example), it might be better to store it in a database table. And, of course, you can use both, splitting the configuration information according to use.

Whatever form you use, the configuration is read into your application as a data structure, normally when the application starts. Commonly, this data structure is made global, the thinking being that this makes it easier for any part of the code to get to the values it holds.

We prefer that you don't do that. Instead, wrap the configuration information behind a (thin) API. This decouples your code from the details of the representation of configuration.

Configuration-As-A-Service

While static configuration is common, we currently favor a different approach. We still want configuration data kept external to the application, but rather than in a flat file or database, we'd like to see it stored behind a service API. This has a number of benefits:

- Multiple applications can share configuration information, with authentication and access control limiting what each can see
- Configuration changes can be made globally
- The configuration data can be maintained via a specialized UI
- The configuration data becomes dynamic

That last point, that configuration should be dynamic, is critical as we move toward highly available applications. The idea that we should have to stop and restart an application to change a single parameter is hopelessly out of touch with modern realities. Using a configuration service, components of the application could register for notifications of updates to parameters they use, and the service could send them messages containing new values if and when they are changed.

Whatever form it takes, configuration data drives the runtime behavior of an application. When configuration values change, there's no need to rebuild the code.

Don't Write Dodo-Code

Without external configuration, your code is not as adaptable or flexible as it could be. Is this a bad thing? Well, out here in the real world, species that don't adapt die.

The dodo didn't adapt to the presence of humans and their livestock on the island of Mauritius, and quickly became extinct.[9] It was the first documented extinction of a species at the hand of man.

Don't let your project (or your career) go the way of the dodo.

Related Sections Include

- Topic 9, *DRY—The Evils of Duplication*, on page 30
- Topic 14, *Domain Languages*, on page 59
- Topic 16, *The Power of Plain Text*, on page 74
- Topic 28, *Decoupling*, on page 130

Image by OpenClipart-Vectors from Pixabay

Don't Overdo It

In the first edition of this book, we suggested using configuration instead of code in a similar fashion, but apparently should have been a little more specific in our instructions. Any advice can be taken to extremes or used inappropriately, so here are a few cautions:

Don't overdo it. One early client of ours decided that every single field in their application should be configurable. As a result, it took weeks to make even the smallest change, as you had to implement both the field and all the admin code to save and edit it. They had some *40,000* configuration variables and a coding nightmare on their hands.

Don't push decisions to configuration out of laziness. If there's genuine debate about whether a feature should work this way or that, or if it should be the users' choice, try it out one way and get feedback on whether the decision was a good one.

---

9. It didn't help that the settlers beat the placid (read: *stupid*) birds to death with clubs for sport.

## CHAPTER 6

Concurrency

Just so we're all on the same page, let's start with some definitions:

Concurrency is when the execution of two or more pieces of code act as if they run at the same time. *Parallelism* is when they *do* run at the same time.

To have concurrency, you need to run code in an environment that can switch execution between different parts of your code when it is running. This is often implemented using things such as fibers, threads, and processes.

To have parallelism, you need hardware that can do two things at once. This might be multiple cores in a CPU, multiple CPUs in a computer, or multiple computers connected together.

Everything Is Concurrent

It's almost impossible to write code in a decent-sized system that doesn't have concurrent aspects to it. They may be explicit, or they may be buried inside a library. Concurrency is a requirement if you want your application to be able to deal with the real world, where things are asynchronous: users are interacting, data is being fetched, external services are being called, all at the same time. If you force this process to be serial, with one thing happening, then the next, and so on, your system feels sluggish and you're probably not taking full advantage of the power of the hardware on which it runs.

In this chapter we'll look at concurrency and parallelism.

Developers often talk about coupling between chunks of code. They're referring to dependencies, and how those dependencies make things hard to change. But there's another form of coupling. *Temporal coupling* happens when your code imposes a sequence on things that is not required to solve the problem at hand. Do you depend on the "tick" coming before the "tock"? Not if you want to stay flexible. Does your code access multiple back-end services sequentially, one after the other? Not if you want to keep your customers. In *Breaking Temporal Coupling*, we'll look at ways of identifying this kind of temporal coupling.

Why is writing concurrent and parallel code so difficult? One reason is that we learned to program using sequential systems, and our languages have features that are relatively safe when used sequentially but become a liability once two things can happen at the same time. One of the biggest culprits here is *shared state*. This doesn't just mean global variables: any time two or more chunks of code hold references to the same piece of mutable data, you have shared state. And *Shared State Is Incorrect State*. The section describes a number of workarounds for this, but ultimately they're all error prone.

If that makes you feed sad, *nil desperandum!* There are better ways to construct concurrent applications. One of these is using the *actor model*, where independent processes, which share no data, communicate over channels using defined, simple, semantics. We talk about both the theory and practice of this approach in *Actors and Processes*.

Finally, we'll look at *Blackboards*. These are systems which act like a combination of an object store and a smart publish/subscribe broker. In their original form, they never really took off. But today we're seeing more and more implementations of middleware layers with blackboard-like semantics. I correctly, these types of systems offer a serious amount of decoupling.

Concurrent and parallel code used to be exotic. Now it is required.

33 Breaking Temporal Coupling

"What is *temporal coupling* all about?", you may ask. It's about time.

Time is an often ignored aspect of software architectures. The only time that preoccupies us is the time on the schedule, the time left until we ship—but this is not what we're talking about here. Instead, we are talking about the role of time as a design element of the software itself. There are two aspects of time that are important to us: concurrency (things happening at the same time) and ordering (the relative positions of things in time).

We don't usually approach programming with either of these aspects in mind. When people first sit down to design an architecture or write a program, things tend to be linear. That's the way most people think—*do this* and then always *do that*. But thinking this way leads to *temporal coupling*: coupling in time. Method A must always be called before method B; only one report can be run at a time; you must wait for the screen to redraw before the button click is received. Tick must happen before tock.

This approach is not very flexible, and not very realistic.

We need to allow for concurrency and to think about decoupling any time or order dependencies. In doing so, we can gain flexibility and reduce any time-based dependencies in many areas of development: workflow analysis, architecture, design, and deployment. The result will be systems that are easier to reason about, that potentially respond faster and more reliably.

Looking for Concurrency

On many projects, we need to model and analyze the application workflows as part of the design. We'd like to find out what *can* happen at the same time, and what *must* happen in a strict order. One way to do this is to capture the workflow using a notation such as the *activity diagram.*[1]

Tip 56	Analyze Workflow to Improve Concurrency

An activity diagram consists of a set of actions drawn as rounded boxes. The arrow leaving an action leads to either another action (which can start once the first action completes) or to a thick line called a *synchronization bar.* Once *all* the actions leading into a synchronization bar are complete, you can then proceed along any arrows leaving the bar. An action with no arrows leading into it can be started at any time.

You can use activity diagrams to maximize parallelism by identifying activities that *could be* performed in parallel, but aren't.

For instance, we may be writing the software for a robotic piña colada maker. We're told that the steps are:

1. Open blender
2. Open piña colada mix
3. Put mix in blender
4. Measure 1/2 cup white rum
5. Pour in rum
6. Add 2 cups of ice
7. Close blender
8. Liquefy for 1 minute
9. Open blender
10. Get glasses
11. Get pink umbrellas
12. Serve

---

1. Although UML has gradually faded, many of its individual diagrams still exist in one form or another, including the very useful *activity diagram.* For more information on all of the UML diagram types, see *UML Distilled: A Brief Guide to the Standard Object Modeling Language [Fow04].*

However, a bartender would lose their job if they followed these steps, one by one, in order. Even though they describe these actions serially, many of them could be performed in parallel. We'll use the following activity diagram to capture and reason about potential concurrency.

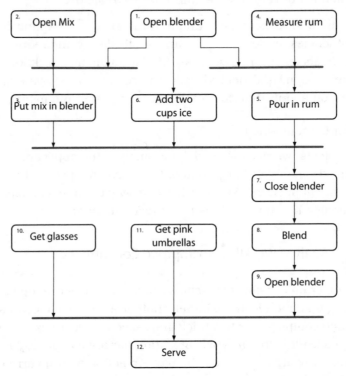

It can be eye-opening to see where the dependencies really exist. In this instance, the top-level tasks (1, 2, 4, 10, and 11) can all happen concurrently, up front. Tasks 3, 5, and 6 can happen in parallel later. If you were in a piña colada-making contest, these optimizations may make all the difference.

Opportunities for Concurrency

Activity diagrams show the potential areas of concurrency, but have nothing to say about whether these areas are worth exploiting. For example, in the piña colada example, a bartender would need five hands to be able to run all the potential initial tasks at once.

And that's where the design part comes in. When we look at the activities, we realize that number 8, liquify, will take a minute. During that time, our bartender can get the glasses and umbrellas (activities 10 and 11) and probably still have time to serve another customer.

Faster Formatting

This book is written in plain text. To build the version to be printed, or an ebook, or whatever, that text is fed through a pipeline of processors. Some look for particular constructs (bibliography citations, index entries, special markup for tips, and so on). Other processors operate on the document as a whole.

Many of the processors in the pipeline have to access external information (reading files, writing files, piping through external programs). All this relatively slow speed work gives us the opportunity to exploit concurrency: in fact each step in the pipeline executes concurrently, reading from the previous step and writing to the next.

In addition, some parts of the process are relatively processor intensive. One of these is the conversion of mathematical formulae. For various historical reasons each equation can take up to 500ms to convert. To speed things up, we take advantage of parallelism. Because each formula is independent of the others, we convert each in its own parallel process and collect the results back into the book as they become available.

As a result, the book builds much, much faster on multicore machines.

(And, yes, we did indeed discover a number of concurrency errors in our pipeline along the way....)

And that's what we're looking for when we're designing for concurrency. We're hoping to find activities that take time, but not time in our code. Querying a database, accessing an external service, waiting for user input: all these things would normally stall our program until they complete. And these are all opportunities to do something more productive than the CPU equivalent of twiddling one's thumbs.

Opportunities for Parallelism

Remember the distinction: concurrency is a software mechanism, and parallelism is a hardware concern. If we have multiple processors, either locally or remotely, then if we can split work out among them we can reduce the overall time things take.

The ideal things to split this way are pieces of work that are relatively independent—where each can proceed without waiting for anything from the others. A common pattern is to take a large piece of work, split it into independent chunks, process each in parallel, then combine the results.

An interesting example of this in practice is the way the compiler for the Elixir language works. When it starts, it splits the project it is building into modules, and compiles each in parallel. Sometimes a module depends on another, in which case its compilation pauses until the results of the other module's build become available. When the top-level module completes, it means that all dependencies have been compiled. The result is a speedy compilation that takes advantage of all the cores available.

Identifying Opportunities Is the Easy Part

Back to your applications. We've identified places where it will benefit from concurrency and parallelism. Now for the tricky part: how can we implement it safely. That's the topic of the rest of the chapter.

Related Sections Include

- Topic 10, *Orthogonality*, on page 39
- Topic 26, *How to Balance Resources*, on page 118
- Topic 28, *Decoupling*, on page 130
- Topic 36, *Blackboards*, on page 187

Challenges

- How many tasks do you perform in parallel when you get ready for work in the morning? Could you express this in a UML activity diagram? Can you find some way to get ready more quickly by increasing concurrency?

---

 34 **Shared State Is Incorrect State**

You're in your favorite diner. You finish your main course, and ask your server if there's any apple pie left. He looks over his shoulder, sees one piece in the display case, and says yes. You order it and sigh contentedly.

Meanwhile, on the other side of the restaurant, another customer asks their server the same question. She also looks, confirms there's a piece, and that customer orders.

One of the customers is going to be disappointed.

Swap the display case for a joint bank account, and turn the waitstaff into point-of-sale devices. You and your partner both decide to buy a new phone at the same time, but there's only enough in the account for one. Someone—the bank, the store, or you—is going to be very unhappy.

Tip 57	Shared State Is Incorrect State

The problem is the shared state. Each server in the restaurant looked into the display case without regard for the other. Each point-of-sale device looked at an account balance without regard for the other.

Nonatomic Updates

Let's look at our diner example as if it were code:

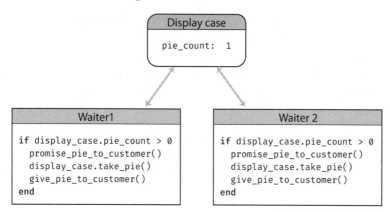

The two waiters operate concurrently (and, in real life, in parallel). Let's look at their code:

```
if display_case.pie_count > 0
  promise_pie_to_customer()
  display_case.take_pie()
  give_pie_to_customer()
end
```

Waiter 1 gets the current pie count, and finds that it is one. He promises the pie to the customer. But at that point, waiter 2 runs. She also sees the pie count is one and makes the same promise to her customer. One of the two then grabs the last piece of pie, and the other waiter enters some kind of error state (which probably involves much grovelling).

The problem here is not that two processes can write to the same memory. The problem is that neither process can guarantee that its view of that memory is consistent. Effectively, when a waiter executes display_case.pie_count(), they copy the value from the display case into their own memory. If the value in the display case changes, their memory (which they are using to make decisions) is now out of date.

This is all because the fetching and then updating the pie count is not an atomic operation: the underlying value can change in the middle.

So how can we make it atomic?

Semaphores and Other Forms of Mutual Exclusion

A semaphore is simply a *thing* that only one person can own at a time. You can create a semaphore and then use it to control access to some other resource. In our example, we could create a semaphore to control access to the pie case, and adopt the convention that anyone who wants to update the pie case contents can only do so if they are holding that semaphore.

Say the diner decides to fix the pie problem with a physical semaphore. They place a plastic Leprechaun on the pie case. Before any waiter can sell a pie, they have to be holding the Leprechaun in their hand. Once their order has been completed (which means delivering the pie to the table) they can return the Leprechaun to its place guarding the treasure of the pies, ready to mediate the next order.

Let's look at this in code. Classically, the operation to grab the semaphore was called *P*, and the operation to release it was called *V*.[2] Today we use terms such as *lock/unlock*, *claim/release*, and so on.

```
case_semaphore.lock()

if display_case.pie_count > 0
  promise_pie_to_customer()
  display_case.take_pie()
  give_pie_to_customer()
end

case_semaphore.unlock()
```

This code assumes that a semaphore has already been created and stored in the variable case_semaphore.

Let's assume both waiters execute the code at the same time. They both try to lock the semaphore, but only one succeeds. The one that gets the semaphore continues to run as normal. The one that doesn't get the semaphore is suspended until the semaphore becomes available (the waiter waits...). When the first waiter completes the order they unlock the semaphore and the second waiter continues running. They now see there's no pie in the case, and apologize to the customer.

There are some problems with this approach. Probably the most significant is that it only works because everyone who accesses the pie case agrees on

---

2. The names P and V come from the initial letters of Dutch words. However there is some discussion about exactly which words. The inventor of the technique, Edsger Dijkstra, has suggested both *passering* and *prolaag* for P, and *vrijgave* and possibly *verhogen* for V.

the convention of using the semaphore. If someone forgets (that is, some developer writes code that doesn't follow the convention) then we're back in chaos.

Make the Resource Transactional

The current design is poor because it delegates responsibility for protecting access to the pie case to the people who use it. Let's change it to centralize that control. To do this, we have to change the API so that waiters can check the count and also take a slice of pie in a single call:

```
slice = display_case.get_pie_if_available()
if slice
  give_pie_to_customer()
end
```

To make this work, we need to write a method that runs as part of the display case itself:

```
def get_pie_if_available()      ####
  if @slices.size > 0            #
    update_sales_data(:pie)      #
    return @slices.shift         #
  else                          #   incorrect code!
    false                       #
  end                           #
end                             ####
```

This code illustrates a common misconception. We've moved the resource access into a central place, but our method can still be called from multiple concurrent threads, so we still need to protect it with a semaphore:

```
def get_pie_if_available()
  @case_semaphore.lock()

  if @slices.size > 0
    update_sales_data(:pie)
    return @slices.shift
  else
    false
  end

  @case_semaphore.unlock()
end
```

Even this code might not be correct. If update_sales_data raises an exception, the semaphore will never get unlocked, and all future access to the pie case will hang indefinitely. We need to handle this:

```
def get_pie_if_available()
  @case_semaphore.lock()

  try {
    if @slices.size > 0
      update_sales_data(:pie)
      return @slices.shift
    else
      false
    end
  }
  ensure {
    @case_semaphore.unlock()
  }
end
```

Because this is such a common mistake, many languages provide libraries that handle this for you:

```
def get_pie_if_available()
  @case_semaphore.protect() {
    if @slices.size > 0
      update_sales_data(:pie)
      return @slices.shift
    else
      false
    end
  }
end
```

Multiple Resource Transactions

Our diner just installed an ice cream freezer. If a customer orders pie *à la mode*, the waiter will need to check that both pie *and* ice cream are available.

We could change the waiter code to something like:

```
slice = display_case.get_pie_if_available()
scoop = freezer.get_ice_cream_if_available()

if slice && scoop
  give_order_to_customer()
end
```

This won't work, though. What happens if we claim a slice of pie, but when we try to get a scoop of ice cream we find out there isn't any? We're now left holding some pie that we can't do anything with (because our customer *must* have ice cream). And the fact we're holding the pie means it isn't in the case, so it isn't available to some other customer who (being a purist) doesn't want ice cream with it.

We could fix this by adding a method to the case that lets us return a slice of pie. We'll need to add exception handling to ensure we don't keep resources if something fails:

```
slice = display_case.get_pie_if_available()

if slice
  try {
      scoop = freezer.get_ice_cream_if_available()
      if scoop
      try {
        give_order_to_customer()
      }
      rescue {
        freezer.give_back(scoop)
      }
      end
  }
  rescue {
    display_case.give_back(slice)
  }
end
```

Again, this is less than ideal. The code is now really ugly: working out what it actually does is difficult: the business logic is buried in all the housekeeping.

Previously we fixed this by moving the resource handling code into the resource itself. Here, though, we have two resources. Should we put the code in the display case or the freezer?

We think the answer is "no" to both options. The pragmatic approach would be to say that "apple pie à la mode" is its own resource. We'd move this code into a new module, and then the client could just say "get me apple pie with ice cream" and it either succeeds or fails.

Of course, in the real world there are likely to be many composite dishes like this, and you wouldn't want to write new modules for each. Instead, you'd probably want some kind of menu item which contained references to its components, and then have a generic get_menu_item method that does the resource dance with each.

Non-Transactional Updates

A lot of attention is given to shared memory as a source of concurrency problems, but in fact the problems can pop up *anywhere* where your application code shares mutable resources: files, databases, external services, and so on. Whenever two or more instances of your code can access some resource at the same time, you're looking at a potential problem.

Sometimes, the resource isn't all that obvious. While writing this edition of the book we updated the toolchain to do more work in parallel using threads. This caused the build to fail, but in bizarre ways and random places. A common thread through all the errors was that files or directories could not be found, even though they were really in exactly the right place.

We tracked this down to a couple of places in the code which temporarily changed the current directory. In the nonparallel version, the fact that this code restored the directory back was good enough. But in the parallel version, one thread would change the directory and then, while in that directory, another thread would start running. That thread would expect to be in the original directory, but because the current directory is shared between threads, that wasn't the case.

The nature of this problem prompts another tip:

Tip 58	Random Failures Are Often Concurrency Issues

Other Kinds of Exclusive Access

Most languages have library support for some kind of exclusive access to shared resources. They may call it mutexes (for mutual exclusion), monitors, or semaphores. These are all implemented as libraries.

However, some languages have concurrency support built into the language itself. Rust, for example, enforces the concept of data ownership; only one variable or parameter can hold a reference to any particular piece of mutable data at a time.

You could also argue that functional languages, with their tendency to make all data immutable, make concurrency simpler. However, they still face the same challenges, because at some point they are forced to step into the real, mutable world.

Doctor, It Hurts...

If you take nothing else away from this section, take this: concurrency in a shared resource environment is difficult, and managing it yourself is fraught with challenges.

Which is why we're recommending the punchline to the old joke:

Doctor, it hurts when I do this.

Then don't do that.

The next couple of sections suggest alternative ways of getting the benefits of concurrency without the pain.

Related Sections Include

- Topic 10, *Orthogonality*, on page 39
- Topic 28, *Decoupling*, on page 130
- Topic 38, *Programming by Coincidence*, on page 197

35 ► Actors and Processes

Without writers, stories would not be written,
Without actors, stories could not be brought to life.

➤ *Angie-Marie Delsante*

Actors and processes offer interesting ways of implementing concurrency without the burden of synchronizing access to shared memory.

Before we get into them, however, we need to define what we mean. And this is going to sound academic. Never fear, we'll be working through it all in a short while.

- An *actor* is an independent virtual processor with its own local (and private) state. Each actor has a mailbox. When a message appears in the mailbox and the actor is idle, it kicks into life and processes the message. When it finishes processing, it processes another message in the mailbox, or, if the mailbox is empty, it goes back to sleep.

  When processing a message, an actor can create other actors, send messages to other actors that it knows about, and create a new state that will become the current state when the next message is processed.

- A *process* is typically a more general-purpose virtual processor, often implemented by the operating system to facilitate concurrency. Processes can be constrained (by convention) to behave like actors, and that's the type of process we mean here.

Actors Can Only Be Concurrent

There are a few things that you *won't* find in the definition of actors:

- There's no single *thing* that's in control. Nothing schedules what happens next, or orchestrates the transfer of information from the raw data to the final output.

- The *only* state in the system is held in messages and in the local state of each actor. Messages cannot be examined except by being read by their recipient, and local state is inaccessible outside the actor.

- All messages are one way—there's no concept of replying. If you want an actor to return a response, you include your own mailbox address in the message you send it, and it will (eventually) send the response as just another message to that mailbox.

- An actor processes each message to completion, and only processes one message at a time.

As a result, actors execute concurrently, asynchronously, and share nothing. If you had enough physical processors, you could run an actor on each. If you have a single processor, then some runtime can handle the switching of context between them. Either way, the code running in the actors is the same.

> | Tip 59 | **Use Actors For Concurrency Without Shared State** |

A Simple Actor

Let's implement our diner using actors. In this case, we'll have three (the customer, the waiter, and the pie case).

The overall message flow will look like this:

- We (as some kind of external, God-like being) tell the customer that they are hungry

- In response, they'll ask the waiter for pie

- The waiter will ask the pie case to get some pie to the customer

- If the pie case has a slice available, it will send it to the customer, and also notify the waiter to add it to the bill

- If there is no pie, the case tells the waiter, and the waiter apologizes to the customer

We've chosen to implement the code in JavaScript using the Nact library.[3] We've added a little wrapper to this that lets us write actors as simple objects, where the keys are the message types that it receives and the values are functions to run when that particular message is received. (Most actor systems have a similar kind of structure, but the details depend on the host language.)

---

3.   https://github.com/ncthbrt/nact

Let's start with the customer. The customer can receive three messages:

- You're hungry (sent by the external context)
- There's pie on the table (sent by the pie case)
- Sorry, there's no pie (sent by the waiter)

Here's the code:

concurrency/actors/index.js
```
const customerActor = {
  'hungry for pie': (msg, ctx, state) => {
    return dispatch(state.waiter,
                    { type: "order", customer: ctx.self, wants: 'pie' })
  },

  'put on table': (msg, ctx, _state) =>
    console.log(`${ctx.self.name} sees "${msg.food}" appear on the table`),

  'no pie left': (_msg, ctx, _state) =>
    console.log(`${ctx.self.name} sulks…`)
}
```

The interesting case is when we receive a "hungry for pie'" message, where we then send a message off to the waiter. (We'll see how the customer knows about the waiter actor shortly.)

Here's the waiter's code:

concurrency/actors/index.js
```
const waiterActor = {
  "order": (msg, ctx, state) => {
    if (msg.wants == "pie") {
      dispatch(state.pieCase,
               { type: "get slice", customer: msg.customer, waiter: ctx.self })
    }
    else {
      console.dir(`Don't know how to order ${msg.wants}`);
    }
  },

  "add to order": (msg, ctx) =>
    console.log(`Waiter adds ${msg.food} to ${msg.customer.name}'s order`),

  "error": (msg, ctx) => {
    dispatch(msg.customer, { type: 'no pie left', msg: msg.msg });
    console.log(`\nThe waiter apologizes to ${msg.customer.name}: ${msg.msg}`)
  }
};
```

When it receives the 'order' message from the customer, it checks to see if the request is for pie. If so, it sends a request to the pie case, passing references both to itself and the customer.

The pie case has state: an array of all the slices of pie it holds. (Again, we see how that gets set up shortly.) When it receives a 'get slice' message from the waiter, it sees if it has any slices left. If it does, it passes the slice to the customer, tells the waiter to update the order, and finally returns an updated state, containing one less slice. Here's the code:

concurrency/actors/index.js

```
const pieCaseActor = {
  'get slice': (msg, context, state) => {
    if (state.slices.length == 0) {
      dispatch(msg.waiter,
              { type: 'error', msg: "no pie left", customer: msg.customer })
      return state
    }
    else {
      var slice = state.slices.shift() + " pie slice";
      dispatch(msg.customer,
              { type: 'put on table', food: slice });
      dispatch(msg.waiter,
              { type: 'add to order', food: slice, customer: msg.customer });
      return state;
    }
  }
}
```

Although you'll often find that actors are started dynamically by other actors, in our case we'll keep it simple and start our actors manually. We will also pass each some initial state:

- The pie case gets the initial list of pie slices it contains
- We'll give the waiter a reference to the pie case
- We'll give the customers a reference to the waiter

concurrency/actors/index.js

```
const actorSystem = start();

let pieCase = start_actor(
  actorSystem,
  'pie-case',
  pieCaseActor,
  { slices: ["apple", "peach", "cherry"] });

let waiter = start_actor(
  actorSystem,
  'waiter',
  waiterActor,
  { pieCase: pieCase });
```

```
let c1 = start_actor(actorSystem,    'customer1',
                     customerActor, { waiter: waiter });
let c2 = start_actor(actorSystem,    'customer2',
                     customerActor, { waiter: waiter });
```

And finally we kick it off. Our customers are greedy. Customer 1 asks for three slices of pie, and customer 2 asks for two:

```
concurrency/actors/index.js
dispatch(c1, { type: 'hungry for pie', waiter: waiter });
dispatch(c2, { type: 'hungry for pie', waiter: waiter });
dispatch(c1, { type: 'hungry for pie', waiter: waiter });
dispatch(c2, { type: 'hungry for pie', waiter: waiter });
dispatch(c1, { type: 'hungry for pie', waiter: waiter });
sleep(500)
  .then(() => {
    stop(actorSystem);
  })
```

When we run it, we can see the actors communicating.[4] The order you see may well be different:

```
$ node index.js
customer1 sees "apple pie slice" appear on the table
customer2 sees "peach pie slice" appear on the table
Waiter adds apple pie slice to customer1's order
Waiter adds peach pie slice to customer2's order
customer1 sees "cherry pie slice" appear on the table
Waiter adds cherry pie slice to customer1's order

The waiter apologizes to customer1: no pie left
customer1 sulks…

The waiter apologizes to customer2: no pie left
customer2 sulks…
```

No Explicit Concurrency

In the actor model, there's no need to write any code to handle concurrency, as there is no shared state. There's also no need to code in explicit end-to-end "do this, do that" logic, as the actors work it out for themselves based on the messages they receive.

There's also no mention of the underlying architecture. This set of components work equally well on a single processor, on multiple cores, or on multiple networked machines.

---

4. In order to run this code you'll also need our wrapper functions, which are not shown here. You can download them from https://media.pragprog.com/titles/tpp20/code/concurrency/actors/index.js

Erlang Sets the Stage

The Erlang language and runtime are great examples of an actor implementation (even though the inventors of Erlang hadn't read the original Actor's paper). Erlang calls actors *processes*, but they aren't regular operating system processes. Instead, just like the actors we've been discussing, Erlang processes are lightweight (you can run millions of them on a single machine), and they communicate by sending messages. Each is isolated from the others, so there is no sharing of state.

In addition, the Erlang runtime implements a *supervision* system, which manages the lifetimes of processes, potentially restarting a process or set of processes in case of failure. And Erlang also offers hot-code loading: you can replace code in a running system without stopping that system. And the Erlang system runs some of the world's most reliable code, often citing nine nines availability.

But Erlang (and it's progeny Elixir) aren't unique—there are actor implementations for most languages. Consider using them for your concurrent implementations.

Related Sections Include

- Topic 28, *Decoupling*, on page 130
- Topic 30, *Transforming Programming*, on page 147
- Topic 36, *Blackboards*, on page 187

Challenges

- Do you currently have code that uses mutual exclusion to protect shared data. Why not try a prototype of the same code written using actors?

- The actor code for the diner only supports ordering slices of pie. Extend it to let customers order pie à la mode, with separate agents managing the pie slices and the scoops of ice cream. Arrange things so that it handles the situation where one or the other runs out.

36 Blackboards

The writing is on the wall...

> ➤ *Daniel 5 (ref)*

Consider how detectives might use a *blackboard* to coordinate and solve a murder investigation. The chief inspector starts off by setting up a large blackboard in the conference room. On it, she writes a single question:

> H. Dumpty (Male, Egg): Accident? Murder?

Did Humpty really fall, or was he pushed? Each detective may make contributions to this potential murder mystery by adding facts, statements from witnesses, any forensic evidence that might arise, and so on. As the data accumulates, a detective might notice a connection and post that observation or speculation as well. This process continues, across all shifts, with many different people and agents, until the case is closed. A sample blackboard is shown in the figure on page 188.

Some key features of the blackboard approach are:

- None of the detectives needs to know of the existence of any other detective—they watch the board for new information, and add their findings.

- The detectives may be trained in different disciplines, may have different levels of education and expertise, and may not even work in the same precinct. They share a desire to solve the case, but that's all.

- Different detectives may come and go during the course of the process, and may work different shifts.

- There are no restrictions on what may be placed on the blackboard. It may be pictures, sentences, physical evidence, and so on.

This is a form of *laissez faire* concurrency. The detectives are independent processes, agents, actors, and so on. Some store facts on the blackboard. Others take facts off the board, maybe combining or processing them, and add more information to the board. Gradually the board helps them come to a conclusion.

Computer-based blackboard systems were originally used in artificial intelligence applications where the problems to be solved were large and complex—speech recognition, knowledge-based reasoning systems, and so on.

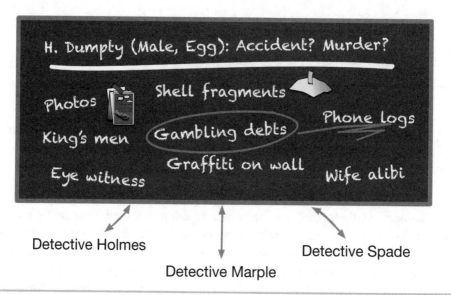

Figure 2— Someone found a connection between Humpty's gambling debts and the phone logs. Perhaps he was getting threatening phone calls.

One of the first blackboard systems was David Gelernter's Linda. It stored facts as typed tuples. Applications could write new tuples into Linda, and query for existing tuples using a form of pattern matching.

Later came distributed blackboard-like systems such as JavaSpaces and T Spaces. With these systems, you can store active Java objects—not just data—on the blackboard, and retrieve them by partial matching of fields (via templates and wildcards) or by subtypes. For example, suppose you had a type Author, which is a subtype of Person. You could search a blackboard containing Person objects by using an Author template with a lastName value of "Shakespeare." You'd get Bill Shakespeare the author, but not Fred Shakespeare the gardener.

These systems never really took off, we believe, in part, because the need for the kind of concurrent cooperative processing hadn't yet developed.

A Blackboard in Action

Suppose we are writing a program to accept and process mortgage or loan applications. The laws that govern this area are odiously complex, with federal, state, and local governments all having their say. The lender must prove they have disclosed certain things, and must ask for certain information—but must *not* ask certain other questions, and so on, and so on.

Beyond the miasma of applicable law, we also have the following problems to contend with:

- Responses can arrive in any order. For instance, queries for a credit check or title search may take a substantial amount of time, while items such as name and address may be available immediately.

- Data gathering may be done by different people, distributed across different offices, in different time zones.

- Some data gathering may be done automatically by other systems. This data may arrive asynchronously as well.

- Nonetheless, certain data may still be dependent on other data. For instance, you may not be able to start the title search for a car until you get proof of ownership or insurance.

- The arrival of new data may raise new questions and policies. Suppose the credit check comes back with a less than glowing report; now you need these five extra forms and perhaps a blood sample.

You can try to handle every possible combination and circumstance using a workflow system. Many such systems exist, but they can be complex and programmer intensive. As regulations change, the workflow must be reorganized: people may have to change their procedures and hard-wired code may have to be rewritten.

A blackboard, in combination with a rules engine that encapsulates the legal requirements, is an elegant solution to the difficulties found here. Order of data arrival is irrelevant: when a fact is posted it can trigger the appropriate rules. Feedback is easily handled as well: the output of any set of rules can post to the blackboard and cause the triggering of yet more applicable rules.

> Tip 60   **Use Blackboards to Coordinate Workflow**

Messaging Systems Can Be Like Blackboards

As we're writing this second edition, many applications are constructed using small, decoupled services, all communicating via some form of messaging system. These messaging systems (such as Kafka and NATS) do far more than simply send data from A to B. In particular, they offer persistence (in the form of an event log) and the ability to retrieve messages through a form of pattern matching. This means you can use them both as a blackboard system and/or as a platform on which you can run a bunch of actors.

But It's Not That Simple...

The actor and/or blackboard and/or microservice approach to architecture removes a whole class of potential concurrency problems from your applications. But that benefit comes at a cost. These approaches are harder to reason about, because a lot of the action is indirect. You'll find it helps to keep a central repository of message formats and/or APIs, particularly if the repository can generate the code and documentation for you. You'll also need good tooling to be able to trace messages and facts as they progress through the system. (A useful technique is to add a unique *trace id* when a particular business function is initiated and then propagate it to all the actors involved. You'll then be able to reconstruct what happens from the log files.)

Finally, these kinds of system can be more troublesome to deploy and manage, as there are more moving parts. To some extent this is offset by the fact that the system is more granular, and can be updated by replacing individual actors, and not the whole system.

Related Sections Include

- Topic 28, *Decoupling*, on page 130
- Topic 29, *Juggling the Real World*, on page 137
- Topic 33, *Breaking Temporal Coupling*, on page 170
- Topic 35, *Actors and Processes*, on page 181

Exercises

Exercise 24 (possible answer on page 302)

Would a blackboard-style system be appropriate for the following applications? Why, or why not?

Image processing. You'd like to have a number of parallel processes grab chunks of an image, process them, and put the completed chunk back.

Group calendaring. You've got people scattered across the globe, in different time zones, and speaking different languages, trying to schedule a meeting.

Network monitoring tool. The system gathers performance statistics and collects trouble reports, which agents use to look for trouble in the system.

Challenges

- Do you use blackboard systems in the real world—the message board by the refrigerator, or the big whiteboard at work? What makes them effective? Are messages ever posted with a consistent format? Does it matter?

## CHAPTER 7

While You Are Coding

Conventional wisdom says that once a project is in the coding phase, the work is mostly mechanical, transcribing the design into executable statements. We think that this attitude is the single biggest reason that software projects fail, and many systems end up ugly, inefficient, poorly structured, unmaintainable, or just plain wrong.

Coding is not mechanical. If it were, all the CASE tools that people pinned their hopes on way back in the early 1980s would have replaced programmers long ago. There are decisions to be made every minute—decisions that require careful thought and judgment if the resulting program is to enjoy a long, accurate, and productive life.

Not all decisions are even conscious. You can better harness your instincts and nonconscious thoughts when you *Listen to Your Lizard Brain*. We'll see how to listen more carefully and look at ways of actively responding to these sometimes niggling thoughts.

But listening to your instincts doesn't mean you can just fly on autopilot. Developers who don't actively think about their code are programming by coincidence—the code might work, but there's no particular reason why. In *Programming by Coincidence*, we advocate a more positive involvement with the coding process.

While most of the code we write executes quickly, we occasionally develop algorithms that have the potential to bog down even the fastest processors. In *Algorithm Speed*, we discuss ways to estimate the speed of code, and we give some tips on how to spot potential problems before they happen.

Pragmatic Programmers think critically about all code, including our own. We constantly see room for improvement in our programs and our designs.

In *Refactoring*, we look at techniques that help us fix up existing code continuously as we go.

Testing is not about finding bugs, it's about getting feedback on your code: aspects of design, the API, coupling, and so on. That means that the major benefits of testing happen when you think about and write the tests, not just when you run them. We'll explore this idea in *Test to Code*.

But of course when you test your own code, you might bring your own biases to the task. In *Property-Based Testing* we'll see how to have the computer do some wide-ranging testing for you and how to handle the inevitable bugs that come up.

It's critical that you write code that is readable and easy to reason about. It's a harsh world out there, filled with bad actors who are actively trying to break into your system and cause harm. We'll discuss some very basic techniques and approaches to help you *Stay Safe Out There*.

Finally, one of the hardest things in software development is *Naming Things*. We have to name a lot of things, and in many ways the names we choose define the reality we create. You need to stay aware of any potential semantic drift while you are coding.

Most of us can drive a car largely on autopilot; we don't explicitly command our foot to press a pedal, or our arm to turn the wheel—we just think "slow down and turn right." However, good, safe drivers are constantly reviewing the situation, checking for potential problems, and putting themselves into good positions in case the unexpected happens. The same is true of coding—it may be largely routine, but keeping your wits about you could well prevent a disaster.

37 Listen to Your Lizard Brain

*Only human beings can look directly at something, have all the
information they need to make an accurate prediction, perhaps
even momentarily make the accurate prediction, and then say that
it isn't so.*

> ➤ Gavin de Becker, The Gift of Fear

Gavin de Becker's life's work is helping people to protect themselves. His book, *The Gift of Fear: And Other Survival Signals That Protect Us from Violence* [de 98], encapsulates his message. One of the key themes running through the book is that as sophisticated humans we have learned to ignore our more animal side; our instincts, our lizard brain. He claims that most people who are attacked in the street are aware of feeling uncomfortable or nervous before the attack. These people just tell themselves they're being silly. Then the figure emerges from the dark doorway....

Instincts are simply a response to patterns packed into our nonconscious brain. Some are innate, others are learned through repetition. As you gain experience as a programmer, your brain is laying down layers of tacit knowledge: things that work, things that don't work, the probable causes of a type of error, all the things you notice throughout your days. This is the part of your brain that hits the *save file* key when you stop to chat with someone, even when you don't realize that you're doing it.

Whatever their source, instincts share one thing: they have no words. Instincts make you feel, not think. And so when an instinct is triggered, you don't see a flashing lightbulb with a banner wrapped around it. Instead, you get nervous, or queasy, or feel like this is just too much work.

The trick is first to notice it is happening, and then to work out why. Let's look first at a couple of common situations in which your inner lizard is trying to tell you something. Then we'll discuss how you can let that instinctive brain out of its protective wrapper.

Fear of the Blank Page

Everyone fears the empty screen, the lonely blinking cursor surrounded by a whole bunch of nothing. Starting a new project (or even a new module in an existing project) can be an unnerving experience. Many of us would prefer to put off making the initial commitment of starting.

We think that there are two problems that cause this, and that both have the same solution.

One problem is that your lizard brain is trying to tell you something; there's some kind of doubt lurking just below the surface of perception. And that's important.

As a developer, you've been trying things and seeing which worked and which didn't. You've been accumulating experience and wisdom. When you feel a nagging doubt, or experience some reluctance when faced with a task, it might be that experience trying to speak to you. Heed it. You may not be able to put your finger on exactly what's wrong, but give it time and your doubts will probably crystallize into something more solid, something you can address. Let your instincts contribute to your performance.

The other problem is a little more prosaic: you might simply be afraid that you'll make a mistake.

And that's a reasonable fear. We developers put a lot of ourselves into our code; we can take errors in that code as reflections on our competence. Perhaps there's an element of *imposter syndrome*, too; we may think that this project is beyond us. We can't see our way through to the end; we'll get so far and then be forced to admit that we're lost.

Fighting Yourself

Sometimes code just flies from your brain into the editor: ideas become bits with seemingly no effort.

Other days, coding feels like walking uphill in mud. Taking each step requires tremendous effort, and every three steps you slide back two.

But, being a professional, you soldier on, taking step after muddy step: you have a job to do. Unfortunately, that's probably the exact opposite of what you should do.

Your code is trying to tell you something. It's saying that this is harder than it should be. Maybe the structure or design is wrong, maybe you're solving the wrong problem, or maybe you're just creating an ant farm's worth of bugs. Whatever the reason, your lizard brain is sensing feedback from the code, and it's desperately trying to get you to listen.

How to Talk Lizard

We talk a lot about listening to your instincts, to your nonconscious, lizard brain. The techniques are always the same.

Tip 61	Listen to Your Inner Lizard

First, stop what you're doing. Give yourself a little time and space to let your brain organize itself. Stop thinking about the code, and do something that is fairly mindless for a while, away from a keyboard. Take a walk, have lunch, chat with someone. Maybe sleep on it. Let the ideas percolate up through the layers of your brain on their own: you can't force it. Eventually they may bubble up to the conscious level, and you have one of those *a ha!* moments.

If that's not working, try externalizing the issue. Make doodles about the code you're writing, or explain it to a coworker (preferably one who isn't a programmer), or to your rubber duck. Expose different parts of your brain to the issue, and see if any of them have a better handle on the thing that's troubling you. We've lost track of the number of conversations we've had where one of us was explaining a problem to the other and suddenly went "Oh! Of course!" and broke off to fix it.

But maybe you've tried these things, and you're still stuck. It's time for action. We need to tell your brain that what you're about to do doesn't matter. And we do that by prototyping.

It's Playtime!

Andy and Dave have both spent hours looking at empty editor buffers. We'll type in some code, then look at the ceiling, then get yet another drink, then type in some more code, then go read a funny story about a cat with two tails, then type some more code, then do select-all/delete and start again. And again. And again.

And over the years we've found a brain hack that seems to work. Tell yourself you need to prototype something. If you're facing a blank screen, then look for some aspect of the project that you want to explore. Maybe you're using a new framework, and want to see how it does data binding. Or maybe it's a new algorithm, and you want to explore how it works on edge cases. Or maybe you want to try a couple of different styles of user interaction.

If you're working on existing code and it's pushing back, then stash it away somewhere and prototype up something similar instead.

Do the following.

1. Write "I'm prototyping" on a sticky note, and stick it on the side of your screen.

2. Remind yourself that prototypes are meant to fail. And remind yourself that prototypes get thrown away, even if they don't fail. There is no downside to doing this.

3. In your empty editor buffer, create a comment describing in one sentence what you want to learn or do.

4. Start coding.

If you start to have doubts, look at the sticky note.

If, in the middle of coding, that nagging doubt suddenly crystallizes into a solid concern, then address it.

If you get to the end of the experiment and you still feel uneasy, start again with the walk and the talk and the time off.

But, in our experience, at some point during the first prototype you will be surprised to find yourself humming along with your music, enjoying the feeling of creating code. The nervousness will have evaporated, replaced by a feeling of urgency: let's get this done!

At this stage, you know what to do. Delete all the prototype code, throw away the sticky note, and fill that empty editor buffer with bright, shiny new code.

Not Just *Your* Code

A large part of our job is dealing with existing code, often written by other people. Those people will have different instincts to you, and so the decisions they made will be different. Not necessarily worse; just different.

You can read their code mechanically, slogging through it making notes on stuff that seems important. It's a chore, but it works.

Or you can try an experiment. When you spot things done in a way that seems strange, jot it down. Continue doing this, and look for patterns. If you can see what drove them to write code that way, you may find that the job of understanding it becomes a lot easier. You'll be able consciously to apply the patterns that they applied tacitly.

And you might just learn something new along the way.

Not Just Code

Learning to listen to your gut when coding is an important skill to foster. But it applies to the bigger picture are well. Sometimes a design just feels wrong, or some requirement makes you feel uneasy. Stop and analyze these feelings. If you're in a supportive environment, express them out loud. Explore them. The chances are that there's something lurking in that dark doorway. Listen to your instincts and avoid the problem before it jumps out at you.

Related Sections Include

- Topic 13, *Prototypes and Post-it Notes*, on page 56
- Topic 22, *Engineering Daybooks*, on page 100
- Topic 46, *Solving Impossible Puzzles*, on page 252

Challenges

- Is there something you know you should do, but have put off because it feels a little scary, or difficult? Apply the techniques in this section. Time box it to an hour, maybe two, and promise yourself that when the bell rings you'll delete what you did. What did you learn?

Programming by Coincidence

Do you ever watch old black-and-white war movies? The weary soldier advances cautiously out of the brush. There's a clearing ahead: are there any land mines, or is it safe to cross? There aren't any indications that it's a minefield—no signs, barbed wire, or craters. The soldier pokes the ground ahead of him with his bayonet and winces, expecting an explosion. There isn't one. So he proceeds painstakingly through the field for a while, prodding and poking as he goes. Eventually, convinced that the field is safe, he straightens up and marches proudly forward, only to be blown to pieces.

The soldier's initial probes for mines revealed nothing, but this was merely lucky. He was led to a false conclusion—with disastrous results.

As developers, we also work in minefields. There are hundreds of traps waiting to catch us each day. Remembering the soldier's tale, we should be wary of drawing false conclusions. We should avoid programming by coincidence—relying on luck and accidental successes—in favor of *programming deliberately*.

How to Program by Coincidence

Suppose Fred is given a programming assignment. Fred types in some code, tries it, and it seems to work. Fred types in some more code, tries it, and it still seems to work. After several weeks of coding this way, the program suddenly stops working, and after hours of trying to fix it, he still doesn't know why. Fred may well spend a significant amount of time chasing this piece of code around without ever being able to fix it. No matter what he does, it just doesn't ever seem to work right.

Fred doesn't know why the code is failing because *he didn't know why it worked in the first place*. It seemed to work, given the limited "testing" that Fred did, but that was just a coincidence. Buoyed by false confidence, Fred charged ahead into oblivion. Now, most intelligent people may know someone like Fred, but *we* know better. We don't rely on coincidences—do we?

Sometimes we might. Sometimes it can be pretty easy to confuse a happy coincidence with a purposeful plan. Let's look at a few examples.

Accidents of Implementation

Accidents of implementation are things that happen simply because that's the way the code is currently written. You end up relying on undocumented error or boundary conditions.

Suppose you call a routine with bad data. The routine responds in a particular way, and you code based on that response. But the author didn't intend for the routine to work that way—it was never even considered. When the routine gets "fixed," your code may break. In the most extreme case, the routine you called may not even be designed to do what you want, but it *seems* to work okay. Calling things in the wrong order, or in the wrong context, is a related problem.

Here it looks like Fred is desperately trying to get something out on the screen using some particular GUI rendering framework:

```
paint();
invalidate();
validate();
revalidate();
repaint();
paintImmediately();
```

But these routines were never designed to be called this way; although they seem to work, that's really just a coincidence.

To add insult to injury, when the scene finally does get drawn, Fred won't try to go back and take out the spurious calls. "It works now, better leave well enough alone...."

It's easy to be fooled by this line of thought. Why should you take the risk of messing with something that's working? Well, we can think of several reasons:

- It may not really be working—it might just look like it is.

- The boundary condition you rely on may be just an accident. In different circumstances (a different screen resolution, more CPU cores), it might behave differently.

- Undocumented behavior may change with the next release of the library.

- Additional and unnecessary calls make your code slower.

- Additional calls increase the risk of introducing new bugs of their own.

For code you write that others will call, the basic principles of good modularization and of hiding implementation behind small, well-documented interfaces can all help. A well-specified contract (see Topic 23, *Design by Contract*, on page 104) can help eliminate misunderstandings.

For routines you call, rely only on documented behavior. If you can't, for whatever reason, then document your assumption well.

Close Enough Isn't

We once worked on a large project that reported on data fed from a very large number of hardware data collection units out in the field. These units spanned states and time zones, and for various logistical and historical reasons, each unit was set to local time.[1] As a result of conflicting time zone interpretations and inconsistencies in Daylight Savings Time policies, results were almost always wrong, but only off by one. The developers on the project had gotten into the habit of just adding one or subtracting one to get the correct answer, reasoning that it was *only* off by one in this one situation. And then the next function would see the value as off by the one the other way, and change it back.

But the fact that it was "only" off by one some of the time was a coincidence, masking a deeper and more fundamental flaw. Without a proper model of time handling, the entire large code base had devolved over time to an untenable mass of +1 and -1 statements. Ultimately, none of it was correct and the project was scrapped.

Phantom Patterns

Human beings are designed to see patterns and causes, even when it's just a coincidence. For example, Russian leaders always alternate between being bald and hairy: a bald (or obviously balding) state leader of Russia has succeeded a non-bald ("hairy") one, and vice versa, for nearly 200 years.[2]

But while you wouldn't write code that depended on the next Russian leader being bald or hairy, in some domains we think that way all the time. Gamblers imagine patterns in lottery numbers, dice games, or roulette, when in fact these are statistically independent events. In finance, stock and bond trading are similarly rife with coincidence instead of actual, discernible patterns.

A log file that shows an intermittent error every 1,000 requests may be a difficult-to-diagnose race condition, or may be a plain old bug. Tests that seem

---

1. Note from the battle-scarred: UTC is there for a reason. Use it.
2. https://en.wikipedia.org/wiki/Correlation_does_not_imply_causation

to pass on your machine but not on the server might indicate a difference between the two environments, or maybe it's just a coincidence.

Don't assume it, prove it.

Accidents of Context

You can have "accidents of context" as well. Suppose you are writing a utility module. Just because you are currently coding for a GUI environment, does the module have to rely on a GUI being present? Are you relying on English-speaking users? Literate users? What else are you relying on that isn't guaranteed?

Are you relying on the current directory being writable? On certain environment variables or configuration files being present? On the time on the server being accurate—within what tolerance? Are you relying on network availability and speed?

When you copied code from the first answer you found on the net, are you sure your context is the same? Or are you building "cargo cult" code, merely imitating form without content?[3]

Finding an answer that happens to fit is not the same as the right answer.

> | Tip 62 | Don't Program by Coincidence |

Implicit Assumptions

Coincidences can mislead at all levels—from generating requirements through to testing. Testing is particularly fraught with false causalities and coincidental outcomes. It's easy to assume that X causes Y, but as we said in Topic 20, *Debugging*, on page 88: don't assume it, prove it.

At all levels, people operate with many assumptions in mind—but these assumptions are rarely documented and are often in conflict between different developers. Assumptions that aren't based on well-established facts are the bane of all projects.

How to Program Deliberately

We want to spend less time churning out code, catch and fix errors as early in the development cycle as possible, and create fewer errors to begin with. It helps if we can program deliberately:

---

3. See Topic 50, *Coconuts Don't Cut It*, on page 270.

- Always be aware of what you are doing. Fred let things get slowly out of hand, until he ended up boiled, like the frog on page 8.

- Can you explain the code, in detail, to a more junior programmer? If not, perhaps you are relying on coincidences.

- Don't code in the dark. Build an application you don't fully grasp, or use a technology you don't understand, and you'll likely be bitten by coincidences. If you're not sure why it works, you won't know why it fails.

- Proceed from a plan, whether that plan is in your head, on the back of a cocktail napkin, or on a whiteboard.

- Rely only on reliable things. Don't depend on assumptions. If you can't tell if something is reliable, assume the worst.

- Document your assumptions. Topic 23, *Design by Contract*, on page 104, can help clarify your assumptions in your own mind, as well as help communicate them to others.

- Don't just test your code, but test your assumptions as well. Don't guess; actually try it. Write an assertion to test your assumptions (see Topic 25, *Assertive Programming*, on page 115). If your assertion is right, you have improved the documentation in your code. If you discover your assumption is wrong, then count yourself lucky.

- Prioritize your effort. Spend time on the important aspects; more than likely, these are the hard parts. If you don't have fundamentals or infrastructure correct, brilliant bells and whistles will be irrelevant.

- Don't be a slave to history. Don't let existing code dictate future code. All code can be replaced if it is no longer appropriate. Even within one program, don't let what you've already done constrain what you do next—be ready to refactor (see Topic 40, *Refactoring*, on page 209). This decision may impact the project schedule. The assumption is that the impact will be less than the cost of *not* making the change.[4]

So next time something seems to work, but you don't know why, make sure it isn't just a coincidence.

---

4. You can also go too far here. We once knew a developer who rewrote all source he was given because he had his own naming conventions.

Related Sections Include

- Topic 4, *Stone Soup and Boiled Frogs*, on page 8
- Topic 9, *DRY—The Evils of Duplication*, on page 30
- Topic 23, *Design by Contract*, on page 104
- Topic 34, *Shared State Is Incorrect State*, on page 174
- Topic 43, *Stay Safe Out There*, on page 231

Exercises

Exercise 25 (possible answer on page 303)

A data feed from a vendor gives you an array of tuples representing key-value pairs. The key of DepositAccount will hold a string of the account number in the corresponding value:

```
[
  ...
  {:DepositAccount, "564-904-143-00"}
  ...
]
```

It worked perfectly in test on the 4-core developer laptops and on the 12-core build machine, but on the production servers running in containers, you keep getting the wrong account numbers. What's going on?

Exercise 26 (possible answer on page 303)

You're coding an autodialer for voice alerts, and have to manage a database of contact information. The ITU specifies that phone numbers should be no longer than 15 digits, so you store the contact's phone number in a numeric field guaranteed to hold at least 15 digits. You've tested in thoroughly throughout North America and everything seems fine, but suddenly you're getting a rash of complaints from other parts of the world. Why?

Exercise 27 (possible answer on page 303)

You have written an app that scales up common recipes for a cruise ship dining room that seats 5,000. But you're getting complaints that the conversions aren't precise. You check, and the code uses the conversion formula of 16 cups to a gallon. That's right, isn't it?

39 Algorithm Speed

In Topic 15, *Estimating*, on page 65, we talked about estimating things such as how long it takes to walk across town, or how long a project will take to finish. However, there is another kind of estimating that Pragmatic Programmers use almost daily: estimating the resources that algorithms use—time, processor, memory, and so on.

This kind of estimating is often crucial. Given a choice between two ways of doing something, which do you pick? You know how long your program runs with 1,000 records, but how will it scale to 1,000,000? What parts of the code need optimizing?

It turns out that these questions can often be answered using common sense, some analysis, and a way of writing approximations called the *Big-O* notation.

What Do We Mean by Estimating Algorithms?

Most nontrivial algorithms handle some kind of variable input—sorting n strings, inverting an $m \times n$ matrix, or decrypting a message with an n-bit key. Normally, the size of this input will affect the algorithm: the larger the input, the longer the running time or the more memory used.

If the relationship were always linear (so that the time increased in direct proportion to the value of n), this section wouldn't be important. However, most significant algorithms are not linear. The good news is that many are sublinear. A binary search, for example, doesn't need to look at every candidate when finding a match. The bad news is that other algorithms are considerably worse than linear; runtimes or memory requirements increase far faster than n. An algorithm that takes a minute to process ten items may take a lifetime to process 100.

We find that whenever we write anything containing loops or recursive calls, we subconsciously check the runtime and memory requirements. This is rarely a formal process, but rather a quick confirmation that what we're doing is sensible in the circumstances. However, we sometimes *do* find ourselves performing a more detailed analysis. That's when Big-O notation comes in handy.

Big-O Notation

The Big-O notation, written $O()$, is a mathematical way of dealing with approximations. When we write that a particular sort routine sorts n records in $O(n^2)$ time, we are simply saying that the worst-case time taken will vary as the square of n. Double the number of records, and the time will increase roughly fourfold. Think of the O as meaning *on the order of*.

The $O()$ notation puts an upper bound on the value of the thing we're measuring (time, memory, and so on). If we say a function takes $O(n^2)$ time, then we know that the upper bound of the time it takes will not grow faster than n^2. Sometimes we come up with fairly complex $O()$ functions, but because the highest-order term will dominate the value as n increases, the convention is to remove all low-order terms, and not to bother showing any constant multiplying factors:

$$O(\frac{n^2}{2} + 3n) \quad \text{is the same as } O(\frac{n^2}{2}) \quad \text{is the same as } O(n^2).$$

This is actually a feature of the $O()$ notation—one $O(n^2)$ algorithm may be 1,000 times faster than another $O(n^2)$ algorithm, but you won't know it from the notation. Big-O is never going to give you actual numbers for time or memory or whatever: it simply tells you how these values will change as the input changes.

Figure 3, *Runtimes of various algorithms*, on page 205 shows several common $O()$ notations you'll come across, along with a graph comparing running times of algorithms in each category. Clearly, things quickly start getting out of hand once we get over $O(n^2)$.

For example, suppose you've got a routine that takes one second to process 100 records. How long will it take to process 1,000? If your code is $O(1)$, then it will still take one second. If it's $O(\lg n)$, then you'll probably be waiting about three seconds. $O(n)$ will show a linear increase to ten seconds, while an $O(n \lg n)$ will take some 33 seconds. If you're unlucky enough to have an $O(n^2)$ routine, then sit back for 100 seconds while it does its stuff. And if you're using an exponential algorithm $O(2^n)$, you might want to make a cup of coffee—your routine should finish in about 10^{263} years. Let us know how the universe ends.

The $O()$ notation doesn't apply just to time; you can use it to represent any other resources used by an algorithm. For example, it is often useful to be able to model memory consumption (see the exercises for an example).

$O(1)$ Constant (access element in array, simple statements)

$O(\lg n)$ Logarithmic (binary search). The base of the logarithm doesn't matter, so this is equivalent $O(\log n)$.

$O(n)$ Linear (sequential search)

$O(n \lg n)$ Worse than linear, but not much worse. (Average runtime of quicksort, heapsort)

$O(n^2)$ Square law (selection and insertion sorts)

$O(n^3)$ Cubic (multiplication of two $n \times n$ matrices)

$O(C^n)$ Exponential (traveling salesman problem, set partitioning)

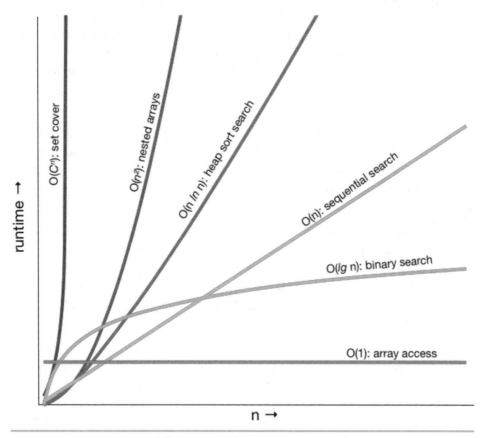

Figure 3—Runtimes of various algorithms

Common Sense Estimation

You can estimate the order of many basic algorithms using common sense.

Simple loops

If a simple loop runs from 1 to n, then the algorithm is likely to be $O(n)$—time increases linearly with n. Examples include exhaustive searches, finding the maximum value in an array, and generating check-sums.

Nested loops

If you nest a loop inside another, then your algorithm becomes $O(m \times n)$, where m and n are the two loops' limits. This commonly occurs in simple sorting algorithms, such as bubble sort, where the outer loop scans each element in the array in turn, and the inner loop works out where to place that element in the sorted result. Such sorting algorithms tend to be $O(n^2)$.

Binary chop

If your algorithm halves the set of things it considers each time around the loop, then it is likely to be logarithmic, $O(\lg n)$. A binary search of a sorted list, traversing a binary tree, and finding the first set bit in a machine word can all be $O(\lg n)$.

Divide and conquer

Algorithms that partition their input work on the two halves independently, and then combine the result can be $O(n \lg n)$. The classic example is quicksort, which works by partitioning the data into two halves and recursively sorting each. Although technically $O(n^2)$, because its behavior degrades when it is fed sorted input, the average runtime of quicksort is $O(n \lg n)$.

Combinatoric

Whenever algorithms start looking at the permutations of things, their running times may get out of hand. This is because permutations involve factorials (there are $5! = 5 \times 4 \times 3 \times 2 \times 1 = 120$ permutations of the digits from 1 to 5). Time a combinatoric algorithm for five elements: it will take six times longer to run it for six, and 42 times longer for seven. Examples include algorithms for many of the acknowledged *hard* problems—the traveling salesman problem, optimally packing things into a container, partitioning a set of numbers so that each set has the same total, and so on. Often, heuristics are used to reduce the running times of these types of algorithms in particular problem domains.

Algorithm Speed in Practice

It's unlikely that you'll spend much time during your career writing sort routines. The ones in the libraries available to you will probably outperform anything you may write without substantial effort. However, the basic kinds of algorithms we've described earlier pop up time and time again. Whenever you find yourself writing a simple loop, you know that you have an $O(n)$ algorithm. If that loop contains an inner loop, then you're looking at $O(m \times n)$. You should be asking yourself how large these values can get. If the numbers are bounded, then you'll know how long the code will take to run. If the numbers depend on external factors (such as the number of records in an overnight batch run, or the number of names in a list of people), then you might want to stop and consider the effect that large values may have on your running time or memory consumption.

> Tip 63   **Estimate the Order of Your Algorithms**

There are some approaches you can take to address potential problems. If you have an algorithm that is $O(n^2)$, try to find a divide-and-conquer approach that will take you down to $O(n\lg n)$.

If you're not sure how long your code will take, or how much memory it will use, try running it, varying the input record count or whatever is likely to impact the runtime. Then plot the results. You should soon get a good idea of the shape of the curve. Is it curving upward, a straight line, or flattening off as the input size increases? Three or four points should give you an idea.

Also consider just what you're doing in the code itself. A simple $O(n^2)$ loop may well perform better than a complex, $O(n\lg n)$ one for smaller values of n, particularly if the $O(n\lg n)$ algorithm has an expensive inner loop.

In the middle of all this theory, don't forget that there are practical considerations as well. Runtime may look like it increases linearly for small input sets. But feed the code millions of records and suddenly the time degrades as the system starts to thrash. If you test a sort routine with random input keys, you may be surprised the first time it encounters ordered input. Try to cover both the theoretical and practical bases. After all this estimating, the only timing that counts is the speed of your code, running in the production environment, with real data. This leads to our next tip.

Tip 64	Test Your Estimates

If it's tricky getting accurate timings, use *code profilers* to count the number of times the different steps in your algorithm get executed, and plot these figures against the size of the input.

Best Isn't Always Best

You also need to be pragmatic about choosing appropriate algorithms—the fastest one is not always the best for the job. Given a small input set, a straightforward insertion sort will perform just as well as a quicksort, and will take you less time to write and debug. You also need to be careful if the algorithm you choose has a high setup cost. For small input sets, this setup may dwarf the running time and make the algorithm inappropriate.

Also be wary of *premature optimization*. It's always a good idea to make sure an algorithm really is a bottleneck before investing your precious time trying to improve it.

Related Sections Include

- Topic 15, *Estimating*, on page 65

Challenges

- Every developer should have a feel for how algorithms are designed and analyzed. Robert Sedgewick has written a series of accessible books on the subject (*Algorithms [SW11]An Introduction to the Analysis of Algorithms [SF13]* and others). We recommend adding one of his books to your collection, and making a point of reading it.

- For those who like more detail than Sedgewick provides, read Donald Knuth's definitive *Art of Computer Programming* books, which analyze a wide range of algorithms.

  - *The Art of Computer Programming, Volume 1: Fundamental Algorithms* [Knu98]
  - *The Art of Computer Programming, Volume 2: Seminumerical Algorithms* [Knu98a]
  - *The Art of Computer Programming, Volume 3: Sorting and Searching* [Knu98b]
  - *The Art of Computer Programming, Volume 4A: Combinatorial Algorithms, Part 1* [Knu11].

- In the first exercise that follows we look at sorting arrays of long integers. What is the impact if the keys are more complex, and the overhead of key comparison is high? Does the key structure affect the efficiency of the sort algorithms, or is the fastest sort always fastest?

Exercises

Exercise 28 (possible answer on page 303)

We coded a set of simple sort routines[5] in Rust. Run them on various machines available to you. Do your figures follow the expected curves? What can you deduce about the relative speeds of your machines? What are the effects of various compiler optimization settings?

Exercise 29 (possible answer on page 304)

In *Common Sense Estimation*, on page 206, we claimed that a binary chop is $O(\lg n)$. Can you prove this?

Exercise 30 (possible answer on page 305)

In Figure 3, *Runtimes of various algorithms*, on page 205, we claimed that $O(\lg n)$ is the same as $O(\log_{10} n)$ (or indeed logarithms to any base). Can you explain why?

---

40 Refactoring

Change and decay in all around I see...

➤ *H. F. Lyte, Abide With Me*

As a program evolves, it will become necessary to rethink earlier decisions and rework portions of the code. This process is perfectly natural. Code needs to evolve; it's not a static thing.

Unfortunately, the most common metaphor for software development is building construction. Bertrand Meyer's classic work *Object-Oriented Software Construction [Mey97]* uses the term "Software Construction," and even your humble authors edited the *Software Construction* column for IEEE Software in the early 2000s.[6]

But using construction as the guiding metaphor implies the following steps:

---

5. https://media-origin.pragprog.com/titles/tpp20/code/algorithm_speed/sort/src/main.rs
6. And yes, we did voice our concerns over the title.

1. An architect draws up blueprints.

2. Contractors dig the foundation, build the superstructure, wire and plumb, and apply finishing touches.

3. The tenants move in and live happily ever after, calling building maintenance to fix any problems.

Well, software doesn't quite work that way. Rather than construction, software is more like *gardening*—it is more organic than concrete. You plant many things in a garden according to an initial plan and conditions. Some thrive, others are destined to end up as compost. You may move plantings relative to each other to take advantage of the interplay of light and shadow, wind and rain. Overgrown plants get split or pruned, and colors that clash may get moved to more aesthetically pleasing locations. You pull weeds, and you fertilize plantings that are in need of some extra help. You constantly monitor the health of the garden, and make adjustments (to the soil, the plants, the layout) as needed.

Business people are comfortable with the metaphor of building construction: it is more scientific than gardening, it's repeatable, there's a rigid reporting hierarchy for management, and so on. But we're not building skyscrapers—we aren't as constrained by the boundaries of physics and the real world.

The gardening metaphor is much closer to the realities of software development. Perhaps a certain routine has grown too large, or is trying to accomplish too much—it needs to be split into two. Things that don't work out as planned need to be weeded or pruned.

Rewriting, reworking, and re-architecting code is collectively known as *restructuring*. But there's a subset of that activity that has become practiced as *refactoring*.

Refactoring [Fow19] is defined by Martin Fowler as a:

> disciplined technique for restructuring an existing body of code, altering its internal structure without changing its external behavior.

The critical parts of this definition are that:

1. The activity is disciplined, not a free-for-all

2. External behavior does not change; this is not the time to add features

Refactoring is not intended to be a special, high-ceremony, once-in-a-while activity, like plowing under the whole garden in order to replant. Instead, refactoring is a day-to-day activity, taking low-risk small steps, more like weeding and raking. Instead of a free-for-all, wholesale rewrite of the codebase, it's a targeted, precision approach to help keep the code easy to change.

In order to guarantee that the external behavior hasn't changed, you need good, automated unit testing that validates the behavior of the code.

When Should You Refactor?

You refactor when you've learned something; when you understand something better than you did last year, yesterday, or even just ten minutes ago.

Perhaps you've come across a stumbling block because the code doesn't quite fit anymore, or you notice two things that should really be merged, or anything else at all strikes you as being "wrong," *don't hesitate to change it.* There's no time like the present. Any number of things may cause code to qualify for refactoring:

Duplication
    You've discovered a violation of the DRY principle.

Nonorthogonal design
    You've discovered something that could be made more orthogonal.

Outdated knowledge
    Things change, requirements drift, and your knowledge of the problem increases. Code needs to keep up.

Usage
    As the system gets used by real people under real circumstances, you realize some features are now more important than previously thought, and "must have" features perhaps weren't.

Performance
    You need to move functionality from one area of the system to another to improve performance.

The Tests Pass
    Yes. Seriously. We did say that refactoring should be a small scale activity, backed up by good tests. So when you've added a small amount of code, and that one extra test passes, you now have a great opportunity to dive in and tidy up what you just wrote.

Refactoring your code—moving functionality around and updating earlier decisions—is really an exercise in *pain management.* Let's face it, changing source code around can be pretty painful: it was working, maybe it's better to leave well enough alone. Many developers are reluctant to go in and re-open a piece of code just because it isn't quite right.

Real-World Complications

So you go to your teammates or client and say, "This code works, but I need another week to completely refactor it."

We can't print their reply.

Time pressure is often used as an excuse for not refactoring. But this excuse just doesn't hold up: fail to refactor now, and there'll be a far greater time investment to fix the problem down the road—when there are more dependencies to reckon with. Will there be more time available then? Nope.

You might want to explain this principle to others by using a medical analogy: think of the code that needs refactoring as "a growth." Removing it requires invasive surgery. You can go in now, and take it out while it is still small. Or, you could wait while it grows and spreads—but removing it then will be both more expensive and more dangerous. Wait even longer, and you may lose the patient entirely.

Tip 65	Refactor Early, Refactor Often

Collateral damage in code can be just as deadly over time (see Topic 3, *Software Entropy*, on page 6). Refactoring, as with most things, is easier to do while the issues are small, as an ongoing activity while coding. You shouldn't need "a week to refactor" a piece of code—that's a full-on rewrite. If that level of disruption is necessary, then you might well not be able to do it immediately. Instead, make sure that it gets placed on the schedule. Make sure that users of the affected code *know* that it is scheduled to be rewritten and how this might affect them.

How Do You Refactor?

Refactoring started out in the Smalltalk community, and had just started to gain a wider audience when we wrote the first edition of this book, probably thanks to the first major book on refactoring (*Refactoring: Improving the Design of Existing Code [Fow19]*, now in its second edition).

At its heart, refactoring is redesign. Anything that you or others on your team designed can be redesigned in light of new facts, deeper understandings, changing requirements, and so on. But if you proceed to rip up vast quantities of code with wild abandon, you may find yourself in a worse position than when you started.

Clearly, refactoring is an activity that needs to be undertaken slowly, deliberately, and carefully. Martin Fowler offers the following simple tips on how to refactor without doing more harm than good:[7]

1. Don't try to refactor and add functionality at the same time.

2. Make sure you have good tests before you begin refactoring. Run the tests as often as possible. That way you will know quickly if your changes have broken anything.

3. Take short, deliberate steps: move a field from one class to another, split a method, rename a variable. Refactoring often involves making many localized changes that result in a larger-scale change. If you keep your steps small, and test after each step, you will avoid prolonged debugging.[8]

Automatic Refactoring

Back in the first edition we noted that, "this technology has yet to appear outside of the Smalltalk world, but this is likely to change...." And indeed, it did, as automatic refactoring is available in many IDEs and for most mainstream languages.

These IDEs can rename variables and methods, split a long routine into smaller ones, automatically propagating the required changes, drag and drop to assist you in moving code, and so on.

We'll talk more about testing at this level in Topic 41, *Test to Code*, on page 214, and larger-scale testing in *Ruthless and Continuous Testing*, on page 275, but Mr. Fowler's point of maintaining good regression tests is the key to refactoring safely.

If you have to go beyond refactoring and end up changing external behavior or interfaces, then it can help to deliberately break the build: old clients of this code should fail to compile. That way you'll know what needs updating. Next time you see a piece of code that isn't quite as it should be, fix it. Manage the pain: if it hurts now, but is going to hurt even more later, you might as well get it over with. Remember the lessons of Topic 3, *Software Entropy*, on page 6: don't live with broken windows.

---

7. Originally spotted in *UML Distilled: A Brief Guide to the Standard Object Modeling Language [Fow00]*.

8. This is excellent advice in general (see Topic 27, *Don't Outrun Your Headlights*, on page 125).

Related Sections Include

- Topic 3, *Software Entropy*, on page 6
- Topic 9, *DRY—The Evils of Duplication*, on page 30
- Topic 12, *Tracer Bullets*, on page 50
- Topic 27, *Don't Outrun Your Headlights*, on page 125
- Topic 44, *Naming Things*, on page 238
- Topic 48, *The Essence of Agility*, on page 259

41 Test to Code

The first edition of this book was written in more primitive times, when most developers wrote no tests—why bother, they thought, the world was going to end in the year 2000 anyway.

In that book, we had a section on how to build code that was easy to test. It was a sneaky way of convincing developers to actually write tests.

These are more enlightened times. If there are any developers still not writing tests, they at least know that they should be.

But there's still a problem. When we ask developers *why* they write tests, they look at us as if we just asked if they still coded using punched cards and they'd say "to make sure the code works," with an unspoken "you dummy" at the end. And we think that's wrong.

So what do *we* think is important about testing? And how do we think you should go about it?

Let's start with the bold statement:

Tip 66	Testing Is Not About Finding Bugs

We believe that the major benefits of testing happen when you think about and write the tests, not when you run them.

Thinking About Tests

It's a Monday morning and you settle in to start work on some new code. You have to write something that queries the database to return a list of people who watch more than 10 videos a week on your "world's funniest dishwashing videos" site.

You fire up your editor, and start by writing the function that performs the query:

```
def return_avid_viewers do
  # ... hmmm ...
end
```

Stop! How do you know that what you're about to do is a good thing?

The answer is that you can't know that. No one can. But thinking about tests can make it more likely. Here's how that works.

Start by imagining that you'd finished writing the function and now had to test it. How would you do that? Well, you'd want to use some test data, which probably means you want to work in a database you control. Now some frameworks can handle that for you, running tests against a test database, but in our case that means we should be passing the database instance into our function rather than using some global one, as that allows us to change it while testing:

```
def return_avid_users(db) do
```

Then we have to think about how we'd populate that test data. The requirement asks for a "list of people who watch more than 10 videos a week." So we look at the database schema for fields that might help. We find two likely fields in a table of who-watched-what: opened_video and completed_video. To write our test data, we need to know which field to use. But we don't know what the requirement means, and our business contact is out. Let's just cheat and pass in the name of the field (which will allow us to test what we have, and potentially change it later):

```
def return_avid_users(db, qualifying_field_name) do
```

We started by thinking about our tests, and without writing a line of code, we've already made two discoveries and used them to change the API of our method.

Tests Drive Coding

In the previous example, thinking about testing made us reduce coupling in our code (by passing in a database connection rather than using a global one) and increase flexibility (by making the name of the field we test a parameter). Thinking about writing a test for our method made us look at it from the outside, as if we were a client of the code, and not its author.

Tip 67 A Test Is the First User of Your Code

We think this is probably the biggest benefit offered by testing: testing is vital feedback that guides your coding.

A function or method that is tightly coupled to other code is hard to test, because you have to set up all that environment before you can even run your method. So making your stuff testable also reduces its coupling.

And before you can test something, you have to understand it. That sounds silly, but in reality we've all launched into a piece of code based on a nebulous understanding of what we had to do. We assure ourselves that we'll work it out as we go along. Oh, and we'll add all the code to support the boundary conditions later, too. Oh, and the error handling. And the code ends up five times longer than it should because it's full of conditional logic and special cases. But shine the light of a test on that code, and things become clearer. If you think about testing boundary conditions and how that will work *before* you start coding, you may well find the patterns in the logic that'll simplify the function. If you think about the error conditions you'll need to test, you'll structure your function accordingly.

Test-Driven Development

There's a school of programming that says that, given all the benefits of thinking about tests up front, why not go ahead and write them up front too? They practice something called *test-driven development* or *TDD*. You'll also see this called *test-first development.*[9]

The basic cycle of TDD is:

1. Decide on a small piece of functionality you want to add.

2. Write a test that will pass once that functionality is implemented.

3. Run all tests. Verify that the only failure is the one you just wrote.

4. Write the smallest amount of code needed to get the test to pass, and verify that the tests now run cleanly.

5. Refactor your code: see if there is a way to improve on what you just wrote (the test or the function). Make sure the tests still pass when you're done.

---

9. Some folks argue that test-first and test-driven development are two different things, saying that the intents of the two are different. However, historically, test-first (which comes from eXtreme Programming) was identical to what people now call TDD.

The idea is that this cycle should be very short: a matter of minutes, so that you're constantly writing tests and then getting them to work.

We see a major benefit in TDD for people just starting out with testing. If you follow the TDD workflow, you'll guarantee that you always have tests for your code. And that means you'll always be thinking about your tests.

However, we've also seen people become slaves to TDD. This manifests itself in a number of ways:

- They spend inordinate amounts of time ensuring that they always have 100% test coverage.

- They have lots of redundant tests. For example, before writing a class for the first time, many TDD adherents will first write a failing test that simply references the class's name. It fails, then they write an empty class definition and it passes. But now you have a test that does absolutely nothing; the next test you write will also reference the class, and so it makes the first unnecessary. There's more stuff to change if the class name changes later. And this is just a trivial example.

- Their designs tend to start at the bottom and work their way up. (See *Bottom-Up vs. Top-Down vs. The Way You Should Do It*, on page 218.)

By all means practice TDD. But, if you do, don't forget to stop every now and then and look at the big picture. It is easy to become seduced by the green "tests passed" message, writing lots of code that doesn't actually get you closer to a solution.

TDD: You Need to Know Where You're Going

The old joke asks "How do you eat an elephant?" The punchline: "One bite at a time." And this idea is often touted as a benefit of TDD. When you can't comprehend the whole problem, take small steps, one test at a time. However, this approach can mislead you, encouraging you to focus on and endlessly polish the easy problems while ignoring the real reason you're coding. An interesting example of this happened in 2006, when Ron Jeffries, a leading figure in the agility movement, started a series of blog posts which documented his test-driven coding of a Sudoko solver.[10] After five posts, he'd refined the representation of the underlying board, refactoring a number of times until he was happy with the object model. But then he abandoned the project. It's interesting to read the blog posts in order, and watch how a clever person can get sidetracked by the minutia, reinforced by the glow of passing tests.

---

10. https://ronjeffries.com/categories/sudoku. A big "thank you" to Ron for letting us use this story.

Bottom-Up vs. Top-Down vs. The Way You Should Do It

Back when computing was young and carefree, there were two schools of design: top-down and bottom-up. The top-down folks said you should start with the overall problem you're trying to solve and break it into a small number of pieces. Then break each of these into smaller pieces, and so on, until you end up with pieces small enough to express in code.

The bottom-up folks build code like you'd build a house. They start at the bottom, producing a layer of code that gives them some abstractions that are closer to the problem they are trying to solve. Then they add another layer, with higher-level abstractions. They keep on until the final layer is an abstraction that solves the problem. "Make it so...."

Neither school actually works, because both ignore one of the most important aspects of software development: we don't know what we're doing when we start. The top-down folks assume they can express the whole requirement up front: they can't. The bottom-up folks assume they can build a list of abstractions which will take them eventually to a single top-level solution, but how can they decide on the functionality of layers when they don't know where they are heading?

| Tip 68 | Build End-to-End, Not Top-Down or Bottom Up |

We strongly believe that the only way to build software is incrementally. Build small pieces of end-to-end functionality, learning about the problem as you go. Apply this learning as you continue to flesh out the code, involve the customer at each step, and have them guide the process.

As a contrast, Peter Norvig describes an alternative approach[11] which feels very different in character: rather than being driven by tests, he starts with a basic understanding of how these kinds of problems are traditionally solved (using constraint propagation), and then focuses on refining his algorithm. He addresses board representation in a dozen lines of code that flow directly from his discussion of notation.

Tests can definitely help drive development. But, as with every drive, unless you have a destination in mind, you can end up going in circles.

---

11. http://norvig.com/sudoku.html

Back to the Code

Component-based development has long been a lofty goal of software development.[12] The idea is that generic software components should be available and combined just as easily as common integrated circuits (ICs) are combined. But this works only if the components you are using are known to be reliable, and if you have common voltages, interconnect standards, timing, and so on.

Chips are designed to be tested—not just at the factory, not just when they are installed, but also in the field when they are deployed. More complex chips and systems may have a full Built-In Self Test (BIST) feature that runs some base-level diagnostics internally, or a Test Access Mechanism (TAM) that provides a test harness that allows the external environment to provide stimuli and collect responses from the chip.

We can do the same thing in software. Like our hardware colleagues, we need to build testability into the software from the very beginning, and test each piece thoroughly before trying to wire them together.

Unit Testing

Chip-level testing for hardware is roughly equivalent to *unit testing* in software—testing done on each module, in isolation, to verify its behavior. We can get a better feeling for how a module will react in the big wide world once we have tested it throughly under controlled (even contrived) conditions.

A software unit test is code that exercises a module. Typically, the unit test will establish some kind of artificial environment, then invoke routines in the module being tested. It then checks the results that are returned, either against known values or against the results from previous runs of the same test (regression testing).

Later, when we assemble our "software ICs" into a complete system, we'll have confidence that the individual parts work as expected, and then we can use the same unit test facilities to test the system as a whole. We talk about this large-scale checking of the system in *Ruthless and Continuous Testing*, on page 275.

Before we get that far, however, we need to decide what to test at the unit level. Historically, programmers threw a few random bits of data at the code, looked at the print statements, and called it tested. We can do much better.

---

12. We've been trying since at least 1986, when Cox and Novobilski coined the term "software IC" in their Objective-C book *Object-Oriented Programming Object-Oriented Programming: An Evolutionary Approach [CN91]*.

Testing Against Contract

We like to think of unit testing as *testing against contract* (see Topic 23, *Design by Contract*, on page 104). We want to write test cases that ensure that a given unit honors its contract. This will tell us two things: whether the code meets the contract, and whether the contract means what we think it means. We want to test that the module delivers the functionality it promises, over a wide range of test cases and boundary conditions.

What does this mean in practice? Let's start with a simple, numerical example: a square root routine. Its documented contract is simple:

```
pre-conditions:
  argument >= 0;

post-conditions:
  ((result * result) - argument).abs <= epsilon*argument;
```

This tells us what to test:

- Pass in a negative argument and ensure that it is rejected.

- Pass in an argument of zero to ensure that it is accepted (this is the boundary value).

- Pass in values between zero and the maximum expressible argument and verify that the difference between the square of the result and the original argument is less than some small fraction of the argument (epsilon).

Armed with this contract, and assuming that our routine does its own pre- and postcondition checking, we can write a basic test script to exercise the square root function.

Then we can call this routine to test our square root function:

```
assertWithinEpsilon(my_sqrt(0), 0)
assertWithinEpsilon(my_sqrt(2.0),    1.4142135624)
assertWithinEpsilon(my_sqrt(64.0),   8.0)
assertWithinEpsilon(my_sqrt(1.0e7), 3162.2776602)
assertRaisesException fn =>  my_sqrt(-4.0) end
```

This is a pretty simple test; in the real world, any nontrivial module is likely to be dependent on a number of other modules, so how do we go about testing the combination?

Suppose we have a module A that uses a DataFeed and a LinearRegression. In order, we would test:

1. DataFeed's contract, in full
2. LinearRegression's contract, in full
3. A's contract, which relies on the other contracts but does not directly expose them

This style of testing requires you to test subcomponents of a module first. Once the subcomponents have been verified, then the module itself can be tested.

If DataFeed and LinearRegression's tests passed, but A's test failed, we can be pretty sure that the problem is in A, or in A's *use* of one of those subcomponents. This technique is a great way to reduce debugging effort: we can quickly concentrate on the likely source of the problem within module A, and not waste time reexamining its subcomponents.

Why do we go to all this trouble? Above all, we want to avoid creating a "time bomb"—something that sits around unnoticed and blows up at an awkward moment later in the project. By emphasizing testing against contract, we can try to avoid as many of those downstream disasters as possible.

> **Tip 69** Design to Test

Ad Hoc Testing

Not to be confused with "odd hack," *ad-hoc* testing is when we run poke at our code manually. This may be as simple as a console.log(), or a piece of code entered interactively in a debugger, IDE environment, or REPL.

At the end of the debugging session, you need to formalize this ad hoc test. If the code broke once, it is likely to break again. Don't just throw away the test you created; add it to the existing unit test arsenal.

Build a Test Window

Even the best sets of tests are unlikely to find all the bugs; there's something about the damp, warm conditions of a production environment that seems to bring them out of the woodwork.

This means you'll often need to test a piece of software once it has been deployed—with real-world data flowing though its veins. Unlike a circuit board or chip, we don't have *test pins* in software, but we *can* provide various views into the internal state of a module, without using the debugger (which may be inconvenient or impossible in a production application).

Log files containing trace messages are one such mechanism. Log messages should be in a regular, consistent format; you may want to parse them automatically to deduce processing time or logic paths that the program took. Poorly or inconsistently formatted diagnostics are just so much "spew"—they are difficult to read and impractical to parse.

Another mechanism for getting inside running code is the "hot-key" sequence or magic URL. When this particular combination of keys is pressed, or the URL is accessed, a diagnostic control window pops up with status messages and so on. This isn't something you normally would reveal to end users, but it can be very handy for the help desk.

More generally, you could use a *feature switch* to enable extra diagnostics for a particular user or class of users.

A Culture of Testing

All software you write *will* be tested—if not by you and your team, then by the eventual users—so you might as well plan on testing it thoroughly. A little forethought can go a long way toward minimizing maintenance costs and help-desk calls.

You really only have a few choices:

- Test First
- Test During
- Test Never

Test First, including Test-Driven Design, is probably your best choice in most circumstances, as it ensures that testing happens. But sometimes that's not as convenient or useful, so Test During coding can be a good fallback, where you write some code, fiddle with it, write the tests for it, then move on to the next bit. The worst choice is often called "Test Later," but who are you kidding? "Test Later" really means "Test Never."

A culture of testing means all the tests pass all the time. Ignore a spew of tests that "always fail" makes it easier to ignore *all* the tests, and the vicious spiral begins (see Topic 3, *Software Entropy*, on page 6).

A Confession

I (Dave) have been known to tell people that I no longer write tests. Partly I do it to shake the faith of those who have turned testing into a religion. And partly I say it because it is (somewhat) true.

I've been coding for 45 years, and writing automated tests for more than 30 of them. Thinking about testing is built in to the way I approach coding. It felt comfortable. And my personality insists that when something starts to feel comfortable I should move on to something else.

In this case I decided to stop writing tests for a couple of months and see what it did to my code. To my surprise, the answer was "not a lot." So I spent some time working out why.

I *believe* the answer is that (for me) most of the benefit of testing comes from thinking about the tests and their impact on the code. And, after doing it for so long, I could do that thinking without actually writing tests. My code was still testable; it just wasn't tested.

But that ignores the fact that tests are also a way of communicating with other developers, so I now *do* write tests on code shared with others or that relies on the peculiarities of external dependencies.

Andy says I shouldn't include this sidebar. He worries it will tempt inexperienced developers not to test. Here's my compromise:

Should you write tests? Yes. But after you've been doing it for 30 years, feel free to experiment a little to see where the benefit lies for you.

Treat test code with the same care as any production code. Keep it decoupled, clean, and robust. Don't rely on unreliable things (see Topic 38, *Programming by Coincidence*, on page 197) like the absolute position of widgets in a GUI system, or exact timestamps in a server log, or the exact wording of error messages. Testing for these sorts of things will result in fragile tests.

> **Tip 70** Test Your Software, or Your Users Will

Make no mistake, testing is part of programming. It's not something left to other departments or staff.

Testing, design, coding—it's all programming.

Related Sections Include

- Topic 27, *Don't Outrun Your Headlights*, on page 125
- Topic 51, *Pragmatic Starter Kit*, on page 273

42 Property-Based Testing

Доверяй, но проверяй   (Trust, but verify)

➤ *Russian proverb*

We recommend writing unit tests for your functions. You do that by thinking about typical things that might be a problem, based on your knowledge of the thing you're testing.

There's a small but potentially significant problem lurking in that paragraph, though. If you write the original code and you write the tests, is it possible that an incorrect assumption could be expressed in both? The code passes the tests, because it does what it is supposed to based on your understanding.

One way around this is to have different people write tests and the code under test, but we don't like this: as we said in Topic 41, *Test to Code*, on page 214, one of the biggest benefits of thinking about tests is the way it informs the code you write. You lose that when the work of testing is split from the coding.

Instead, we favor an alternative, where the computer, which doesn't share your preconceptions, does some testing for you.

Contracts, Invariants, and Properties

In Topic 23, *Design by Contract*, on page 104, we talked about the idea that code has *contracts* that it meets: you meet the conditions when you feed it input, and it will make certain guarantees about the outputs it produces.

There are also code *invariants*, things that remain true about some piece of state when it's passed through a function. For example, if you sort a list, the result will have the same number of elements as the original—the length is invariant.

Once we work out our contracts and invariants (which we're going to lump together and call *properties*) we can use them to automate our testing. What we end up doing is called *property-based testing*.

> Tip 71   Use Property-Based Tests to Validate Your Assumptions

As an artificial example, we can build some tests for our sorted list. We've already established one property: the sorted list is the same size as the original. We can also state that no element in the result can be greater than the one that follows it.

We can now express that in code. Most languages have some kind of property-based testing framework. This example is in Python, and uses the Hypothesis tool and pytest, but the principles are pretty universal.

Here is the full source of the tests:

```
proptest/sort.py
from    hypothesis import given
import hypothesis.strategies as some

@given(some.lists(some.integers()))
def test_list_size_is_invariant_across_sorting(a_list):
    original_length = len(a_list)
    a_list.sort()
    assert len(a_list) == original_length

@given(some.lists(some.text()))
def test_sorted_result_is_ordered(a_list):
    a_list.sort()
    for i in range(len(a_list) - 1):
        assert a_list[i] <= a_list[i + 1]
```

Here's what happens when we run it:

```
$ pytest  sort.py
======================= test session starts =========================
...
plugins: hypothesis-4.14.0

sort.py ..                                                    [100%]

===================== 2 passed in 0.95 seconds =====================
```

Not much drama there. But, behind the scenes, Hypothesis ran both of our tests one hundred times, passing in a different list each time. The lists will have varying lengths, and will have different contents. It's as if we'd cooked up 200 individual tests with 200 random lists.

Test Data Generation

Like most property-based testing libraries, Hypothesis gives you a minilanguage for describing the data it should generate. The language is based around calls to functions in the hypothesis.strategies module, which we aliased as some, just because it reads better.

If we wrote:

```
@given(some.integers())
```

Our test function would run multiple times. Each time, it would be passed a different integer. If instead we wrote the following:

```
@given(some.integers(min_value=5, max_value=10).map(lambda x: x * 2))
```

then we'd get the even numbers between 10 and 20.

You can also compose types, so that

```
@given(some.lists(some.integers(min_value=1), max_size=100))
```

will be lists of natural numbers that are at most 100 elements long.

This isn't supposed to be a tutorial on any particular framework, so we'll skip a bunch of cool details and instead look at a real-world example.

Finding Bad Assumptions

We're writing a simple order processing and stock control system (because there's always room for one more). It models the stock levels with a Warehouse object. We can query a warehouse to see if something is in stock, remove things from stock, and get the current stock levels.

Here's the code:

proptest/stock.py
```python
class Warehouse:
    def __init__(self, stock):
        self.stock = stock

    def in_stock(self, item_name):
        return (item_name in self.stock) and (self.stock[item_name] > 0)

    def take_from_stock(self, item_name, quantity):
        if quantity <= self.stock[item_name]:
            self.stock[item_name] -= quantity
        else:
            raise Exception("Oversold {}".format(item_name))

    def stock_count(self, item_name):
        return self.stock[item_name]
```

We wrote a basic unit test, which passes:

proptest/stock.py
```python
def test_warehouse():
    wh = Warehouse({"shoes": 10, "hats": 2, "umbrellas": 0})
    assert wh.in_stock("shoes")
    assert wh.in_stock("hats")
    assert not wh.in_stock("umbrellas")

    wh.take_from_stock("shoes", 2)
    assert wh.in_stock("shoes")

    wh.take_from_stock("hats", 2)
    assert not wh.in_stock("hats")
```

Then we wrote a function that processes a request to order items from the warehouse. It returns a tuple where the first element is either "ok" or "not available", followed by the item and requested quantity. We also wrote some tests, and they pass:

```
proptest/stock.py
def order(warehouse, item, quantity):
    if warehouse.in_stock(item):
        warehouse.take_from_stock(item, quantity)
        return ( "ok", item, quantity )
    else:
        return ( "not available", item, quantity )
```

```
proptest/stock.py
def test_order_in_stock():
    wh = Warehouse({"shoes": 10, "hats": 2, "umbrellas": 0})
    status, item, quantity = order(wh, "hats", 1)
    assert status   == "ok"
    assert item     == "hats"
    assert quantity == 1
    assert wh.stock_count("hats") == 1

def test_order_not_in_stock():
    wh = Warehouse({"shoes": 10, "hats": 2, "umbrellas": 0})
    status, item, quantity = order(wh, "umbrellas", 1)
    assert status   == "not available"
    assert item     == "umbrellas"
    assert quantity == 1
    assert wh.stock_count("umbrellas") == 0

def test_order_unknown_item():
    wh = Warehouse({"shoes": 10, "hats": 2, "umbrellas": 0})
    status, item, quantity = order(wh, "bagel", 1)
    assert status   == "not available"
    assert item     == "bagel"
    assert quantity == 1
```

On the surface, everything looks fine. But before we ship the code, let's add some property tests.

One thing we know is that stock cannot appear and disappear across our transaction. This means that if we take some items from the warehouse, the number we took plus the number currently in the warehouse should be the same as the number originally in the warehouse. In the following test, we run our test with the item parameter chosen randomly from "hat" or "shoe" and the quantity chosen from 1 to 4:

```
proptest/stock.py
@given(item      = some.sampled_from(["shoes", "hats"]),
       quantity = some.integers(min_value=1, max_value=4))

def test_stock_level_plus_quantity_equals_original_stock_level(item, quantity):
    wh = Warehouse({"shoes": 10, "hats": 2, "umbrellas": 0})
    initial_stock_level = wh.stock_count(item)
    (status, item, quantity) = order(wh, item, quantity)
    if status == "ok":
        assert wh.stock_count(item) + quantity == initial_stock_level
```

Let's run it:

```
$ pytest stock.py
. . .
stock.py:72:
- - - - - - - - - - - - - - - - - - - - - - - - - - - - - - - - - -
stock.py:76: in test_stock_level_plus_quantity_equals_original_stock_level
    (status, item, quantity) = order(wh, item, quantity)
stock.py:40: in order
    warehouse.take_from_stock(item, quantity)
- - - - - - - - - - - - - - - - - - - - - - - - - - - - - - - - - -
self = <stock.Warehouse object at 0x10cf97cf8>, item_name = 'hats'
quantity = 3

    def take_from_stock(self, item_name, quantity):
      if quantity <= self.stock[item_name]:
        self.stock[item_name] -= quantity
      else:
>       raise Exception("Oversold {}".format(item_name))
E       Exception: Oversold hats

stock.py:16: Exception
-------------------------- Hypothesis --------------------------
Falsifying example:
 test_stock_level_plus_quantity_equals_original_stock_level(
     item='hats', quantity=3)
```

It blew up in warehouse.take_from_stock: we tried to remove three hats from the warehouse, but it only has two in stock.

Our property testing found a faulty assumption: our in_stock function only checks that there's at least one of the given item in stock. Instead we need to make sure we have enough to fill the order:

```
proptest/stock1.py
def in_stock(self, item_name, quantity):
    return (item_name in self.stock) and (self.stock[item_name] >= quantity)
```

And we change the order function, too:

```
proptest/stock1.py
def order(warehouse, item, quantity):
    if warehouse.in_stock(item, quantity):
        warehouse.take_from_stock(item, quantity)
        return ( "ok", item, quantity )
    else:
        return ( "not available", item, quantity )
```

And now our property test passes.

Property-Based Tests Often Surprise You

In the previous example, we used a property-based test to check that stock levels were adjusted properly. The test found a bug, but it wasn't to do with stock level adjustment. Instead, it found a bug in our in_stock function.

This is both the power and the frustration of property-based testing. It's powerful because you set up some rules for generating inputs, set up some assertions for validating output, and then just let it rip. You never quite know what will happen. The test may pass. An assertion may fail. Or the code may fail totally because it couldn't handle the inputs it was given.

The frustration is that it can be tricky to pin down what failed.

Our suggestion is that when a property-based test fails, find out what parameters it was passing to the test function, and then use those values to create a separate, regular, unit test. That unit test does two things for you. First, it lets you focus in on the problem without all the additional calls being made into your code by the property-based testing framework. Second, that unit test acts as a *regression test*. Because property-based tests generate random values that get passed to your test, there's no guarantee that the same values will be used the next time you run tests. Having a unit test that forces those values to be used ensures that this bug won't slip through.

Property-Based Tests Also Help Your Design

When we talked about unit testing, we said that one of the major benefits was the way it made you think about your code: a unit test is the first client of your API.

The same is true of property-based tests, but in a slightly different way. They make you think about your code in terms of invariants and contracts; you think about what must not change, and what must be true. This extra insight has a magical effect on your code, removing edge cases and highlighting functions that leave data in an inconsistent state.

We believe that property-based testing is complementary to unit testing: they address different concerns, and each brings its own benefits. If you're not currently using them, give them a go.

Related Sections Include

- Topic 23, *Design by Contract*, on page 104
- Topic 25, *Assertive Programming*, on page 115
- Topic 45, *The Requirements Pit*, on page 244

Exercises

Exercise 31 (possible answer on page 305)

Look back at the warehouse example. Are there any other properties that you can test?

Exercise 32 (possible answer on page 305)

Your company ships machinery. Each machine comes in a crate, and each crate is rectangular. The crates vary in size. Your job is to write some code to pack as many crates as possible in a single layer that fits in the delivery truck. The output of your code is a list of all the crates. For each crate, the list gives the location in the truck, along with the width and height. What properties of the output could be tested?

Challenges

Think about the code you're currently working on. What are the properties: the contracts and invariants? Can you use property-based testing framework to verify these automatically?

Stay Safe Out There

Good fences make good neighbors.

➤ Robert Frost, *Mending Wall*

In the first edition's discussion of code coupling we made a bold and naive statement: "we don't need to be as paranoid as spies or dissidents." We were wrong. In fact, you *do* need to be that paranoid, every day.

As we write this, the daily news is filled with stories of devastating data breaches, hijacked systems, and cyberfraud. Hundreds of millions of records stolen at once, billions and billions of dollars in losses and remediation—and these numbers are growing rapidly each year. In the vast majority of cases, it's not because the attackers were terribly clever, or even vaguely competent.

It's because the developers were careless.

The Other 90%

When coding, you may go through several cycles of "it works!" and "why isn't that working?" with the occasional "there's no way that could have happened…"[13] After several hills and bumps on this uphill climb, it's easy to say to yourself, "phew, it all works!" and proclaim the code done. Of course, it's not done yet. You're 90% done, but now you have the *other* 90% to consider.

The next thing you have to do is analyze the code for ways it can go wrong and add those to your test suite. You'll consider things such as passing in bad parameters, leaking or unavailable resources; that sort of thing.

In the good old days, this evaluation of internal errors may have been sufficient. But today that's only the beginning, because in addition to errors from internal causes, you need to consider how an external actor could deliberately screw up the system. But perhaps you protest, "Oh, no one will care about this code, it's not important, no one even knows about this server…" It's a big world out there, and most of it is connected. Whether it's a bored kid on the other side of the planet, state-sponsored terrorism, criminal gangs, corporate espionage, or even a vengeful ex, they are out there and aiming for you. The survival time of an unpatched, outdated system on the open net is measured in minutes—or even less.

Security through obscurity just doesn't work.

---

13. See *Debugging*.

Security Basic Principles

Pragmatic Programmers have a healthy amount of paranoia. We know we have faults and limitations, and that external attackers will seize on *any* opening we leave to compromise our systems. Your particular development and deployment environments will have their own security-centric needs, but there are a handful of basic principles that you should always bear in mind:

1. Minimize Attack Surface Area
2. Principle of Least Privilege
3. Secure Defaults
4. Encrypt Sensitive Data
5. Maintain Security Updates

Let's take a look at each of these.

Minimize Attack Surface Area

The *attack surface area* of a system is the sum of all access points where an attacker can enter data, extract data, or invoke execution of a service. Here are a few examples:

Code complexity leads to attack vectors

Code complexity makes the attack surface larger, with more opportunities for unanticipated side effects. Think of complex code as making the surface area more porous and open to infection. Once again, simple, smaller code is better. Less code means fewer bugs, fewer opportunities for a crippling security hole. Simpler, tighter, less complex code is easier to reason about, easier to spot potential weaknesses.

Input data is an attack vector

Never trust data from an external entity, always sanitize it before passing it on to a database, view rendering, or other processing.[14] Some languages can help with this. In Ruby, for example, variables holding external input are *tainted*, which limits what operations can be performed on them. For example, this code apparently uses the wc utility to report on the number of characters in a file whose name is supplied at runtime:

```ruby
safety/taint.rb
puts "Enter a file name to count: "
name = gets
system("wc -c #{name}")
```

---

14. Remember our good friend, little Bobby Tables (https://xkcd.com/327)? While you're reminiscing have a look at https://bobby-tables.com, which lists ways of sanitizing data passed to database queries.

A nefarious user could do damage like this:

```
Enter a file name to count:
test.dat; rm -rf /
```

However, setting the SAFE level to 1 will taint external data, which means it can't be used in dangerous contexts:

```
safety/taint.rb
```
➤ `$SAFE = 1`

```
puts "Enter a file name to count: "
name = gets
system("wc -c #{name}")
```

~~~ session $ ruby taint.rb Enter a file name to count: test.dat; rm -rf /

code/safety/taint.rb:5:in system': Insecure operation - system (SecurityError) from code/safety/taint.rb:5:in main' ~~~

Unauthenticated services are an attack vector
By their very nature, any user anywhere in the world can call unauthenticated services, so barring any other handling or limiting you've immediately created an opportunity for a *denial-of-service* attack at the very least. Quite a few of highly public data breaches recently were caused by developers accidentally putting data in unauthenticated, publicly readable data stores in the cloud.

Authenticated services are an attack vector
Keep the number of authorized users at an absolute minimum. Cull unused, old, or outdated users and services. Many net-enabled devices have been found to contain simple default passwords or unused, unprotected administrative accounts. If an account with deployment credentials is compromised, your entire product is compromised.

Output data is an attack vector
There's a (possibly apocryphal) story about a system that dutifully reported the error message Password is used by another user. Don't give away information. Make sure that the data you report is appropriate for the authorization of that user. Truncate or obfuscate potentially risky information such as Social Security or other government ID numbers.

Debugging info is an attack vector

There's nothing as heartwarming as seeing a full stack trace with data on your local ATM machine, an airport kiosk, or crashing web page. Information designed to make debugging easier can make breaking in easier as well. Make sure any "test window" (discussed on page 221) and runtime exception reporting is protected from spying eyes.[15]

| Tip 72 | Keep It Simple and Minimize Attack Surfaces |

Principle of Least Privilege

Another key principle is to use the *least* amount of privilege for the *shortest* time you can get away with. In other words, don't automatically grab the highest permission level, such as root or Administrator. If that high level *is* needed, take it, do the minimum amount of work, and relinquish your permission quickly to reduce the risk. This principle dates back to the early 1970s:

> Every program and every privileged user of the system should operate using the least amount of privilege necessary to complete the job.— Jerome Saltzer, Communications of the ACM, 1974.

Take the login program on Unix-derived systems. It initially executes with root privileges. As soon as it finishes authenticating the correct user, though, it drops the high level privilege to that of the user.

This doesn't just apply to operating system privilege levels. Does your application implement different levels of access? Is it a blunt tool, such as "administrator" vs. "user?" If so, consider something more finely grained, where your sensitive resources are partitioned into different categories, and individual users have permissions for only certain of those categories.

This technique follows the same sort of idea as minimizing surface area—reducing the scope of attack vectors, both by time and by privilege level. In this case, less is indeed more.

Secure Defaults

The default settings on your app, or for your users on your site, should be the *most* secure values. These might not be the most user-friendly or convenient values, but it's better to let each individual decide for themselves the trade-offs between security and convenience.

---

15. This technique has proven to be successful at the CPU chip level, where well-known exploits target debugging and administrative facilities. Once cracked, the entire machine is left exposed.

For example, the default for password entry might be to hide the password as entered, replacing each character with an asterisk. If you're entering a password in a crowded public place, or projected before a large audience, that's a sensible default. But some users might want to see the password spelled out, perhaps for accessibility. If there's little risk someone is looking over their shoulder, that's a reasonable choice for them.

Encrypt Sensitive Data

Don't leave personally identifiable information, financial data, passwords, or other credentials in plain text, whether in a database or some other external file. If the data gets exposed, encryption offers an additional level of safety.

In *Version Control* we strongly recommend putting everything needed for the project under version control. Well, *almost* everything. Here's one major exception to that rule:

Don't check in secrets, API keys, SSH keys, encryption passwords or other credentials alongside your source code in version control.

Keys and secrets need to be managed separately, generally via config files or environment variables as part of build and deployment.

Maintain Security Updates

Updating computer systems can be a huge pain. You need that security patch, but as a side effect it breaks some portion of your application. You could decide to wait, and defer the update until later. That's a terrible idea, because now your system is vulnerable to a known exploit.

Tip 73	Apply Security Patches Quickly

This tip affects every net-connected device, including phones, cars, appliances, personal laptops, developer machines, build machines, production servers, and cloud images. Everything. And if you think that this doesn't really matter, just remember that the largest data breaches in history (so far) were caused by systems that were behind on their updates.

Don't let it happen to you.

Password Antipatterns

One of the fundamental problems with security is that oftentimes good security runs counter to common sense or common practice. For example, you might think that strict password requirements would increase security for your application or site. You'd be wrong.

Strict password policies will actually *lower* your security. Here's a short list of very bad ideas, along with some recommendations from the NIST:[a]

- Do not restrict password length to less than 64 characters. NIST recommends 256 as a good maximum length.

- Do not truncate the user's chosen password.

- Do not restrict special characters such as [](){};&%$# or /. See the note about Bobby Tables earlier in this section. If special characters in your password will compromise your system, you have bigger problems. The NIST says to accept all printing ASCII characters, space, and Unicode.

- Do not provide password hints to unauthenticated users, or prompt for specific types of information (e.g., "what was the name of your first pet?").

- Do not disable the paste function in the browser. Crippling the functionality of the browser and password managers does not make your system more secure, in fact it drives users to create simpler, shorter passwords that are much easier to compromise. Both the NIST in the US and the National Cyber Security Centre in the UK specifically require verifiers to allow paste functionality for this reason.

- Do not impose other composition rules. For example, do not mandate any particular mix of upper and lower case, numerics, or special characters, or prohibit repeating characters, and so on.

- Do not arbitrarily require users to change their passwords after some length of time. Only do this for a valid reason (e.g., if there has been a breach).

You want to encourage long, random passwords with a high degree of entropy. Putting artificial constraints limits entropy and encourages bad password habits, leaving your user's accounts vulnerable to takeover.

---

a. *NIST Special Publication 800-63B: Digital Identity Guidelines: Authentication and Lifecycle Management*, available free online at https://doi.org/10.6028/NIST.SP.800-63b

Common Sense vs. Crypto

It's important to keep in mind that common sense may fail you when it comes to matters of cryptography. The first and most important rule when it comes to crypto is *never do it yourself*.[16] Even for something as simple as passwords, common practices are wrongheaded (see the sidebar *Password Antipatterns*, on page 236). Once you get into the world of crypto, even the tiniest, most insignificant-looking error can compromise everything: your clever new, home-made encryption algorithm can probably be broken by an expert in minutes. You don't want to do encryption yourself.

As we've said elsewhere, rely only on reliable things: well-vetted, thoroughly examined, well-maintained, frequently updated, preferably open source libraries and frameworks.

Beyond simple encryption tasks, take a hard look at other security-related features of your site or application. Take authentication, for instance.

In order to implement your own login with password or biometric authentication, you need to understand how hashes and salts work, how crackers use things like Rainbow tables, why you shouldn't use MD5 or SHA1, and a host of other concerns. And even if you get all that right, at the end of the day you're still responsible for holding onto the data and keeping it secure, subject to whatever new legislation and legal obligations come up.

Or, you could take the Pragmatic approach and let someone else worry about it and use a third-party authentication provider. This may be an off-the-shelf service you run in-house, or it could be a third party in the cloud. Authentication services are often available from email, phone, or social media providers, which may or may not be appropriate for your application. In any case, these folks spend all their days keeping their systems secure, and they're better at it than you are.

Stay safe out there.

Related Sections Include

- Topic 23, *Design by Contract*, on page 104
- Topic 24, *Dead Programs Tell No Lies*, on page 112
- Topic 25, *Assertive Programming*, on page 115
- Topic 38, *Programming by Coincidence*, on page 197
- Topic 45, *The Requirements Pit*, on page 244

---

16. Unless you have a PhD in cryptography, and even then only with major peer review, extensive field trials with a bug bounty, and budget for long-term maintenance.

44 ▶ Naming Things

The beginning of wisdom is to call things by their proper name.

➤ *Confucius*

What's in a name? When we're programming, the answer is "everything!"

We create names for applications, subsystems, modules, functions, variables—we're constantly creating new things and bestowing names on them. And those names are very, very important, because they reveal a lot about your intent and belief.

We believe that things should be named according to the role they play in your code. This means that, whenever you create something, you need to pause and think "what is my motivation to create this?"

This is a powerful question, because it takes you out of the immediate problem-solving mindset and makes you look at the bigger picture. When you consider the role of a variable or function, you're thinking about what is special about it, about what it can do, and what it interacts with. Often, we find ourselves realizing that what we were about to do made no sense, all because we couldn't come up with an appropriate name.

There's some science behind the idea that names are deeply meaningful. It turns out that the brain can read and understand words really fast: faster than many other activities. This means that words have a certain priority when we try to make sense of something. This can be demonstrated using the Stroop effect.[17]

Look at the following panel. It has a list of color names or shades, and each is shown in a color or shade. But the names and colors don't necessarily match. Here's part one of the challenge—say aloud the name of each color as written:[18]

---

17. *Studies of Interference in Serial Verbal Reactions [Str35]*
18. We have two versions of this panel. One uses different colors, and the other uses shades of gray. If you're seeing this in black and white and want the color version, or if you're having trouble distinguishing colors and want to try the grayscale version, pop over to https://pragprog.com/the-pragmatic-programmer/stroop-effect.

WHITE	WHITE	GRAY
WHITE	GRAY	GRAY
GRAY	WHITE	BLACK
BLACK	WHITE	WHITE
BLACK	GRAY	GRAY

Now repeat this, but instead say aloud the color used to draw the word. Harder, eh? It's easy to be fluent when reading, but way harder when trying to recognize colors.

Your brain treats written words as something to be respected. We need to make sure the names we use live up to this.

Let's look at a couple of examples:

- We're authenticating people who access our site that sells jewelry made from old graphics cards:

```
let user = authenticate(credentials)
```

The variable is user because it's *always* user. But why? It means nothing. How about customer, or buyer? That way we get constant reminders as we code of what this person is trying to do, and what that means to us.

- We have an instance method that discounts an order:

```
public void deductPercent(double amount)
    // ...
```

Two things here. First, deductPercent is *what it does* and not *why it does it*. Then the name of the parameter amount is at best misleading: is it an absolute amount, a percentage?

Perhaps this would be better:

```
public void applyDiscount(Percentage discount)
    // ...
```

The method name now makes its intent clear. We've also changed the parameter from a double to a Percentage, a type we've defined. We don't know about you, but when dealing with percentages we never know if the value is supposed to be between 0 and 100 or 0.0 and 1.0. Using a type documents what the function expects.

- We have a module that does interesting things with Fibonacci numbers. One of those things is to calculate the nth number in the sequence. Stop and think what you'd call this function.

Most people we ask would call it fib. Seems reasonable, but remember it will normally be called in the context of its module, so the call would be Fib.fib(n). How about calling it of or nth instead:

```
Fib.of(0)    # => 0
Fib.nth(20)  # => 4181
```

When naming things, you're constantly looking for ways of clarifying what you mean, and that act of clarification will lead you to a better understanding of your code *as you write it*.

However, not all names have to be candidates for a literary prize.

The Exception That Proves the Rule

While we strive for clarity in code, branding is a different matter entirely.

There's a well-established tradition that projects and project teams should have obscure, "clever" names. Names of Pokémon, Marvel superheroes, cute mammals, *Lord of the Rings* characters, you name it.

Literally.

Honor the Culture

There are only two hard things in computer science: cache invalidation and naming things.

Most introductory computer texts will admonish you never to use single letter variables such as i, j, or k.[19]

We think they're wrong. Sort of.

In fact, it depends on the culture of that particular programming language or environment. In the C programming language, i, j, and k are traditionally used as loop increment variables, s is used for a character string, and so on. If you program in that environment, that's what you are used to seeing and it would be jarring (and hence wrong) to violate that norm. On the other hand,

---

19. Do you know *why* i is commonly used as a loop variable? The answer comes from over 60 years ago, when variables starting with I through N were integers in the original FORTRAN. And FORTRAN was in turn influenced by algebra.

using that convention in a different environment where it's *not* expected is just as wrong. You'd never do something heinous like this Clojure example which assigns a string to variable i:

```
(let [i "Hello World"]
     (println i))
```

Some language communities prefer camelCase, with embedded capital letters, while others prefer snake_case with embedded underscores to separate words. The languages themselves will of course accept either, but that doesn't make it right. Honor the local culture.

Some languages allow a subset of Unicode in names. Get a sense of what the community expects before going all cute with names like ɹǝsn or εξέρχεται.

Consistency

Emerson is famous for writing "A foolish consistency is the hobgoblin of little minds...," but Emerson wasn't on a team of programmers.

Every project has its own vocabulary: jargon words that have a special meaning to the team. "Order" means one thing to a team creating an online store, and something very different to a team whose app charts the lineage of religious groups. It's important that everyone on the team knows what these words mean, and that they use them consistently.

One way is to encourage a lot of communication. If everyone pair programs, and pairs switch frequently, then jargon will spread osmotically.

Another way is to have a project glossary, listing the terms that have special meaning to the team. This is an informal document, possibly maintained on a wiki, possibly just index cards on a wall somewhere.

After a while, the project jargon will take on a life of its own. As everyone gets comfortable with the vocabulary, you'll be able to use the jargon as a shorthand, expressing a lot of meaning accurately and concisely. (This is exactly what a *pattern language* is.)

Renaming Is Even Harder

There are two hard problems in computer science: cache invalidation, naming things, and off-by-one errors.

No matter how much effort you put in up front, things change. Code is refactored, usage shifts, meaning becomes subtly altered. If you aren't vigilant about updating names as you go, you can quickly descend into a nightmare much worse than meaningless names: *misleading* names. Have you ever had someone explain inconsistencies in code such as, "The routine called getData really writes data to an archive file"?

As we discuss in *Software Entropy*, when you spot a problem, fix it—right here and now. When you see a name that no longer expresses the intent, or is misleading or confusing, fix it. You've got full regression tests, so you'll spot any instances you may have missed.

Tip 74	Name Well; Rename When Needed

If for some reason you can't change the now-wrong name, then you've got a bigger problem: an ETC violation (see *The Essence of Good Design*). Fix that first, then change the offending name. Make renaming easy, and do it often.

Otherwise you'll have to explain to the new folks on the team that getData really writes data to a file, and you'll have to do it with a straight face.

Related Sections Include

- Topic 3, *Software Entropy*, on page 6
- Topic 40, *Refactoring*, on page 209
- Topic 45, *The Requirements Pit*, on page 244

Challenges

- When you find a function or method with an overly generic name, try and rename it to express all the things it really does. Now it's an easier target for refactoring.

- In our examples, we suggested using more specific names such as *buyer* instead of the more traditional and generic *user*. What other names do you habitually use that could be better?

- Are the names in your system congruent with user terms from the domain? If not, why? Does this cause a Stroop-effect style cognitive dissonance for the team?

- Are names in your system hard to change? What can you do to fix that particular broken window?

## CHAPTER 8

Before the Project

At the very beginning of a project, you and the team need to learn the requirements. Simply being told what to do or listening to users is not enough: read *The Requirements Pit* and learn how to avoid the common traps and pitfalls.

Conventional wisdom and constraint management are the topics of *Solving Impossible Puzzles*. Whether you are performing requirements, analysis, coding, or testing, difficult problems will crop up. Most of the time, they won't be as difficult as they first appear to be.

And when that impossible project comes up, we like to turn to our secret weapon: *Working Together*. And by "working together" we don't mean sharing a massive requirements document, flinging heavily cc'd emails or enduring endless meetings. We mean solving problems together while coding. We'll show you who you need and how to start.

Even though the Agile Manifesto begins with "Individuals and interactions over processes and tools," virtually all "agile" projects begin with an ironic discussion of which process and which tools they'll use. But no matter how well thought out it is, and regardless of which "best practices" it includes, no method can replace *thinking*. You don't need any particular process or tool, what you do need is the *The Essence of Agility*.

With these critical issues sorted out *before* the project gets under way, you can be better positioned to avoid "analysis paralysis" and actually begin—and complete—your successful project.

45 ▶ The Requirements Pit

Perfection is achieved, not when there is nothing left to add
but when there is nothing left to take away...

> ➤ Antoine de St. Exupery, Wind, Sand, and Stars, 1939

Many books and tutorials refer to *requirements gathering* as an early phase of the project. The word "gathering" seems to imply a tribe of happy analysts, foraging for nuggets of wisdom that are lying on the ground all around them while the Pastoral Symphony plays gently in the background. "Gathering" implies that the requirements are already there—you need merely find them, place them in your basket, and be merrily on your way.

It doesn't quite work that way. Requirements rarely lie on the surface. Normally, they're buried deep beneath layers of assumptions, misconceptions, and politics. Even worse, often they don't really exist at all.

Tip 75	No One Knows Exactly What They Want

The Requirements Myth

In the early days of software, computers were more valuable (in terms of amortized cost per hour) than the people who worked with them. We saved money by trying to get things correct the first time. Part of that process was trying to specify exactly what we were going to get the machine to do. We'd start by getting a specification of the requirements, parlay that into a design document, then into flowcharts and pseudo code, and finally into code. Before feeding it into a computer, though, we'd spend time desk checking it.

It cost a lot of money. And that cost meant that people only tried to automate something when they knew exactly what they wanted. As early machines were fairly limited, the scope of problems they solved was constrained: it was actually *possible* to understand the whole problem before you started.

But that is not the real world. The real world is messy, conflicted, and unknown. In that world, exact specifications of anything are rare, if not downright impossible.

That's where we programmers come in. Our job is to help people understand what they want. In fact, that's probably our most valuable attribute. And it's worth repeating:

Tip 76	Programmers Help People Understand What They Want

Programming as Therapy

Let's call the people who ask us to write software our clients.

The typical client comes to us with a need. The need may be strategic, but it is just as likely to be a tactical issue: a response to a current problem. The need may be for a change to an existing system or it may ask for something new. The need will sometimes be expressed in business terms, and sometimes in technical ones.

The mistake new developers often make is to take this statement of need and implement a solution for it.

In our experience, this initial statement of need is not an absolute requirement. The client may not realize this, but it is really an invitation to explore.

Let's take a simple example.

You work for a publisher of paper and electronic books. You're given a new requirement:

> Shipping should be free on all orders costing $50 or more.

Stop for a second and imagine yourself in that position. What's the first thing that comes to mind?

The chances are very good that you had questions:

- Does the $50 include tax?
- Does the $50 include current shipping charges?
- Does the $50 have to be for paper books, or can the order also include ebooks?
- What kind of shipping is offered? Priority? Ground?
- What about international orders?
- How often will the $50 limit change in the future?

That's what we do. When given something that seems simple, we annoy people by looking for edge cases and asking about them.

The chances are the client will have already thought of some of these, and just assumed that the implementation would work that way. Asking the question just flushes that information out.

But other questions will likely be things that the client hadn't previously considered. That's where things get interesting, and where a good developer learns to be diplomatic.

> **You:** We were wondering about the $50 total. Does that include what we'd normally charge for shipping?
>
> **Client:** Of course. It's the total they'd pay us.
>
> **You:** That's nice and simple for our customers to understand: I can see the attraction. But I can see some less scrupulous customers trying to game that system.
>
> **Client:** How so?
>
> **You:** Well, let's say they buy a book for $25, and then select overnight shipping, the most expensive option. That'll likely be about $30, making the whole order $55. We'd then make the shipping free, and they'd get overnight shipping on a $25 book for just $25.
>
> (At this point the experienced developer stops. Deliver facts, and let the client make the decisions.)
>
> **Client:** Ouch. That certainly wasn't what I intended; we'd lose money on those orders. What are the options?

And this starts an exploration. Your role in this is to interpret what the client says and to feed back to them the implications. This is both an intellectual process and a creative one: you're thinking on your feet and you're contributing to a solution that is likely to be better than one that either you or the client would have produced alone.

Requirements Are a Process

In the previous example, the developer took the requirements and fed-back a consequence to the client. This initiated the exploration. During that exploration, you are likely to come up with more feedback as the client plays with different solutions. This is the reality of all requirements gathering:

> Tip 77   Requirements Are Learned in a Feedback Loop

Your job is to help the client understand the consequences of their stated requirements. You do that by generating feedback, and letting them use that feedback to refine their thinking.

In the previous example, the feedback was easy to express in words. Sometimes that's not the case. And sometimes you honestly won't know enough about the domain to be as specific as that.

In those cases, Pragmatic Programmers rely on the "is this what you meant?" school of feedback. We produce mockups and prototypes, and let the client play with them. Ideally the things we produce are flexible enough that we can change them during our discussions with the client, letting us respond to "that isn't what I meant" with "so more like this?"

Sometimes these mockups can be thrown together in an hour or so. They are obviously just hacks to get an idea across.

But the reality is that *all* of the work we do is actually some form of mockup. Even at the end of a project we're still interpreting what our client wants. In fact, by that point we're likely to have more clients: the QA people, operations, marketing, and maybe even test groups of customers.

So the Pragmatic Programmer looks at *all* of the project as a requirements gathering exercise. That's why we prefer short iterations; ones that end with direct client feedback. This keeps us on track, and makes sure that if we *do* go in the wrong direction, the amount of time lost is minimized.

Walk in Your Client's Shoes

There's a simple technique for getting inside your clients' heads that isn't used often enough: become a client. Are you writing a system for the help desk? Spend a couple of days monitoring the phones with an experienced support person. Are you automating a manual stock control system? Work in the warehouse for a week.[1]

As well as giving you insight into how the system will *really* be used, you'd be amazed at how the request "May I sit in for a week while you do your job?" helps build trust and establishes a basis for communication with your clients. Just remember not to get in the way!

| Tip 78 | Work with a User to Think Like a User |

Gathering feedback is also the time to start to build a rapport with your client base, learning their expectations and hopes for the system you are building. See Topic 52, *Delight Your Users*, on page 280, for more.

---

1. Does a week sound like a long time? It really isn't, particularly when you're looking at processes in which management and workers occupy different worlds. Management will give you one view of how things operate, but when you get down on the floor, you'll find a very different reality—one that will take time to assimilate.

Requirements vs. Policy

Let's imagine that while discussing a Human Resources system, a client says "Only an employee's supervisors and the personnel department may view that employee's records." Is this statement truly a requirement? Perhaps today, but it embeds business policy in an absolute statement.

Business policy? Requirement? It's a relatively subtle distinction, but it's one that will have profound implications for the developers. If the requirement is stated as "Only supervisors and personnel can view an employee record," the developer may end up coding an explicit test every time the application accesses this data. However, if the statement is "Only authorized users may access an employee record," the developer will probably design and implement some kind of access control system. When policy changes (and it will), only the metadata for that system will need to be updated. In fact, gathering requirements in this way naturally leads you to a system that is well factored to support metadata.

In fact, there's a general rule here:

Tip 79	Policy Is Metadata

Implement the general case, with the policy information as an example of the type of thing the system needs to support.

Requirements vs. Reality

In a January 1999 *Wired* magazine article,[2] producer and musician Brian Eno described an incredible piece of technology—the ultimate mixing board. It does anything to sound that can be done. And yet, instead of letting musicians make better music, or produce a recording faster or less expensively, it gets in the way; it disrupts the creative process.

To see why, you have to look at how recording engineers work. They balance sounds intuitively. Over the years, they develop an innate feedback loop between their ears and their fingertips—sliding faders, rotating knobs, and so on. However, the interface to the new mixer didn't leverage off those abilities. Instead, it forced its users to type on a keyboard or click a mouse. The functions it provided were comprehensive, but they were packaged in unfamiliar and exotic ways. The functions the engineers needed were sometimes

---

2.   https://www.wired.com/1999/01/eno/

hidden behind obscure names, or were achieved with nonintuitive combinations of basic facilities.

This example also illustrates our belief that successful tools adapt to the hands that use them. Successful requirements gathering takes this into account. And this is why early feedback, with prototypes or tracer bullets, will let your clients say "yes, it does *what* I want, but not *how* I want."

Documenting Requirements

We believe that the best requirements documentation, perhaps the *only* requirements documentation, is working code.

But that doesn't mean that you can get away without documenting your understanding of what the client wants. It just means that those documents are not a deliverable: they are not something that you give to a client to sign off on. Instead, they are simply mileposts to help guide the implementation process.

Requirements Documents Are Not for Clients

In the past, both Andy and Dave have been on projects that produced incredibly detailed requirements. These substantial documents expanded on the client's initial two-minute explanation of what was wanted, producing inch-thick masterpieces full of diagrams and tables. Things were specified to the point where there was almost no room for ambiguity in the implementation. Given sufficiently powerful tools, the document could actually *be* the final program.

Creating these documents was a mistake for two reasons. First, as we've discussed, the client doesn't really know what they want up front. So when we take what they say and expand it into what is almost a legal document, we are building an incredibly complex castle on quicksand.

You might say "but then we take the document to the client and they sign off on it. We're getting feedback." And that leads us to the second problem with these requirement specifications: the client never reads them.

The client uses programmers because, while the client is motivated by solving a high-level and somewhat nebulous problem, programmers are interested in all the details and nuances. The requirements document is written for developers, and contains information and subtleties that are sometimes incomprehensible and frequently boring to the client.

Submit a 200-page requirements document, and the client will likely heft it to decide if it weighs enough to be important, they may read the first couple of paragraphs (which is why the first two paragraphs are always titled *Management Summary*), and they may flick through the rest, sometimes stopping when there's a neat diagram.

This isn't putting the client down. But giving them a large technical document is like giving the average developer a copy of the *Iliad* in Homeric Greek and asking them to code the video game from it.

Requirements Documents Are for Planning

So we don't believe in the monolithic, heavy-enough-to-stun-an-ox, requirements document. We do, however, know that requirements have to be written down, simply because developers on a team need to know what they'll be doing.

What form does this take? We favor something that can fit on a real (or virtual) index card. These short descriptions are often called *user stories*. They describe what a small portion of the application should do from the perspective of a user of that functionality.

When written this way, the requirements can be placed on a board and moved around to show both status and priority.

You might think that a single index card can't hold the information needed to implement a component of the application. You'd be right. And that's part of the point. By keeping this statement of requirements short, you're encouraging developers to ask clarifying questions. You're enhancing the feedback process between clients and coders before and during the creation of each piece of code.

Overspecification

Another big danger in producing a requirements document is being too specific. Good requirements are abstract. Where requirements are concerned, the simplest statement that accurately reflects the business need is best. This doesn't mean you can be vague—you must capture the underlying semantic invariants as requirements, and document the specific or current work practices as policy.

Requirements are not architecture. Requirements are not design, nor are they the user interface. Requirements are *need*.

Just One More Wafer-Thin Mint…

Many project failures are blamed on an increase in scope—also known as feature bloat, creeping featurism, or requirements creep. This is an aspect of the boiled-frog syndrome from Topic 4, *Stone Soup and Boiled Frogs*, on page 8. What can we do to prevent requirements from creeping up on us?

The answer (again) is feedback. If you're working with the client in iterations with constant feedback, then the client will experience first-hand the impact of "just one more feature." They'll see another story card go up on the board, and they'll get to help choose another card to move into the next iteration to make room. Feedback works both ways.

Maintain a Glossary

As soon as you start discussing requirements, users and domain experts will use certain terms that have specific meaning to them. They may differentiate between a "client" and a "customer," for example. It would then be inappropriate to use either word casually in the system.

Create and maintain a *project glossary*—one place that defines all the specific terms and vocabulary used in a project. All participants in the project, from end users to support staff, should use the glossary to ensure consistency. This implies that the glossary needs to be widely accessible—a good argument for online documentation.

Tip 80	Use a Project Glossary

It's hard to succeed on a project if users and developers call the same thing by different names or, even worse, refer to different things by the same name.

Related Sections Include

- Topic 5, *Good-Enough Software*, on page 11
- Topic 7, *Communicate!*, on page 19
- Topic 11, *Reversibility*, on page 47
- Topic 13, *Prototypes and Post-it Notes*, on page 56
- Topic 23, *Design by Contract*, on page 104
- Topic 43, *Stay Safe Out There*, on page 231
- Topic 44, *Naming Things*, on page 238
- Topic 46, *Solving Impossible Puzzles*, on page 252
- Topic 52, *Delight Your Users*, on page 280

Exercises

Exercise 33 (possible answer on page 305)

Which of the following are probably genuine requirements? Restate those that are not to make them more useful (if possible).

1. The response time must be less than ~500ms.
2. Modal windows will have a gray background.
3. The application will be organized as a number of front-end processes and a back-end server.
4. If a user enters non-numeric characters in a numeric field, the system will flash the field background and not accept them.
5. The code and data for this embedded application must fit within 32Mb.

Challenges

- Can you use the software you are writing? Is it possible to have a good feel for requirements *without* being able to use the software yourself?

- Pick a non-computer-related problem you currently need to solve. Generate requirements for a noncomputer solution.

---

46 ▶ ## Solving Impossible Puzzles

Gordius, the King of Phrygia, once tied a knot that no one could untie. It was said that whoever solved the riddle of the Gordian Knot would rule all of Asia. So along comes Alexander the Great, who chops the knot to bits with his sword. Just a little different interpretation of the requirements, that's all.... And he did end up ruling most of Asia.

Every now and again, you will find yourself embroiled in the middle of a project when a really tough puzzle comes up: some piece of engineering that you just can't get a handle on, or perhaps some bit of code that is turning out to be much harder to write than you thought. Maybe it looks impossible. But is it really as hard as it seems?

Consider real-world puzzles—those devious little bits of wood, wrought iron, or plastic that seem to turn up as Christmas presents or at garage sales. All you have to do is remove the ring, or fit the T-shaped pieces in the box, or whatever.

So you pull on the ring, or try to put the Ts in the box, and quickly discover that the obvious solutions just don't work. The puzzle can't be solved that way. But even though it's obvious, that doesn't stop people from trying the same thing—over and over—thinking there must be a way.

Of course, there isn't. The solution lies elsewhere. The secret to solving the puzzle is to identify the real (not imagined) constraints, and find a solution therein. Some constraints are *absolute*; others are merely *preconceived notions*. Absolute constraints *must* be honored, however distasteful or stupid they may appear to be.

On the other hand, as Alexander proved, some apparent constraints may not be real constraints at all. Many software problems can be just as sneaky.

Degrees of Freedom

The popular buzz-phrase "thinking outside the box" encourages us to recognize constraints that might not be applicable and to ignore them. But this phrase isn't entirely accurate. If the "box" is the boundary of constraints and conditions, then the trick is to *find* the box, which may be considerably larger than you think.

The key to solving puzzles is both to recognize the constraints placed on you and to recognize the degrees of freedom you *do* have, for in those you'll find your solution. This is why some puzzles are so effective; you may dismiss potential solutions too readily.

For example, can you connect all of the dots in the following puzzle and return to the starting point with just three straight lines—without lifting your pen from the paper or retracing your steps (*Math Puzzles & Games [Hol92]*)?

You must challenge any preconceived notions and evaluate whether or not they are real, hard-and-fast constraints.

It's not whether you think inside the box or outside the box. The problem lies in *finding* the box—identifying the real constraints.

Tip 81	Don't Think Outside the Box—*Find* the Box

When faced with an intractable problem, enumerate *all* the possible avenues you have before you. Don't dismiss anything, no matter how unusable or stupid it sounds. Now go through the list and explain why a certain path cannot be taken. Are you sure? Can you *prove* it?

Consider the Trojan horse—a novel solution to an intractable problem. How do you get troops into a walled city without being discovered? You can bet that "through the front door" was initially dismissed as suicide.

Categorize and prioritize your constraints. When woodworkers begin a project, they cut the longest pieces first, then cut the smaller pieces out of the remaining wood. In the same manner, we want to identify the most restrictive constraints first, and fit the remaining constraints within them.

By the way, a solution to the Four Posts puzzle is shown at the end of the book on page 306.

Get Out of Your Own Way!

Sometimes you will find yourself working on a problem that seems much harder than you thought it should be. Maybe it feels like you're going down the wrong path—that there must be an easier way than this! Perhaps you are running late on the schedule now, or even despair of ever getting the system to work because this particular problem is "impossible."

This is an ideal time to do something else for a while. Work on something different. Go walk the dog. Sleep on it.

Your conscious brain is aware of the problem, but your conscious brain is really pretty dumb (no offense). So it's time to give your real brain, that amazing associative neural net that lurks below your consciousness, some space. You'll be amazed how often the answer will just pop into your head when you deliberately distract yourself.

If that sounds too mystical for you, it isn't. *Psychology Today*[3] reports:

> To put it plainly—people who were distracted did better on a complex problem-solving task than people who put in conscious effort.

---

3.   https://www.psychologytoday.com/us/blog/your-brain-work/201209/stop-trying-solve-problems

If you're still not willing to drop the problem for a while, the next best thing is probably finding someone to explain it to. Often, the distraction of simply talking about it will lead you to enlightenment.

Have them ask you questions such as:

- Why are you solving this problem?

- What's the benefit of solving it?

- Are the problems you're having related to edge cases? Can you eliminate them?

- Is there a simpler, related problem you can solve?

This is another example of Rubber Ducking in practice.

Fortune Favors the Prepared Mind

Louis Pasteur is reported to have said:

> Dans les champs de l'observation le hasard ne favorise que les esprits préparés.
> *(When it comes to observation, fortune favors the prepared mind.)*

That is true for problem solving, too. In order to have those *eureka!* moments, your nonconscious brain needs to have plenty of raw material; prior experiences that can contribute to an answer.

A great way to feed your brain is to give it feedback on what works and what doesn't work as you do your daily job. And we describe a great way to do that using an Engineering Daybook (Topic 22, *Engineering Daybooks*, on page 100).

And always remember the advice on the cover of *The Hitchhiker's Guide to the Galaxy*: DON'T PANIC.

Related Sections Include

- Topic 5, *Good-Enough Software*, on page 11
- Topic 37, *Listen to Your Lizard Brain*, on page 192
- Topic 45, *The Requirements Pit*, on page 244
- Andy wrote an entire book about this kind of thing: *Pragmatic Thinking and Learning: Refactor Your Wetware [Hun08]*.

Challenges

- Take a hard look at whatever difficult problem you are embroiled in today. Can you cut the Gordian knot? Do you have to do it this way? Do you have to do it at all?

- Were you handed a set of constraints when you signed on to your current project? Are they all still applicable, and is the interpretation of them still valid?

Working Together

I've never met a human being who would want to read 17,000 pages of documentation, and if there was, I'd kill him to get him out of the gene pool.

> Joseph Costello, President of Cadence

It was one of those "impossible" projects, the kind you hear about that sounds both exhilarating and terrifying at the same time. An ancient system was approaching end-of-life, the hardware was physically going away, and a brand-new system had to be crafted that would match the (often undocumented) behavior *exactly*. Many hundreds of millions of dollars of other people's money would pass through this system, and the deadline from inception to deployment was on the order of months.

And that is where Andy and Dave first met. An impossible project with a ridiculous deadline. There was only one thing that made the project a roaring success. The expert who had managed this system for years was sitting right there in her office, just across the hall from our broom closet–sized development room. Continuously available for questions, clarifications, decisions, and demos.

Throughout this book we recommend working closely with users; they are part of your team. On that first project together, we practiced what now might be called *pair programming* or *mob programming*: one person typing code while one or more other team members comment, ponder, and solve problems together. It's a powerful way of working together that transcends endless meetings, memos, and overstuffed legalistic documentation prized for weight over usefulness.

And that's what we really mean by "working with": not just asking questions, having discussions, and taking notes, but asking questions and having discussions *while you're actually coding*.

Conway's Law

In 1967, Melvin Conway introduced an idea in *How do Committees Invent? [Con68]* which would become known as Conway's Law:

> Organizations which design systems are constrained to produce designs which are copies of the communication structures of these organizations.

That is, the social structures and communication pathways of the team and the organization will be mirrored in the application, website, or product being developed. Various studies have shown strong support for this idea. We've witnessed it first-hand countless times—for example, in teams where no one talks to each other at all, resulting in siloed, "stove-pipe" systems. Or teams that were split into two, resulting in a client/server or frontend/backend division.

Studies also offer support for the reverse principle: you can deliberately structure your team the way you want your code to look. For example, geographically distributed teams are shown to tend toward more modular, distributed software.

But most importantly, development teams that include users will produce software that clearly reflects that involvement, and teams that don't bother will reflect that, too.

Pair Programming

Pair programming is one of the practices of eXtreme Programming that has become popular outside of XP itself. In pair programming, one developer operates the keyboard, and the other does not. Both work on the problem together, and can switch typing duties as needed.

There are many benefits to pair programming. Different people bring different backgrounds and experience, different problem-solving techniques and approaches, and differing levels of focus and attention to any given problem. The developer acting as typist must focus on the low-level details of syntax and coding style, while the other developer is free to consider higher-level issues and scope. While that might sound like a small distinction, remember that we humans have only so much brain bandwidth. Fiddling around with typing esoteric words and symbols that the compiler will grudgingly accept takes a fair bit of our own processing power. Having a second developer's full brain available during the task brings a lot more mental power to bear.

The inherent peer-pressure of a second person helps against moments of weakness and bad habits of naming variables foo and such. You're less inclined to take a potentially embarrassing shortcut when someone is actively watching, which also results in higher-quality software.

Mob Programming

And if two heads are better than one, what about having a dozen diverse people all working on the same problem at the same time, with one typist?

Mob programming, despite the name, does not involve torches or pitchforks. It's an extension of pair programming that involves more than just two developers. Proponents report great results using mobs to solve hard problems. Mobs can easily include people not usually considered part of the development team, including users, project sponsors, and testers. In fact, in our first "impossible" project together, it was a common sight for one of us to be typing while the other discussed the issue with our business expert. It was a small mob of three.

You might think of mob programming as *tight collaboration with live coding.*

What Should I Do?

If you're currently only programming solo, maybe try pair programming. Give it a minimum of two weeks, only a few hours at a time, as it will feel strange at first. To brainstorm new ideas or diagnose thorny issues, perhaps try a mob programming session.

If you are already pairing or mobbing, who's included? Is it just developers, or do you allow members of your extended team to participate: users, testers, sponsors…?

And as with all collaboration, you need to manage the human aspects of it as well as the technical. Here are just a few tips to get started:

- Build the code, not your ego. It's not about who's brightest; we all have our moments, good and bad.
- Start small. Mob with only 4-5 people, or start with just a few pairs, in short sessions.
- Criticize the code, not the person. "Let's look at this block" sounds much better than "you're wrong."
- Listen and try to understand others' viewpoints. Different isn't wrong.
- Conduct frequent retrospectives to try and improve for next time.

Coding in the same office or remote, alone, in pairs, or in mobs, are all effective ways of working together to solve problems. If you and your team have only ever done it one way, you might want to experiment with a different style. But don't just jump in with a naive approach: there are rules, suggestions, and guidelines for each of these development styles. For instance, with mob programming you swap out the typist every 5-10 minutes.

Do some reading and research, from both textbook and experience reports, and get a feel for the advantages and pitfalls you may encounter. You might want to start by coding a simple exercise, and not just jump straight into your toughest production code.

But however you go about it, let us suggest one final piece of advice:

Tip 82	Don't Go into the Code Alone

48 ▸ The Essence of Agility

You keep using that word, I do not think it means
what you think it means.

> ➤ Inigo Montoya, *The Princess Bride*

Agile is an adjective: it's how you do something. You can be an agile developer. You can be on a team that adopts agile practices, a team that responds to change and setbacks with agility. Agility is your style, not you.

Tip 83	Agile Is Not a Noun; Agile Is How You Do Things

As we write this, almost 20 years after the inception of the Manifesto for Agile Software Development,[4] we see many, many developers successfully applying its values. We see many fantastic teams who find ways to take these values and use them to guide what they do, and how they change what they do.

But we also see another side of agility. We see teams and companies eager for off-the-shelf solutions: Agile-in-a-Box. And we see many consultants and companies all too happy to sell them what they want. We see companies adopting more layers of management, more formal reporting, more specialized developers, and more fancy job titles which just mean "someone with a clipboard and a stopwatch."[5]

We feel that many people have lost sight of the true meaning of agility, and we'd like to see folks return to the basics.

---

4.   https://agilemanifesto.org
5.   For more on just how bad that approach can be, see *The Tyranny of Metrics* [Mul18].

Remember the values from the manifesto:

> We are uncovering better ways of developing software by doing it and helping others do it. Through this work we have come to value:
>
> - **Individuals and interactions** over processes and tools
> - **Working software** over comprehensive documentation
> - **Customer collaboration** over contract negotiation
> - **Responding to change** over following a plan
>
> That is, while there is value in the items on the right, we value the items on the left more.

Anyone selling you something that increases the importance on things on the right over things on the left clearly doesn't value the same things that we and the other manifesto writers did.

And anyone selling you a solution-in-a-box hasn't read the introductory statement. The values are motivated and informed by the continuous act of uncovering better ways to produce software. This is not a static document. It's suggestions for a generative process.

There Can Never Be an Agile Process

In fact, whenever someone says "do this, and you'll be agile," they are wrong. By definition.

Because agility, both in the physical world and in software development, is all about responding to change, responding to the unknowns you encounter after you set out. A running gazelle doesn't go in a straight line. A gymnast makes hundreds of corrections a second as they respond to changes in their environment and minor errors in their foot placement.

So it is with teams and individual developers. There is no single plan you can follow when you develop software. Three of the four values tell you that. They're all about gathering and responding to feedback.

The values don't tell you what to do. They tell you what to look for when you decide for yourself what to do.

These decisions are always contextual: they depend on who you are, the nature of your team, your application, your tooling, your company, your customer, the outside world; an incredibly large number of factors, some major and some trivial. No fixed, static plan can survive this uncertainty.

So What Do We Do?

No one can tell you *what* to do. But we think we can tell you something about the spirit with which you do it. It all boils down to how you deal with uncertainty. The manifesto suggests that you do this by gathering and acting on feedback. So here's our recipe for working in an agile way:

1. Work out where you are.

2. Make the smallest meaningful step towards where you want to be.

3. Evaluate where you end up, and fix anything you broke.

Repeat these steps until you're done. And use them recursively, at every level of everything you do.

Sometimes even the most trivial-seeming decision becomes important when you gather feedback.

"Now my code needs to get the account owner.

```
let user = accountOwner(accountID);
```

Hmmm… user is a useless name. I'll make it owner.

```
let owner = accountOwner(accountID);
```

But now that feels a little redundant. What am I actually trying to do here? The story says that I'm sending this person an email, so I need to find their email address. Maybe I don't need the whole account owner at all.

```
let email = emailOfAccountOwner(accountID);
```

By applying the feedback loop at a really low level (the naming of a variable) we've actually improved the design of the overall system, reducing the coupling between this code and the code that deals with accounts.

The feedback loop also applies at the highest level of a project. Some of our most successful work has happened when we started working on a client's requirements, took a single step, and realized that what we were about to do wasn't necessary, that the best solution didn't even involve software.

This loop applies outside the scope of a single project. Teams should apply it to review their process and how well it worked. A team that doesn't continuously experiment with their process is not an agile team.

And This Drives Design

In Topic 8, *The Essence of Good Design*, on page 28 we assert that the measure of design is how easy the result of that design is to change: a good design produces something that's easier to change than a bad design.

And this discussion about agility explains *why* that's the case.

You make a change, and discover you don't like it. Step 3 in our list says we have to be able to fix what we break. To make our feedback loop efficient, this fix has to be as painless as possible. If it isn't, we'll be tempted to shrug it off and leave it unfixed. We talk about this effect in Topic 3, *Software Entropy*, on page 6. To make this whole agile thing work, we need to practice good design, because good design makes things easy to change. And if it's easy to change, we can adjust, at every level, without any hesitation.

That is agility.

Related Sections Include

- Topic 27, *Don't Outrun Your Headlights*, on page 125
- Topic 40, *Refactoring*, on page 209
- Topic 50, *Coconuts Don't Cut It*, on page 270

Challenges

The simple feedback loop isn't just for software. Think of other decisions you've made recently. Could any of them have been improved by thinking about how you might be able to undo them if things didn't take you in the direction you were going? Can you think of ways you can improve what you do by gathering and acting on feedback?

## CHAPTER 9

Pragmatic Projects

As your project gets under way, we need to move away from issues of individual philosophy and coding to talk about larger, project-sized issues. We aren't going to go into specifics of project management, but we will talk about a handful of critical areas that can make or break any project.

As soon as you have more than one person working on a project, you need to establish some ground rules and delegate parts of the project accordingly. In *Pragmatic Teams*, we'll show how to do this while honoring the Pragmatic philosophy.

The purpose of a software development method is to help people work together. Are you and your team doing what works well for you, or are you only investing in the trivial surface artifacts, and not getting the real benefits you deserve? We'll see why *Coconuts Don't Cut It* and offer the true secret to success.

And of course none of that matters if you can't deliver software consistently and reliably. That's the basis of the magic trio of version control, testing, and automation: the *Pragmatic Starter Kit*.

Ultimately, though, success is in the eye of the beholder—the sponsor of the project. The perception of success is what counts, and in *Delight Your Users* we'll show you how to delight every project's sponsor.

The last tip in the book is a direct consequence of all the rest. In *Pride and Prejudice*, we ask you to sign your work, and to take pride in what you do.

49 ▶ Pragmatic Teams

At Group L, Stoffel oversees six first-rate programmers, a manage-
rial challenge roughly comparable to herding cats.

> ➤ *The Washington Post Magazine, June 9, 1985*

Even in 1985, the joke about herding cats was getting old. By the time of the first edition at the turn of the century, it was positively ancient. Yet it persists, because it has a ring of truth to it. Programmers are a bit like cats: intelligent, strong willed, opinionated, independent, and often worshiped by the net.

So far in this book we've looked at pragmatic techniques that help an individual be a better programmer. Can these methods work for teams as well, even for teams of strong-willed, independent people? The answer is a resounding "yes!" There are advantages to being a pragmatic individual, but these advantages are multiplied manyfold if the individual is working on a pragmatic team.

A team, in our view, is a small, mostly stable entity of its own. Fifty people aren't a team, they're a horde.[1] Teams where members are constantly being pulled onto other assignments and no one knows each other aren't a team either, they are merely strangers temporarily sharing a bus stop in the rain.

A pragmatic team is small, under 10-12 or so members. Members come and go rarely. Everyone knows everyone well, trusts each other, and depends on each other.

Tip 84	Maintain Small, Stable Teams

In this section we'll look briefly at how pragmatic techniques can be applied to teams as a whole. These notes are only a start. Once you've got a group of pragmatic developers working in an enabling environment, they'll quickly develop and refine their own team dynamics that work for them.

Let's recast some of the previous sections in terms of teams.

---

1. As team size grows, communication paths grow at the rate of $O(n^2)$, where n is the number of team members. On larger teams, communication begins to break down and becomes ineffective.

No Broken Windows

Quality is a team issue. The most diligent developer placed on a team that just doesn't care will find it difficult to maintain the enthusiasm needed to fix niggling problems. The problem is further exacerbated if the team actively discourages the developer from spending time on these fixes.

Teams as a whole should not tolerate broken windows—those small imperfections that no one fixes. The team *must* take responsibility for the quality of the product, supporting developers who understand the *no broken windows* philosophy we describe in Topic 3, *Software Entropy*, on page 6, and encouraging those who haven't yet discovered it.

Some team methodologies have a "quality officer"—someone to whom the team delegates the responsibility for the quality of the deliverable. This is clearly ridiculous: quality can come only from the individual contributions of *all* team members. Quality is built in, not bolted on.

Boiled Frogs

Remember the apocryphal frog in the pan of water, back in Topic 4, *Stone Soup and Boiled Frogs*, on page 8? It doesn't notice the gradual change in its environment, and ends up cooked. The same can happen to individuals who aren't vigilant. It can be difficult to keep an eye on your overall environment in the heat of project development.

It's even easier for teams as a whole to get boiled. People assume that someone else is handling an issue, or that the team leader must have OK'd a change that your user is requesting. Even the best-intentioned teams can be oblivious to significant changes in their projects.

Fight this. Encourage everyone to actively monitor the environment for changes. Stay awake and aware for increased scope, decreased time scales, additional features, new environments—anything that wasn't in the original understanding. Keep metrics on new requirements.[2] The team needn't reject changes out of hand—you simply need to be aware that they're happening. Otherwise, it'll be *you* in the hot water.

---

2. A *burnup* chart is better for this than the more usual *burndown* chart. With a burnup chart, you can clearly see how the additional features move the goalposts.

Schedule Your Knowledge Portfolio

In Topic 6, *Your Knowledge Portfolio*, on page 13 we looked at ways you should invest in your personal Knowledge Portfolio on your own time. Teams that want to succeed need to consider their knowledge and skill investments as well.

If your team is serious about improvement and innovation, you need to schedule it. Trying to get things done "whenever there's a free moment" means *they will never happen*. Whatever sort of backlog or task list or flow you're working with, don't reserve it for only feature development. The team works on more than just new features. Some possible examples include:

Old Systems Maintenance
While we love working on the shiny new system, there's likely maintenance work that needs to be done on the old system. We've met teams who try and shove this work in the corner. If the team is charged with doing these tasks, then do them—for real.

Process Reflection and Refinement
Continuous improvement can only happen when you take the time to look around, figure out what's working and not, and then make changes (see Topic 48, *The Essence of Agility*, on page 259). Too many teams are so busy bailing out water that they don't have time to fix the leak. Schedule it. Fix it.

New tech experiments
Don't adopt new tech, frameworks, or libraries just because "everyone is doing it," or based on something you saw at a conference or read online. Deliberately vet candidate technologies with prototypes. Put tasks on the schedule to try the new things and analyze results.

Learning and skill improvements
Personal learning and improvements are a great start, but many skills are more effective when spread team-wide. Plan to do it, whether it's the informal brown-bag lunch or more formal training sessions.

| Tip 85 | Schedule It to Make It Happen |

Communicate Team Presence

It's obvious that developers in a team must talk to each other. We gave some suggestions to facilitate this in Topic 7, *Communicate!*, on page 19. However, it's easy to forget that the team itself has a presence within the organization. The team as an entity needs to communicate clearly with the rest of the world.

To outsiders, the worst project teams are those that appear sullen and reticent. They hold meetings with no structure, where no one wants to talk. Their emails and project documents are a mess: no two look the same, and each uses different terminology.

Great project teams have a distinct personality. People look forward to meetings with them, because they know that they'll see a well-prepared performance that makes everyone feel good. The documentation they produce is crisp, accurate, and consistent. The team speaks with one voice.[3] They may even have a sense of humor.

There is a simple marketing trick that helps teams communicate as one: generate a brand. When you start a project, come up with a name for it, ideally something off-the-wall. (In the past, we've named projects after things such as killer parrots that prey on sheep, optical illusions, gerbils, cartoon characters, and mythical cities.) Spend 30 minutes coming up with a zany logo, and use it. Use your team's name liberally when talking with people. It sounds silly, but it gives your team an identity to build on, and the world something memorable to associate with your work.

Don't Repeat Yourselves

In Topic 9, *DRY—The Evils of Duplication*, on page 30, we talked about the difficulties of eliminating duplicated work between members of a team. This duplication leads to wasted effort, and can result in a maintenance nightmare. "Stovepipe" or "siloed" systems are common in these teams, with little sharing and a lot of duplicated functionality.

Good communication is key to avoiding these problems. And by "good" we mean *instant* and *frictionless*.

You should be able to ask a question of team members and get a more-or-less instant reply. If the team is co-located, this might be as simple as poking your head over the cube wall or down the hall. For remote teams, you may have to rely on a messaging app or other electronic means.

---

3. The team speaks with one voice—externally. Internally, we strongly encourage lively, robust debate. Good developers tend to be passionate about their work.

If you have to wait a week for the team meeting to ask your question or share your status, that's an awful lot of friction.[4] Frictionless means it's easy and low-ceremony to ask questions, share your progress, your problems, your insights and learnings, and to stay aware of what your teammates are doing.

Maintain awareness to stay DRY.

Team Tracer Bullets

A project team has to accomplish many different tasks in different areas of the project, touching a lot of different technologies. Understanding requirements, designing architecture, coding for frontend and server, testing, all have to happen. But it's a common misconception that these activities and tasks can happen separately, in isolation. They can't.

Some methodologies advocate all sort of different roles and titles within the team, or create separate specialized teams entirely. But the problem with that approach is that it introduces *gates* and *handoffs*. Now instead of a smooth flow from the team to deployment, you have artificial gates where the work stops. Handoffs that have to wait to be accepted. Approvals. Paperwork. The Lean folks call this *waste*, and strive to actively eliminate it.

All of these different roles and activities are actually different views of the same problem, and artificially separating them can cause a boatload of trouble. For example, programmers who are two or three levels removed from the actual users of their code are unlikely to be aware of the context in which their work is used. They will not be able to make informed decisions.

With *Tracer Bullets*, we recommend developing individual features, however small and limited initially, that go end-to-end through the entire system. That means that you need all the skills to do that within the team: frontend, UI/UX, server, DBA, QA, etc., all comfortable and accustomed to working with each other. With a tracer bullet approach, you can implement very small bits of functionality very quickly, and get immediate feedback on how well your team communicates and delivers. That creates an environment where you can make changes and tune your team and process quickly and easily.

Tip 86	Organize Fully Functional Teams

Build teams so you can build code end-to-end, incrementally and iteratively.

---

4. Andy has met teams who conduct their daily Scrum standups on Fridays.

Automation

A great way to ensure both consistency and accuracy is to automate everything the team does. Why struggle with code formatting standards when your editor or IDE can do it for you automatically? Why do manual testing when the continuous build can run tests automatically? Why deploy by hand when automation can do it the same way every time, repeatably and reliably?

Automation is an essential component of every project team. Make sure the team has skills at *tool building* to construct and deploy the tools that automate the project development and production deployment.

Know When to Stop Adding Paint

Remember that teams are made up of individuals. Give each member the ability to shine in their own way. Give them just enough structure to support them and to ensure that the project delivers value. Then, like the painter in *Good-Enough Software*, resist the temptation to add more paint.

Related Sections Include

- Topic 2, *The Cat Ate My Source Code*, on page 3
- Topic 7, *Communicate!*, on page 19
- Topic 12, *Tracer Bullets*, on page 50
- Topic 19, *Version Control*, on page 84
- Topic 50, *Coconuts Don't Cut It*, on page 270
- Topic 51, *Pragmatic Starter Kit*, on page 273

Challenges

- Look around for successful teams outside the area of software development. What makes them successful? Do they use any of the processes discussed in this section?

- Next time you start a project, try convincing people to brand it. Give your organization time to become used to the idea, and then do a quick audit to see what difference it made, both within the team and externally.

- You were probably once given problems such as "If it takes 4 workers 6 hours to dig a ditch, how long would it take 8 workers?" In real life, however, what factors affect the answer if the workers were writing code instead? In how many scenarios is the time actually reduced?

- Read *The Mythical Man Month [Bro96]* by Frederick Brooks. For extra credit, buy two copies so you can read it twice as fast.

50 Coconuts Don't Cut It

The native islanders had never seen an airplane before, or met people such as these strangers. In return for use of their land, the strangers provided mechanical birds that flew in and out all day long on a "runway," bringing incredible material wealth to their island home. The strangers mentioned something about war and fighting. One day it was over and they all left, taking their strange riches with them.

The islanders were desperate to restore their good fortunes, and re-built a facsimile of the airport, control tower, and equipment using local materials: vines, coconut shells, palm fronds, and such. But for some reason, even though they had everything in place, the planes didn't come. They had imitated the form, but not the content. Anthropologists call this a *cargo cult*.

All too often, *we* are the islanders.

It's easy and tempting to fall into the cargo cult trap: by investing in and building up the easily-visible artifacts, you hope to attract the underlying, working magic. But as with the original cargo cults of Melanesia,[5] a fake airport made out of coconut shells is no substitute for the real thing.

For example, we have personally seen teams that claim to be using Scrum. But, upon closer examination, it turned out they were doing a daily stand up meeting once a week, with four-week iterations that often turned into six- or eight-week iterations. They felt that this was okay because they were using a popular "agile" scheduling tool. They were only investing in the superficial artifacts—and even then, often in name only, as if "stand up" or "iteration" were some sort of incantation for the superstitious. Unsurprisingly, they, too, failed to attract the real magic.

Context Matters

Have you or your team fallen in this trap? Ask yourself, why are you even using that particular development method? Or that framework? Or that testing technique? Is it actually well-suited for the job at hand? Does it work well for you? Or was it adopted just because it was being used by the latest internet-fueled success story?

---

5. See https://en.wikipedia.org/wiki/Cargo_cult.

There's a current trend to adopt the policies and processes of successful companies such as Spotify, Netflix, Stripe, GitLab, and others. Each have their own unique take on software development and management. But consider the context: are you in the same market, with the same constraints and opportunities, similar expertise and organization size, similar management, and similar culture? Similar user base and requirements?

Don't fall for it. Particular artifacts, superficial structures, policies, processes, and methods are not enough.

Tip 87	Do What Works, Not What's Fashionable

How do you know "what works"? You rely on that most fundamental of Pragmatic techniques:

Try it.

Pilot the idea with a small team or set of teams. Keep the good bits that seem to work well, and discard anything else as waste or overhead. No one will downgrade your organization because it operates differently from Spotify or Netflix, because even they didn't follow their current processes while they were growing. And years from now, as those companies mature and pivot and continue to thrive, they'll be doing something different yet again.

That's the actual secret to their success.

One Size Fits No One Well

The purpose of a software development methodology is to help people work together. As we discuss in *The Essence of Agility*, there is no single plan you can follow when you develop software, especially not a plan that someone *else* came up with at another company.

Many certification programs are actually even worse than that: they are predicated on the student being able to memorize and follow the rules. But that's not what you want. You need the ability to see beyond the existing rules and exploit possibilities for advantage. That's a very different mindset from "but Scrum/Lean/Kanban/XP/agile does it this way…" and so on.

Instead, you want to take the best pieces from any particular methodology and adapt them for use. No one size fits all, and current methods are far from complete, so you'll need to look at more than just one popular method.

For example, Scrum defines some project management practices, but Scrum by itself doesn't provide enough guidance at the technical level for teams or at the portfolio/governance level for leadership. So where do you start?

Be Like Them!

We frequently hear software development leaders tell their staff, "We should operate like Netflix" (or one of these other leading companies). Of course you *could* do that.

First, get yourself a few hundred thousand servers and tens of millions of users...

The Real Goal

The goal of course isn't to "do Scrum," "do agile," "do Lean," or what-have-you. The goal is to be in a position to deliver working software that gives the users some new capability *at a moment's notice*. Not weeks, months, or years from now, but *now*. For many teams and organizations, continuous delivery feels like a lofty, unattainable goal, especially if you're saddled with a process that restricts delivery to months, or even weeks. But as with any goal, the key is to keep aiming in the right direction.

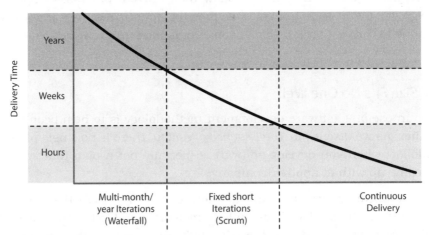

If you're delivering in years, try and shorten the cycle to months. From months, cut it down to weeks. From a four-week sprint, try two. From a two week sprint, try one. Then daily. Then, finally, on demand. Note that being able to deliver on demand does not mean you are forced to deliver every minute of every day. You deliver when the users need it, when it makes business sense to do so.

| Tip 88 | Deliver When Users Need It |

In order to move to this style of continuous development, you need a rock-solid infrastructure, which we discuss in the next topic, *Pragmatic Starter Kit*. You do development in the main trunk of your version control system, not in branches, and use techniques such as *feature switches* to roll out test features to users selectively.

Once your infrastructure is in order, you need to decide how to organize the work. Beginners might want to start with Scrum for project management, plus the technical practices from eXtreme Programming (XP). More disciplined and experienced teams might look to Kanban and Lean techniques, both for the team and perhaps for larger governance issues.

But don't take our word for it, investigate and try these approaches for yourself. Be careful, though, in overdoing it. Overly investing in any particular methodology can leave you blind to alternatives. You get used to it. Soon it becomes hard to see any other way. You've become calcified, and now you can't adapt quickly anymore.

Might as well be using coconuts.

Related Sections Include

- Topic 12, *Tracer Bullets*, on page 50
- Topic 27, *Don't Outrun Your Headlights*, on page 125
- Topic 48, *The Essence of Agility*, on page 259
- Topic 49, *Pragmatic Teams*, on page 264
- Topic 51, *Pragmatic Starter Kit*, on page 273

---

51 Pragmatic Starter Kit

Civilization advances by extending the number of important operations we can perform without thinking.

> ➤ *Alfred North Whitehead*

Back when cars were a novelty, the instructions for starting a Model-T Ford were more than two pages long. With modern cars, you just push a button—the starting procedure is automatic and foolproof. A person following a list of instructions might flood the engine, but the automatic starter won't.

Although software development is still an industry at the Model-T stage, we can't afford to go through two pages of instructions again and again for some common operation. Whether it is the build and release procedure, testing, project paperwork, or any other recurring task on the project, it has to be automatic and repeatable on any capable machine.

In addition, we want to ensure consistency and repeatability on the project. Manual procedures leave consistency up to chance; repeatability isn't guaranteed, especially if aspects of the procedure are open to interpretation by different people.

After we wrote the first edition of *The Pragmatic Programmer*, we wanted to create more books to help teams develop software. We figured we should start at the beginning: what are the most basic, most important elements that *every* team needs regardless of methodology, language, or technology stack. And so the idea of the *Pragmatic Starter Kit* was born, covering these three critical and interrelated topics:

- Version Control
- Regression Testing
- Full Automation

These are the three legs that support every project. Here's how.

Drive with Version Control

As we said in *Version Control*, you want to keep everything needed to build your project under version control. That idea becomes even more important in the context of the project itself.

First, it allows build machines to be ephemeral. Instead of one hallowed, creaky machine in the corner of the office that everyone is afraid to touch,[6] build machines and/or clusters are created on demand as spot instances in the cloud. Deployment configuration is under version control as well, so releasing to production can be handled automatically.

And that's the important part: at the project level, version control *drives* the build and release process.

> Tip 89   **Use Version Control to Drive Builds, Tests, and Releases**

---

6.   We've seen this first-hand more times than you'd think.

That is, build, test, and deployment are triggered via commits or pushes to version control, and built in a container in the cloud. Release to staging or production is specified by using a tag in your version control system. Releases then become a much more low-ceremony part of every day life—true continuous delivery, not tied to any one build machine or developer's machine.

Ruthless and Continuous Testing

Many developers test gently, subconsciously knowing where the code will break and avoiding the weak spots. Pragmatic Programmers are different. We are *driven* to find our bugs *now*, so we don't have to endure the shame of others finding our bugs later.

Finding bugs is somewhat like fishing with a net. We use fine, small nets (unit tests) to catch the minnows, and big, coarse nets (integration tests) to catch the killer sharks. Sometimes the fish manage to escape, so we patch any holes that we find, in hopes of catching more and more slippery defects that are swimming about in our project pool.

> **Tip 90**   Test Early, Test Often, Test Automatically

We want to start testing as soon as we have code. Those tiny minnows have a nasty habit of becoming giant, man-eating sharks pretty fast, and catching a shark is quite a bit harder. So we write unit tests. A lot of unit tests.

In fact, a good project may well have *more* test code than production code. The time it takes to produce this test code is worth the effort. It ends up being much cheaper in the long run, and you actually stand a chance of producing a product with close to zero defects.

Additionally, knowing that you've passed the test gives you a high degree of confidence that a piece of code is "done."

> **Tip 91**   Coding Ain't Done 'Til All the Tests Run

The automatic build runs all available tests. It's important to aim to "test for real," in other words, the test environment should match the production environment closely. Any gaps are where bugs breed.

The build may cover several major types of software testing: unit testing; integration testing; validation and verification; and performance testing.

This list is by no means complete, and some specialized projects will require various other types of testing as well. But it gives us a good starting point.

Unit Testing

A *unit test* is code that exercises a module. We covered this in Topic 41, *Test to Code*, on page 214. Unit testing is the foundation of all the other forms of testing that we'll discuss in this section. If the parts don't work by themselves, they probably won't work well together. All of the modules you are using must pass their own unit tests before you can proceed.

Once all of the pertinent modules have passed their individual tests, you're ready for the next stage. You need to test how all the modules use and interact with each other throughout the system.

Integration Testing

Integration testing shows that the major subsystems that make up the project work and play well with each other. With good contracts in place and well tested, any integration issues can be detected easily. Otherwise, integration becomes a fertile breeding ground for bugs. In fact, it is often the single largest source of bugs in the system.

Integration testing is really just an extension of the unit testing we've described—you're just testing how entire subsystems honor their contracts.

Validation and Verification

As soon as you have an executable user interface or prototype, you need to answer an all-important question: the users told you what they wanted, but is it what they need?

Does it meet the functional requirements of the system? This, too, needs to be tested. A bug-free system that answers the wrong question isn't very useful. Be conscious of end-user access patterns and how they differ from developer test data (for an example, see the story about brush strokes on page 90).

Performance Testing

Performance or stress testing may be important aspects of the project as well.

Ask yourself if the software meets the performance requirements under real-world conditions—with the expected number of users, or connections, or transactions per second. Is it scalable?

For some applications, you may need specialized testing hardware or software to simulate the load realistically.

Testing the Tests

Because we can't write perfect software, it follows that we can't write perfect test software either. We need to test the tests.

Think of our set of test suites as an elaborate security system, designed to sound the alarm when a bug shows up. How better to test a security system than to try to break in?

After you have written a test to detect a particular bug, *cause* the bug deliberately and make sure the test complains. This ensures that the test will catch the bug if it happens for real.

> **Tip 92** Use Saboteurs to Test Your Testing

If you are *really* serious about testing, take a separate branch of the source tree, introduce bugs on purpose, and verify that the tests will catch them. At a higher level, you can use something like Netflix's *Chaos Monkey*[7] to disrupt (i.e., "kill") services and test your application's resilience.

When writing tests, make sure that alarms sound when they should.

Testing Thoroughly

Once you are confident that your tests are correct, and are finding bugs you create, how do you know if you have tested the code base thoroughly enough?

The short answer is "you don't," and you never will. You might look to try *coverage analysis* tools that watch your code during testing and keep track of which lines of code have been executed and which haven't. These tools help give you a general feel for how comprehensive your testing is, but don't expect to see 100% coverage.[8]

Even if you do happen to hit every line of code, that's not the whole picture. What *is* important is the number of states that your program may have. States are not equivalent to lines of code. For instance, suppose you have a function that takes two integers, each of which can be a number from 0 to 999:

```
int test(int a, int b) {
  return a / (a + b);
}
```

---

7. https://netflix.github.io/chaosmonkey
8. For an interesting study of the correlation between test coverage and defects, see *Mythical Unit Test Coverage [ADSS18]*.

In theory, this three-line function has 1,000,000 logical states, 999,999 of which will work correctly and one that will not (when a+b equals zero). Simply knowing that you executed this line of code doesn't tell you that—you would need to identify all possible states of the program. Unfortunately, in general this is a *really hard* problem. Hard as in, "The sun will be a cold hard lump before you can solve it."

> **Tip 93**　Test State Coverage, Not Code Coverage

Property-Based Testing

A great way to explore how your code handles unexpected states is to have a computer generate those states.

Use *property-based* testing techniques to generate test data according to the contracts and invariants of the code under test. We cover this topic in detail in Topic 42, *Property-Based Testing*, on page 224.

Tightening the Net

Finally, we'd like to reveal the single most important concept in testing. It is an obvious one, and virtually every textbook says to do it this way. But for some reason, most projects still do not.

If a bug slips through the net of existing tests, you need to add a new test to trap it next time.

> **Tip 94**　Find Bugs Once

Once a human tester finds a bug, it should be the *last* time a human tester finds that bug. The automated tests should be modified to check for that particular bug from then on, every time, with no exceptions, no matter how trivial, and no matter how much the developer complains and says, "Oh, that will never happen again."

Because it will happen again. And we just don't have the time to go chasing after bugs that the automated tests could have found for us. We have to spend our time writing new code—and new bugs.

Full Automation

As we said at the beginning of this section, modern development relies on scripted, automatic procedures. Whether you use something as simple as shell scripts with rsync and ssh, or full-featured solutions such as Ansible, Puppet, Chef, or Salt, just don't rely on any manual intervention.

Once upon a time, we were at a client site where all the developers were using the same IDE. Their system administrator gave each developer a set of instructions on installing add-on packages to the IDE. These instructions filled many pages—pages full of click here, scroll there, drag this, double-click that, and do it again.

Not surprisingly, every developer's machine was loaded slightly differently. Subtle differences in the application's behavior occurred when different developers ran the same code. Bugs would appear on one machine but not on others. Tracking down version differences of any one component usually revealed a surprise.

Tip 95	Don't Use Manual Procedures

People just aren't as repeatable as computers are. Nor should we expect them to be. A shell script or program will execute the same instructions, in the same order, time after time. It is under version control itself, so you can examine changes to the build/release procedures over time as well ("but it *used* to work...").

Everything depends on automation. You can't build the project on an anonymous cloud server unless the build is fully automatic. You can't deploy automatically if there are manual steps involved. And once you introduce manual steps ("just for this one part...") you've broken a very large window.[9]

With these three legs of version control, ruthless testing, and full automation, your project will have the firm foundation you need so you can concentrate on the hard part: delighting users.

Related Sections Include

- Topic 11, *Reversibility*, on page 47
- Topic 12, *Tracer Bullets*, on page 50
- Topic 17, *Shell Games*, on page 78
- Topic 19, *Version Control*, on page 84
- Topic 41, *Test to Code*, on page 214
- Topic 49, *Pragmatic Teams*, on page 264
- Topic 50, *Coconuts Don't Cut It*, on page 270

---

9. Always remember *Software Entropy*. Always.

Challenges

- Are your nightly or continuous builds automatic, but deploying to production isn't? Why? What's special about that server?

- Can you automatically test your project completely? Many teams are forced to answer "no." Why? Is it too hard to define the acceptable results? Won't this make it hard to prove to the sponsors that the project is "done"?

- Is it too hard to test the application logic independent of the GUI? What does this say about the GUI? About coupling?

Delight Your Users

When you enchant people, your goal is not to make money
from them or to get them to do what you want, but
to fill them with great delight.

➤ *Guy Kawasaki*

Our goal as developers is to *delight users.* That's why we're here. Not to mine them for their data, or count their eyeballs or empty their wallets. Nefarious goals aside, even delivering working software in a timely manner isn't enough. That alone won't delight them.

Your users are not particularly motivated by code. Instead, they have a business problem that needs solving within the context of their objectives and budget. Their belief is that by working with your team they'll be able to do this.

Their expectations are not software related. They aren't even implicit in any specification they give you (because that specification will be incomplete until your team has iterated through it with them several times).

How do you unearth their expectations, then? Ask a simple question:

> How will you know that we've all been successful a month (or a year, or whatever) after this project is done?

You may well be surprised by the answer. A project to improve product recommendations might actually be judged in terms of customer retention; a project to consolidate two databases might be judged in terms of data quality, or it might be about cost savings. But it's these expectations of business value that really count—not just the software project itself. The software is only a means to these ends.

And now that you've surfaced some of the underlying expectations of value behind the project, you can start thinking about how you can deliver against them:

- Make sure everyone on the team is totally clear about these expectations.

- When making decisions, think about which path forward moves closer to those expectations.

- Critically analyze the user requirements in light of the expectations. On many projects we've discovered that the stated "requirement" was in fact just a guess at what could be done by technology: it was actually an amateur implementation plan dressed up as a requirements document. Don't be afraid to make suggestions that change the requirement if you can demonstrate that they will move the project closer to the objective.

- Continue to think about these expectations as you progress through the project.

We've found that as our knowledge of the domain increases, we're better able to make suggestions on other things that could be done to address the underlying business issues. We strongly believe that developers, who are exposed to many different aspects of an organization, can often see ways of weaving different parts of the business together that aren't always obvious to individual departments.

> **Tip 96** Delight Users, Don't Just Deliver Code

If you want to delight your client, forge a relationship with them where you can actively help solve their problems. Even though your title might be some variation of "Software Developer" or "Software Engineer," in truth it should be "Problem Solver." That's what we do, and that's the essence of a Pragmatic Programmer.

We solve problems.

Related Sections Include

- Topic 12, *Tracer Bullets*, on page 50
- Topic 13, *Prototypes and Post-it Notes*, on page 56
- Topic 45, *The Requirements Pit*, on page 244

53 ▶ Pride and Prejudice

You have delighted us long enough.

> ➤ *Jane Austen, Pride and Prejudice*

Pragmatic Programmers don't shirk from responsibility. Instead, we rejoice in accepting challenges and in making our expertise well known. If we are responsible for a design, or a piece of code, we do a job we can be proud of.

> **Tip 97** Sign Your Work

Artisans of an earlier age were proud to sign their work. You should be, too.

Project teams are still made up of people, however, and this rule can cause trouble. On some projects, the idea of *code ownership* can cause cooperation problems. People may become territorial, or unwilling to work on common foundation elements. The project may end up like a bunch of insular little fiefdoms. You become prejudiced in favor of your code and against your coworkers.

That's not what we want. You shouldn't jealously defend your code against interlopers; by the same token, you should treat other people's code with respect. The Golden Rule ("Do unto others as you would have them do unto you") and a foundation of mutual respect among the developers is critical to make this tip work.

Anonymity, especially on large projects, can provide a breeding ground for sloppiness, mistakes, sloth, and bad code. It becomes too easy to see yourself as just a cog in the wheel, producing lame excuses in endless status reports instead of good code.

While code must be owned, it doesn't have to be owned by an individual. In fact, Kent Beck's eXtreme Programming[10] recommends communal ownership of code (but this also requires additional practices, such as pair programming, to guard against the dangers of anonymity).

---

10. http://www.extremeprogramming.org

We want to see pride of ownership. "I wrote this, and I stand behind my work." Your signature should come to be recognized as an indicator of quality. People should see your name on a piece of code and expect it to be solid, well written, tested, and documented. A really professional job. Written by a professional.

A Pragmatic Programmer.

Thank you.

Dave Andy

Postface

In the twenty years leading up to the first edition, we were part of the evolution of the computer from a peripheral curiosity to a modern imperative for businesses. In the twenty years since then, software has grown beyond mere business machines and has truly taken over the world. But what does that really mean for us?

In *The Mythical Man-Month: Essays on Software Engineering [Bro96]*, Fred Brooks said "The programmer, like the poet, works only slightly removed from pure thought-stuff. He builds his castles in the air, from air, creating by exertion of the imagination." We start with a blank page, and we can create pretty much anything we can imagine. And the things we create can change the world.

From Twitter helping people plan revolutions, to the processor in your car working to stop you skidding, to the smartphone which means we no longer have to remember pesky daily details, our programs are everywhere. Our imagination is everywhere.

We developers are incredibly privileged. We are truly building the future. It's an extraordinary amount of power. And with that power comes an extraordinary responsibility.

How often do we stop to think about that? How often do we discuss, both among ourselves and with a more general audience, what this means?

Embedded devices use an order of magnitude more computers than those used in laptops, desktops, and data centers. These embedded computers often control life-critical systems, from power plants to cars to medical equipment. Even a simple central heating control system or home appliance can kill someone if it is poorly designed or implemented. When you develop for these devices, you take on a staggering responsibility.

Many nonembedded systems can also do both great good and great harm. Social media can promote peaceful revolution or foment ugly hate. Big data can make shopping easier, and it can destroy any vestige of privacy you might think you have. Banking systems make loan decisions that change people's lives. And just about any system can be used to snoop on its users.

We've seen hints of the possibilities of a utopian future, and examples of unintended consequences leading to nightmare dystopias. The difference between the two outcomes might be more subtle than you think. And it's all in your hands.

The Moral Compass

The price of this unexpected power is vigilance. Our actions directly affect people. No longer the hobby program on the 8-bit CPU in the garage, the isolated batch business process on the mainframe in the data center, or even just the desktop PC; our software weaves the very fabric of daily modern life.

We have a duty to ask ourselves two questions about every piece of code we deliver:

1. Have I protected the user?

2. Would I use this myself?

First, you should ask "Have I done my best to protect the users of this code from harm?" Have I made provisions to apply ongoing security patches to that simple baby monitor? Have I ensured that *however* the automatic central heating thermostat fails the customer will still have manual control? Am I storing only the data I need, and encrypting anything personal?

No one is perfect; everyone misses things now and then. But if you can't truthfully say that you tried to list all the consequences, and made sure to protect the users from them, then you bear some responsibility when things go bad.

> Tip 98   First, Do No Harm

Second, there's a judgment related to the Golden Rule: would I be happy to be a user of this software? Do I want my details shared? Do I want my movements to be given to retail outlets? Would I be happy to be driven by this autonomous vehicle? Am I comfortable doing this?

Some inventive ideas begin to skirt the bounds of ethical behavior, and if you're involved in that project, you are just as responsible as the sponsors.

No matter how many degrees of separation you might rationalize, one rule remains true:

Tip 99	Don't Enable Scumbags

Imagine the Future you Want

It's up to you. It's your imagination, your hopes, your concerns that provide the pure thought-stuff that builds the next twenty years and beyond.

You are building the future, for yourselves and for your descendants. Your duty is to make it a future that we'd all want to inhabit. Recognize when you're doing something against this ideal, and have the courage to say "no!" Envision the future we *could* have, and have the courage to create it. Build castles in the air every day.

We all have an amazing life.

Tip 100	It's Your Life. Share it. Celebrate it. Build it. AND HAVE FUN!

Bibliography

[ADSS18]   Vard Antinyan, Jesper Derehag, Anna Sandberg, and Miroslaw Staron. Mythical Unit Test Coverage. *IEEE Software.* 35:73-79, 2018.

[And10]   Jackie Andrade. What does doodling do? *Applied Cognitive Psychology.* 24(1):100-106, 2010, January.

[Arm07]   Joe Armstrong. *Programming Erlang: Software for a Concurrent World.* The Pragmatic Bookshelf, Raleigh, NC, 2007.

[BR89]   Albert J. Bernstein and Sydney Craft Rozen. *Dinosaur Brains: Dealing with All Those Impossible People at Work.* John Wiley & Sons, New York, NY, 1989.

[Bro96]   Frederick P. Brooks, Jr. *The Mythical Man-Month: Essays on Software Engineering.* Addison-Wesley, Reading, MA, Anniversary, 1996.

[CN91]   Brad J. Cox and Andrew J. Novobilski. *Object-Oriented Programming: An Evolutionary Approach.* Addison-Wesley, Reading, MA, Second, 1991.

[Con68]   Melvin E. Conway. How do Committees Invent? *Datamation.* 14(5):28-31, 1968, April.

[de 98]   Gavin de Becker. *The Gift of Fear: And Other Survival Signals That Protect Us from Violence.* Dell Publishing, New York City, 1998.

[DL13]   Tom DeMacro and Tim Lister. *Peopleware: Productive Projects and Teams.* Addison-Wesley, Boston, MA, Third, 2013.

[Fow00]   Martin Fowler. *UML Distilled: A Brief Guide to the Standard Object Modeling Language.* Addison-Wesley, Boston, MA, Second, 2000.

[Fow04]   Martin Fowler. *UML Distilled: A Brief Guide to the Standard Object Modeling Language.* Addison-Wesley, Boston, MA, Third, 2004.

[Fow19]   Martin Fowler. *Refactoring: Improving the Design of Existing Code.* Addison-Wesley, Boston, MA, Second, 2019.

[GHJV95]   Erich Gamma, Richard Helm, Ralph Johnson, and John Vlissides. *Design Patterns: Elements of Reusable Object-Oriented Software*. Addison-Wesley, Reading, MA, 1995.

[Hol92]   Michael Holt. *Math Puzzles & Games*. Dorset House, New York, NY, 1992.

[Hun08]   Andy Hunt. *Pragmatic Thinking and Learning: Refactor Your Wetware*. The Pragmatic Bookshelf, Raleigh, NC, 2008.

[Joi94]   T.E. Joiner. Contagious depression: Existence, specificity to depressed symptoms, and the role of reassurance seeking. *Journal of Personality and Social Psychology*. 67(2):287–296, 1994, August.

[Knu11]   Donald E. Knuth. *The Art of Computer Programming, Volume 4A: Combinatorial Algorithms, Part 1*. Addison-Wesley, Boston, MA, 2011.

[Knu98]   Donald E. Knuth. *The Art of Computer Programming, Volume 1: Fundamental Algorithms*. Addison-Wesley, Reading, MA, Third, 1998.

[Knu98a]   Donald E. Knuth. *The Art of Computer Programming, Volume 2: Seminumerical Algorithms*. Addison-Wesley, Reading, MA, Third, 1998.

[Knu98b]   Donald E. Knuth. *The Art of Computer Programming, Volume 3: Sorting and Searching*. Addison-Wesley, Reading, MA, Second, 1998.

[KP99]   Brian W. Kernighan and Rob Pike. *The Practice of Programming*. Addison-Wesley, Reading, MA, 1999.

[Mey97]   Bertrand Meyer. *Object-Oriented Software Construction*. Prentice Hall, Upper Saddle River, NJ, Second, 1997.

[Mul18]   Jerry Z. Muller. *The Tyranny of Metrics*. Princeton University Press, Princeton NJ, 2018.

[SF13]   Robert Sedgewick and Phillipe Flajolet. *An Introduction to the Analysis of Algorithms*. Addison-Wesley, Boston, MA, Second, 2013.

[Str35]   James Ridley Stroop. Studies of Interference in Serial Verbal Reactions. *Journal of Experimental Psychology*. 18:643–662, 1935.

[SW11]   Robert Sedgewick and Kevin Wayne. *Algorithms*. Addison-Wesley, Boston, MA, Fourth, 2011.

[Tal10]   Nassim Nicholas Taleb. *The Black Swan: Second Edition: The Impact of the Highly Improbable*. Random House, New York, NY, Second, 2010.

[WH82]   James Q. Wilson and George Helling. The police and neighborhood safety. *The Atlantic Monthly*. 249[3]:29–38, 1982, March.

[YC79]   Edward Yourdon and Larry L. Constantine. *Structured Design: Fundamentals of a Discipline of Computer Program and Systems Design.* Prentice Hall, Englewood Cliffs, NJ, 1979.

[You95]   Edward Yourdon. When good-enough software is best. *IEEE Software.* 1995, May.

I would rather have questions that can't be answered than answers that can't be questioned.

➤ *Richard Feynman*

Possible Answers to the Exercises

Answer 1 (from exercise 1 on page 46)

To our way of thinking, class Split2 is more orthogonal. It concentrates on its own task, splitting lines, and ignores details such as where the lines are coming from. Not only does this make the code easier to develop, but it also makes it more flexible. Split2 can split lines read from a file, generated by another routine, or passed in via the environment.

Answer 2 (from exercise 2 on page 46)

Let's start with an assertion: you can write good, orthogonal code in just about any language. At the same time, every language has temptations: features that can lead to increased coupling and decreased orthogonality.

In OO languages, features such as multiple inheritance, exceptions, operator overloading, and parent-method overriding (via subclassing) provide ample opportunity to increase coupling in nonobvious ways. There is also a kind of coupling because a class couples code to data. This is normally a good thing (when coupling is good, we call it cohesion). But if you don't make your classes focused enough, it can lead to some pretty ugly interfaces.

In functional languages, you're encouraged to write lots of small, decoupled functions, and to combine them in different ways to solve your problem. In theory this sounds good. In practice it often is. But there's a form of coupling that can happen here, too. These functions typically transform data, which means the result of one function can become the input to another. If you're not careful, making a change to the data format a function generates can result in a failure somewhere down the transformational stream. Languages with good type systems can help mitigate this.

Answer 3 (from exercise 3 on page 59)

Low-tech to the rescue! Draw a few cartoons with markers on a whiteboard—a car, a phone, and a house. It doesn't have to be great art; stick-figure outlines are fine. Put Post-it notes that describe the contents of target pages on the clickable areas. As the meeting progresses, you can refine the drawings and placements of the Post-it notes.

Answer 4 (from exercise 4 on page 64)

Because we want to make the language extendable, we'll make the parser table driven. Each entry in the table contains the command letter, a flag to say whether an argument is required, and the name of the routine to call to handle that particular command.

lang/turtle.c
```
typedef struct {
  char   cmd;              /* the command letter */
  int hasArg;              /* does it take an argument */
  void (*func)(int, int); /* routine to call */
} Command;

static Command cmds[] = {
  { 'P',  ARG,     doSelectPen },
  { 'U',  NO_ARG,  doPenUp },
  { 'D',  NO_ARG,  doPenDown },
  { 'N',  ARG,     doPenDir },
  { 'E',  ARG,     doPenDir },
  { 'S',  ARG,     doPenDir },
  { 'W',  ARG,     doPenDir }
};
```

The main program is pretty simple: read a line, look up the command, get the argument if required, then call the handler function.

lang/turtle.c
```
while (fgets(buff, sizeof(buff), stdin)) {

  Command *cmd = findCommand(*buff);

  if (cmd) {
    int   arg = 0;

    if (cmd->hasArg && !getArg(buff+1, &arg)) {
      fprintf(stderr, "'%c' needs an argument\n", *buff);
      continue;
    }

    cmd->func(*buff, arg);
  }
}
```

The function that looks up a command performs a linear search of the table, returning either the matching entry or NULL.

lang/turtle.c

```
Command *findCommand(int cmd) {
  int i;

  for (i = 0; i < ARRAY_SIZE(cmds); i++) {
    if (cmds[i].cmd == cmd)
      return cmds + i;
  }

  fprintf(stderr, "Unknown command '%c'\n", cmd);
  return 0;
}
```

Finally, reading the numeric argument is pretty simple using sscanf.

lang/turtle.c

```
int getArg(const char *buff, int *result) {
  return sscanf(buff, "%d", result) == 1;
}
```

Answer 5 (from exercise 5 on page 65)

Actually, you've already solved this problem in the previous exercise, where you wrote an interpreter for the external language, will contain the internal interpreter. In the case of our sample code, this is the doXxx functions.

Answer 6 (from exercise 6 on page 65)

Using BNF, a time specification could be

time	::=	*hour ampm*	*hour* : *minute ampm*	*hour* : *minute*
ampm	::=	am	pm
hour	::=	*digit*	*digit digit*
minute	::=	*digit digit*
digit	::=	0	1	2	3	4	5	6	7	8	9

A better definition of *hour* and *minute* would take into account that an hours can only be from 00 to 23, and a minute from 00 to 59:

hour	::=	*h-tens digit*	*digit*
minute	::=	*m-tens digit*
h-tens	::=	0	1
m-tens	::=	0	1	2	3	4	5
digit	::=	0	1	2	3	4	5	6	7	8	9

Answer 7 (from exercise 7 on page 65)

Here's the parser written using the Pegjs JavaScript library:

```
lang/peg_parser/time_parser.pegjs
time
   = h:hour offset:ampm                { return h + offset }
   / h:hour ":" m:minute offset:ampm   { return h + m + offset }
   / h:hour ":" m:minute               { return h + m }

ampm
   = "am" { return 0 }
   / "pm" { return 12*60 }

hour
   = h:two_hour_digits { return h*60 }
   / h:digit           { return h*60 }

minute
   = d1:[0-5] d2:[0-9] { return parseInt(d1+d2, 10); }

digit
   = digit:[0-9] { return parseInt(digit, 10); }

two_hour_digits
   = d1:[01] d2:[0-9 ] { return parseInt(d1+d2, 10); }
   / d1:[2]  d2:[0-3]  { return parseInt(d1+d2, 10); }
```

The tests show it in use:

```
lang/peg_parser/test_time_parser.js
let test = require('tape');
let time_parser = require('./time_parser.js');

// time    ::= hour ampm            |
//             hour : minute ampm   |
//             hour : minute
//
// ampm    ::= am | pm
//
// hour    ::= digit | digit digit
//
// minute  ::= digit digit
//
// digit   ::= 0 |1 | 2 | 3 | 4 | 5 | 6 | 7 | 8 | 9

const h  = (val) => val*60;
const m  = (val) => val;
const am = (val) => val;
const pm = (val) => val + h(12);

let tests = {
  "1am": h(1),
  "1pm": pm(h(1)),
```

```
  "2:30": h(2) + m(30),
  "14:30": pm(h(2)) + m(30),
  "2:30pm": pm(h(2)) + m(30),
}

test('time parsing', function (t) {
    for (const string in tests) {
      let result = time_parser.parse(string)
      t.equal(result, tests[string], string);
    }
    t.end()
});
```

Answer 8 (from exercise 8 on page 65)

Here's a possible solution in Ruby:

```
lang/re_parser/time_parser.rb
TIME_RE = %r{
(?<digit>[0-9]){0}
(?<h_ten>[0-1]){0}
(?<m_ten>[0-6]){0}
(?<ampm> am | pm){0}
(?<hour>   (\g<h_ten> \g<digit>) | \g<digit>){0}
(?<minute> \g<m_ten>  \g<digit>){0}

\A(
    ( \g<hour> \g<ampm> )
  | ( \g<hour> : \g<minute> \g<ampm> )
  | ( \g<hour> : \g<minute> )
)\Z

}x

def parse_time(string)
  result = TIME_RE.match(string)
  if result
    result[:hour].to_i * 60 +
    (result[:minute] || "0").to_i +
    (result[:ampm] == "pm" ? 12*60 : 0)
  end
end
```

(This code uses the trick of defining named patterns at the start of the regular expression, and then referencing them as subpatterns in the actual match.)

Answer 9 (from exercise 9 on page 71)

Our answer must be couched in several assumptions:

- The storage device contains the information we need to be transferred.
- We know the speed at which the person walks.
- We know the distance between the machines.

- We are not accounting for the time it takes to transfer information to and from the storage device.
- The overhead of storing data is roughly equal to the overhead of sending it over a communications line.

Answer 10 (from exercise 10 on page 71)

Subject to the caveats in the previous answer: A 1TGB tape contains 8×2^{40}, or 2^{43} bits, so a 1Gbps line would have to pump data for about 9,000 seconds, or roughly 2½ hours, to transfer the equivalent amount of information. If the person is walking at a constant 3½ mph, then our two machines would need to be almost 9 miles apart for the communications line to outperform our courier. Otherwise, the person wins.

Answer 14 (from exercise 14 on page 112)

We'll show the function signatures in Java, with the pre- and postconditions in comments.

First, the invariant for the class:

```
/**
 * @invariant getSpeed() > 0
 *         implies isFull()              // Don't run empty
 *
 * @invariant getSpeed() >= 0 &&
 *         getSpeed() < 10               // Range check
 */
```

Next, the pre- and postconditions:

```
/**
 * @pre Math.abs(getSpeed() - x) <= 1 // Only change by one
 * @pre x >= 0 && x < 10               // Range check
 * @post getSpeed() == x               // Honor requested speed
 */
public void setSpeed(final int x)

/**
 * @pre !isFull()                      // Don't fill it twice
 * @post isFull()                      // Ensure it was done
 */
void fill()

/**
 * @pre isFull()                       // Don't empty it twice
 * @post !isFull()                     // Ensure it was done
 */
void empty()
```

Answer 15 (from exercise 15 on page 112)

There are 21 terms in the series. If you said 20, you just experienced a fence-post error (not knowing whether to count the fenceposts or the spaces between them).

Answer 16 (from exercise 16 on page 118)

- September, 1752 had only 19 days. This was done to synchronize calendars as part of the Gregorian Reformation.

- The directory could have been removed by another process, you might not have permission to read it, the drive might not be mounted, ...; you get the picture.

- We sneakily didn't specify the types of a and b. Operator overloading might have defined +, =, or != to have unexpected behavior. Also, a and b may be aliases for the same variable, so the second assignment will overwrite the value stored in the first. Also, if the program is concurrent and badly written, a might have been updated by the time the addition takes place.

- In non-Euclidean geometry, the sum of the angles of a triangle will not add up to 180°. Think of a triangle mapped on the surface of a sphere.

- Leap minutes may have 61 or 62 seconds.

- Depending on the language, numeric overflow may leave the result of a+1 negative.

Answer 17 (from exercise 17 on page 125)

In most C and C++ implementations, there is no way of checking that a pointer actually points to valid memory. A common mistake is to deallocate a block of memory and reference that memory later in the program. By then, the memory pointed to may well have been reallocated to some other purpose. By setting the pointer to NULL, the programmers hope to prevent these rogue references—in most cases, dereferencing a NULL pointer will generate a runtime error.

Answer 18 (from exercise 18 on page 125)

By setting the reference to NULL, you reduce the number of pointers to the referenced object by one. Once this count reaches zero, the object is eligible for garbage collection. Setting the references to NULL can be significant for long-running programs, where the programmers need to ensure that memory utilization doesn't increase over time.

Answer 19 (from exercise 19 on page 146)

A simple implementation could be:

```
event/strings_ex_1.rb
class FSM
  def initialize(transitions, initial_state)
    @transitions = transitions
    @state       = initial_state
  end
  def accept(event)
    @state, action = TRANSITIONS[@state][event] || TRANSITIONS[@state][:default]
  end
end
```

(Download this file to get the updated code that uses this new FSM class.)

Answer 20 (from exercise 20 on page 147)

- ...three *network interface down* events within five minutes

  This *could* be implemented using a state machine, but it would be trickier than it might first appear: if you get events at minutes 1, 4, 7, and 8, then you should trigger the warning on the fourth event, which means the state machine needs to be able to handle reseting itself.

  For this reason, event streams would seem to be the technology of choice. There's a reactive function named buffer with size and offset parameters that would let you return each group of three incoming events. You could then look at the timestamps of the first and last event in a group to determine if the alarm should be triggered.

- ...after sunset, and there is motion detected at the bottom of the stairs followed by motion detected at the top of the stairs...

  This could probably be implemented using a combination of pubsub and state machines. You could use pubsub to disseminate events to any number of state machines, and then have the state machines determine what to do.

- ...notify various reporting systems that an order was completed.

  This is probably best handled using pubsub. You might want to use streams, but that would require that the systems being notified were also stream based.

- ...three backend services and wait for the responses.

  This is similar to our example that used streams to fetch user data.

Answer 21 (from exercise 21 on page 157)

1. Shipping and sales tax are added to an order:

```
basic order → finalized order
```

   In conventional code, it's likely you'd have a function that calculated shipping costs and another that calculated tax. But we're thinking about transformations here, so we transform an order with just items into a new kind of thing: an order that can be shipped.

2. Your application loads configuration information from a named file:

```
file name → configuration structure
```

3. Someone logs in to a web application:

```
user credentials → session
```

Answer 22 (from exercise 22 on page 158)

The high-level transformation:

```
field contents as string
    → [validate & convert]
        → {:ok, value} | {:error, reason}
```

could be broken down into:

```
field contents as string
    → [convert string to integer]
    → [check value >= 18]
    → [check value <= 150]
        → {:ok, value} | {:error, reason}
```

This assumes that you have an error-handling pipeline.

Answer 23 (from exercise 23 on page 158)

Let's answer the second part first: we prefer the first piece of code.

In the second chunk of code, each step returns an object that implements the next function we call: the object returned by content_of must implement find_matching_lines, and so on.

This means that the object returned by content_of is coupled to our code. Imagine the requirement changed, and we have to ignore lines starting with a # character. In the transformation style, that would be easy:

```
const content      = File.read(file_name);
const no_comments = remove_comments(content)
const lines        = find_matching_lines(no_comments, pattern)
const result       = truncate_lines(lines)
```

We could event swap the order of remove_comments and find_matching_lines and it would still work.

But in the chained style, this would be more difficult. Where should our remove_comments method live: in the object returned by content_of or the object returned by find_matching_lines? And what other code will we break if we change that object? This coupling is why the method chaining style is sometimes called a *train wreck*.

Answer 24 (from exercise 24 on page 190)

Image processing.

> For simple scheduling of a workload among the parallel processes, a shared work queue may be more than adequate. You might want to consider a blackboard system if there is feedback involved—that is, if the results of one processed chunk affect other chunks, as in machine vision applications, or complex 3D image-warp transforms.

Group calendaring

> This might be a good fit. You can post scheduled meetings and availability to the blackboard. You have entities functioning autonomously, feedback from decisions is important, and participants may come and go.

> You might want to consider partitioning this kind of blackboard system depending on who is searching: junior staff may care about only the immediate office, human resources may want only English-speaking offices worldwide, and the CEO may want the whole enchilada.

> There is also some flexibility on data formats: we are free to ignore formats or languages we don't understand. We have to understand different formats only for those offices that have meetings with each other, and we do not need to expose all participants to a full transitive closure of all possible formats. This reduces coupling to where it is necessary, and does not constrain us artificially.

Network monitoring tool

> This is very similar to the mortgage/loan application program on page 188. You've got trouble reports sent in by users and statistics reported automatically, all posting to the blackboard. A human or software agent can analyze the blackboard to diagnose network failures: two errors on a line might just be cosmic rays, but 20,000 errors and you've got a hardware problem. Just as the detectives solve the murder mystery, you can have multiple entities analyzing and contributing ideas to solve the network problems.

Answer 25 (from exercise 25 on page 202)

The assumption with a list of key-value pairs is generally that the key is unique, and hash libraries typically enforce that either by the behavior of the hash itself or with explicit error messages for duplicated keys. However, an array typically does not have those constraints, and will happily store duplicate keys unless you code it specifically not to. So in this case, the first key found that matches DepositAccount wins, and any remaining matching entries are ignored. The order of entries is not guaranteed, so sometimes it works and sometimes it doesn't.

And what about the difference in machines from development and production? It's just a coincidence.

Answer 26 (from exercise 26 on page 202)

The fact that a purely numeric field works in the US, Canada, and the Caribbean is a coincidence. Per the ITU spec, international call format starts with a literal + sign. The * character is also used in some locales, and more commonly, leading zeros can be a part of the number. Never store a phone number in a numeric field.

Answer 27 (from exercise 27 on page 202)

Depends on where you are. In the US, volume measures are based on the gallon, which is the volume of a cylinder 6 inches high and 7 inches in diameter, rounded to the nearest cubic inch.

In Canada, "one cup" in a recipe could mean any of

- 1/5 of an imperial quart, or 227ml
- 1/4 of a US quart, or 236ml
- 16 metric tablespoons, or 240ml
- 1/4 of a liter, or 250ml

Unless you're talking about a rice cooker, in which case "one cup" is 180ml. That derives from the *koku*, which was the estimated volume of dry rice required to feed one person for one year: apparently, around 180L. Rice cooker cups are 1 *gō*, which is 1/1000 of a koku. So, roughly the amount of rice a person would eat at a single meal.[1]

Answer 28 (from exercise 28 on page 209)

Clearly, we can't give any absolute answers to this exercise. However, we can give you a couple of pointers.

---

1.   Thanks for this bit of trivia goes to Avi Bryant (@avibryant)

If you find that your results don't follow a smooth curve, you might want to check to see if some other activity is using some of your processor's power. You probably won't get good figures if background processes periodically take cycles away from your programs. You might also want to check memory: if the application starts using swap space, performance will nose dive.

Here's a graph of the results of running the code on one of our machines:

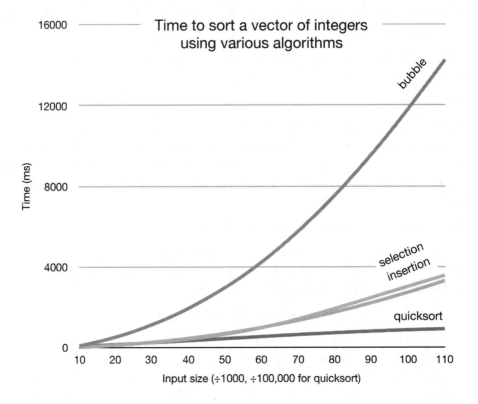

Answer 29 (from exercise 29 on page 209)

There are a couple of ways of getting there. One is to turn the problem on its head. If the array has just one element, we don't iterate around the loop. Each additional iteration doubles the size of the array we can search. The general formula for the array size is therefore $n = 2^m$, where m is the number of iterations. If you take logs to the base 2 of each side, you get $\lg n = \lg 2^m$, which by the definition of logs becomes $\lg n = m$.

Answer 30 (from exercise 30 on page 209)

This is probably too much of a flashback to secondary school math, but the formula for converting a logarithm in base a to one in base b is:

$$\log_b x = \frac{\log_a x}{\log_a b}$$

Because $\log_a b$ is a constant, then we can ignore it inside a Big-O result.

Answer 31 (from exercise 31 on page 230)

One property we can test is that an order succeeds if the warehouse has enough items on hand. We can generate orders for random quantities of items, and verify that an "OK" tuple is returned if the warehouse had stock.

Answer 32 (from exercise 32 on page 230)

This is a good use of property-based testing. The unit tests can focus on individual cases where you've worked out the result by some other means, and the property tests can focus on things like:

- Do any two crates overlap?
- Does any part of any crate exceed the width or length of the truck?
- Is the packing density (area used by crates divided by the area of the truck bed) less than or equal to 1?
- If it's part of the requirement, does the packing density exceed the minimum acceptable density?

Answer 33 (from exercise 33 on page 252)

1. This statement sounds like a real requirement: there may be constraints placed on the application by its environment.

2. On its own, this statement isn't really a requirement. But to find out what's *really* required, you have to ask the magic question, "Why?"

   It may be that this is a corporate standard, in which case the actual requirement should be something like "all UI elements must conform to the MegaCorp User Interface Standards, V12.76."

   It may be that this is a color that the design team happen to like. In that case, you should think about the way the design team also likes to change their minds, and phrase the requirement as "the background color of all modal windows must be configurable. As shipped, the color will be gray." Even better would be the broader statement "All visual elements of the application (colors, fonts, and languages) must be configurable."

Or it may simply mean that the user needs to be able to distinguish modal and nonmodal windows. If that's the case, some more discussions are needed.

3. This statement is not a requirement, it's architecture. When faced with something like this, you have to dig deep to find out what the user is thinking. Is this a scaling issue? Or performance? Cost? Security? The answers will inform your design.

4. The underlying requirement is probably something closer to "The system will prevent the user from making invalid entries in fields, and will warn the user when these entries are made."

5. This statement is probably a hard requirement, based on some hardware limitation.

And here's a solution to the four-dots problem:

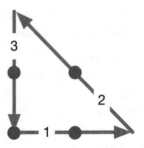

Connect the four dots with three lines, returning to the starting point, without lifting the pen.

Index

SYMBOLS

%>% operator, 151
-> operator, 151
->> operator, 151
|> (pipe operator), 151

A

absolute constraints, 253
abstraction layers
    bottom-up code, 218
    orthogonal design, 41
    reversibility and, 49
accessor functions, 36
accidents
    of context, 200
    implementation, 198
accuracy
    bug reports, 90
    estimates, 66–67, 71
actions, finite state machines, 139–141
activity diagrams, 171–174
actor model, 170, 181–186, 190
ad hoc testing, 221
adaptability, programmers, xx, *see also* changeability
administrative accounts, 233
agency, 1–2
agents, design by contract, 111
agility, 243, 259–262, 266
Algorithms, 208
algorithms
    assertions for, 115
    challenges, 208
    dividing, 207
    speed, 191, 203–209
aliases for shell functions, 80

and_then function, 157
anonymity, 282
Ansible, 61–62
antipatterns
    exceptions, 123
    passwords, 236
ANTLR, 63
APIs
    delegation, 163
    DRY principle, 37
    hiding for reversibility, 49
    repositories, 37, 190
    wrapping configuration in, 167
    wrapping global data in, 136
applications
    parameterizing with configuration, 166–168
    responsive, 137–147
architecture
    concurrency in, 170, 185, 190
    flexible, 48
    prototyping, 57–58
    vs. requirements, 250
    reversibility, 48–49
    tracer bullets, 52–55
archives, version control advantages, 85
Armstrong, Joe, 114
arrays, algorithm runtimes, 204, 206
Art of Computer Programming series, 208
The Art of Enbugging, 137
artificial intelligence, blackboard systems and, 187
assertions
    debugging with, 104, 115–118

with design by contract, 201
    vs. design by contract, 108
    vs. error handling, 115
    optional, 117
    side effects, 116
assets, expiring, 14
assumptions
    in debugging, 96, 201
    documenting, 199, 201
    implicit, 200
    programming by coincidence, 198, 200–201
    programming deliberately, 201
    testing and programming by coincidence, 200–201
    testing with assertions, 104, 115–118, 201
    testing, property-based, 224–230
attack surface area, minimizing, 232–234
audience, *see also* users
    involving in communications, 22
    listening to, 22
    understanding in communications, 20, 24
audits, version control advantages, 85
authentication, 237
automation
    challenges, 280
    communication, 19
    project management with, 263, 274, 278
    property-based testing, 224–230
    refactoring, 213

repository hosting tools, 87
shell advantages, 78
shell challenge, 80
teams and, 269
testing, 275, 278, 280
autorepeat, 83
awk, 98

B

backups, version control, 84, 86, 88
balancing resources, 104, 118–125
Beck, Kent, 282
benefit question, 18
bias, 127
Big-O notation, 93, 203–208
binary chop, 92–93, 204, 206, 209
binary formats
    challenge, 78
    disadvantages, 74, 76
    Unix, 77
binary search, *see* binary chop
bind functions, 157
bison, 63
The Black Swan, 127
blackboards, 170, 187–190
blame, 4, 89
BNF grammar, 65
Bobby Tables, 232, 236
body language, 20
Boiled Frogs
    feature bloat, 251
    programming deliberately and, 201
    reacting to change, 1, 10
    teams and, 265
Booleans, assertions, 115
bottom-up design, 217–218
boundary conditions, 91, 198
bounds, Big-O notation, 204, 207
branches, 85, 87
branding, 240, 267, 269
Brasseur, VM (Vicky), xviii
breaks
    listening to lizard brain, 194
    puzzle solving, 254

broken windows
    avoiding, 1, 6–8, 265
    challenges, 8
    failing tests and, 222
    manual procedures and, 279
    naming things, 242
    refactoring and, 212–213
    teams, 265
Brooks, Frederick, 269, 285
bubble sorts, 206
build machines, 274
builds
    breaking for rewriting, 213
    repository hosting tools, 87
    running all available tests in, 275
    version control and, 274
burnup charts, 265
butterfly effect, 47

C

C
    assertions, 115, 117
    naming conventions and culture, 240
    NULL pointer, 125
    resource allocation, 124–125
C++
    assertions, 115, 117
    inheritance, 159, 161
    NULL pointer, 125
calendaring blackboard exercise, 190
camelCase
    naming conventions and culture, 241
    text manipulation exercise, 100
career advancement
    agency of programmers, 1–2
    knowledge portfolio, 1, 13–19, 266
    taking responsibility for, 3
cargo cults, 263, 270–273
case
    naming conventions and culture, 241
    text manipulation exercise, 100
certification programs, 271

challenges
    about, xvi
    actors, 186
    agility and, 262
    automation, 280
    balancing resources, 125
    blackboards, 190
    Boiled Frogs, 11
    broken windows, 8
    change strategies, 10
    communication, 24
    concurrency, 174
    deployment, 280
    design, 29
    design by contract, 111
    domain languages, 64
    editors, 81, 83
    entropy, 8
    estimating algorithms, 208
    estimating time, 71
    ETC principle, 29
    good-enough software, 13
    inheritance, 46, 166
    knowledge portfolio, 19
    listening to lizard brain, 197
    naming, 242
    orthogonality, 46
    parallelism, 174
    plain text, 78
    property-based testing, 230
    puzzle solving, 256
    requirements, 252
    responsibility, 5
    reversibility, 50
    shell, 80
    Stone Soup strategy, 10
    teams, 269
    testing, 230, 280
    version control, 88
change, *see also* changeability
    agility and, 260
    be a catalyst for, 9
    Boiled Frogs, 1, 10, 201, 265
    challenges, 10
    inevitability of, 47–48, 129
    resistance to, 1–2
    situational awareness, 11
    Stone Soup strategy, 1, 9–11
    strategies for, 1, 9–11
changeability, *see also* change
    configuring for, 129, 166–168
    decoupling and, 129–136

DRY principle, 30–38
ETC principle, 27–30
exercises, 146
finite state machines, 138–141, 146
good vs. bad design, 28
inheritance and, 129, 158–166
observer pattern, 138, 142
orthogonality and, 40
publish/subscribe strategy, 138, 143
reacting to events, 129, 137–147
reactive programming, 138, 143–147
reversibility, 27, 47–50
streams, 138, 143–147
tracer bullets, 53
transformations, 129, 147–158
channels, publish/subscribe strategy, 143
Chaos Monkey, 277
checklist, debugging, 97
checksums, 206
chips
  security, 234
  testing, 219
circuits, integrated, 219
class invariants, design by contract, 105, 107, 109
classes
  delegation, 161–162, 166
  design by contract, 105, 107, 109
  encapsulating resources in, 122
  inheritance, 129, 136, 158–166
  interfaces and protocols, 161, 166
  mixins, 161, 164–166
  prefix classes, 158
classes for knowledge portfolios, 16
Clojure
  -> operator, 151
  ->> operator, 151
  assertions, 117
  design by contract support, 106
  naming conventions and culture, 240
cloud services
  automation and, 279

publish/subscribe in, 143
version control and, 84, 274
cluster names, in configuration data, 166
code
  analyzing other people's code, 196
  for this book, xvii, 185
  code duplication examples, 32–34
  complexity and security, 232
  decoupling configuration from, 167
  good-enough software, 1, 11–13, 269
  hot-code loading, 186
  ownership, 282
  shy, 43, 136
  wrapper code for actor model example, 185
code ownership, 282
code profilers, 208
code reviews, 38
cognitive biases, 127
cohesion, 40, 126
coincidence, programming by, 108, 191, 197–202, 223
collaboration
  agility and, 260
  trust and taking responsibility, 3
collaboration, component, prototyping, 58
color themes, 79
combinatoric algorithms, 204, 206
command completion, shell, 80
command line, see also shells
  repository hosting tools, 87
  utilities, 46
comments
  design by contract in, 108
  documentation from, 23
  DRY principle, 23, 34
  prototypes, 57
communication
  audience, involving, 22
  audience, listening to, 22
  audience, understanding, 20, 24

challenges, 24
  consistency in jargon, 241
  Conway's Law, 257
  documentation as, 23
  DRY principle, 19, 38, 267
  feedback from, 126
  online, 25
  planning content, 20
  repository hosting tools, 87
  resources on, 24
  strategies, 2, 19–24
  team, 38, 257, 267
  tracer bullets, 53
community participation, knowledge portfolios, 16, 19
compilers
  design by contract, 108
  parallelism, 173
  type checking, 154
  warnings as debugging starting points, 90
completeness in prototyping, 57
completion, command/file, 80
components in model-building, 67
concurrency
  activity diagrams, 171–174
  actor model, 170, 181–186, 190
  blackboards, 170, 187–190
  challenges, 174
  defined, 169
  identifying, 171–174
  laissez faire, 187
  language support for exclusive access, 180
  mutual exclusion strategies, 176–181
  non-transactional, 179
  opportunities for, 173
  processes, 170, 181, 186
  random failures as concurrency failures, 180
  shared state, 170, 174–181
  temporal coupling, 169–174
  transactional resources, 177–180

ubiquity of, 169
version control advantages, 85
configuring
cautions, 168
for changeability, 129, 166–168
configuration-as-a-service, 167
shell, 79
static configuration, 166
consistency in names, 241
constant algorithms, 204, 206
constraints
absolute, 253
prototyping, 58
puzzle solving, 253
construction metaphor, 209
context
accidents of, 200
cargo cults, 270
critical thinking, 18
estimating time and, 66
specific command completion, 80
thinking about, 1
continuous delivery, 275
continuous improvement, xxii, 266
Conway's Law, 257
Conway, Melvin, 257
correctness in prototyping, 57
costs
algorithms, 208
prototypes, 56, 59
refactoring, 201
tracer bullets, 54
coupling, *see also* decoupling
about, 129–130
error handling, 113
examples, 131–136
exposing data structure, 36
global data, 131, 135
hiding data, 153
inheritance, 131, 136, 160–166
in pipelines, 135
in prototyping, 58
resource allocation, 119
strategies for, 130–136
symptoms of, 131
temporal, 169–174
train wrecks, 131–135
coverage analysis tools, 277
Cox, Brad, 219

craft
caring about, xxi
programming as, xix, xxi–xxii
creativity, trust and taking responsibility, 3
credentials, in configuration data, 166
creep, requirements, 251, 265
critical thinking
instincts, 193–196
knowledge portfolio, 17
listening to lizard brain, 191–197
need for, xxi
questions for, 18
cryptography, 237
CSV, 63
cubic algorithms, 204, 206
Cucumber, 60, 62
cults, cargo, 263, 270–273
Cuthbert, Nick, xviii

D

data
access to, 58
blackboards, 187–190
debugging strategies, 92, 96
design by contract, 105
DRY principle, 35, 37
encrypting, 232, 235
events as data in streams, 144
exposing data structure, 36
finite state machines as, 139–141
hiding and coupling, 153
ownership in Rust, 180
plain-text advantages, 74–75
programming as transformation of, 147, 149
prototyping, 57–58
resource allocation and dynamic data structures, 124
security, 232–233, 235
tainted, 232
test data, 225, 276
truncating/obfuscating, 233
day books, *see* engineering daybooks
daybook, 100

de Becker, Gavin, 192
deadlocks, 121
debugging
about, 74
with assertions, 115–118, 201
with binary chop, 92–93
checklist, 97
feedback, 117
finding bugs only once, 278
Heisenbugs, 116
learning from, 96
mindset, 89
orthogonality and, 44
as problem solving, 89
process of elimination, 95
programming by coincidence, 198
with property-based testing, 229
psychology of, 89
reading error message, 92, 113
refactoring, 213
reproducing bugs, 91
rubber ducking, 94
security and, 234
starting points, 90
strategies for, 91–97
surprise in, 96
tracer bullets advantages, 53
tracing statements, 94
unit testing and, 221
version control advantages, 85
Decorator Pattern, 43
decoupling, *see also* coupling
about, 129
asynchronous events with pubsub, 143
asynchronous events with streams, 146
configuration from code, 167
ETC principle, 28
examples, 131–136
global data, 131, 135
incremental approach, 126
inheritance, 131, 136, 160–166
orthogonality, 39–46
strategies for, 130–136
Tell, Don't Ask principle, 132

test code, 135, 223
train wrecks, 131–135
defaults, security, 232, 234
defensive coding
    assertions, 104, 115–118
    balancing resources,
        104, 118–125
    design by contract, 103–
        112
    don't outrun your head-
        lights, 104, 125–127,
        213
    failing fast, 104, 112–114
    impossibility of perfect
        software, 103
delegation
    as alternative to inheri-
        tance, 161–162, 166
    vs. inheritance, 46
delighting users, 263, 280–
    281
delivery
    continuous, 275
    good-enough software, 13
    as real goal, 272
Demeter Project, 133
Demeter, Law of, 43, 133
demos, 54, 126
denial
    assumptions, 115
    debugging, 89, 112
denial of service, 233
deployment
    automation and, 269,
        279
    blackboards and, 190
    challenges, 280
    design by contract and,
        108
    flexibility in, 48
    security, 235
    test windows, 221
    version control and, 84,
        87, 274
design, see also design by
    contract; DRY principle;
    prototypes
    agility and, 262
    bottom-up, 217–218
    challenges, 29, 111
    changeability of good de-
        sign, 28
    for concurrency, 173
    domain languages and,
        27, 59–65
    end-to-end, 218

ETC principle, 27–30,
    242
exercises, 112
incremental approach,
    126
listening to lizard brain,
    196
orthogonality, 27, 39–46,
    211
for parallelism, 173
property-based testing
    and, 229
refactoring as redesign,
    212
reversibility, 27, 47–50
time as element of, 170
top-down, 218
tracer bullets, 27, 50–55,
    249, 268
design by contract
    vs. assertions, 108
    with assertions, 201
    avoiding programming by
        coincidence, 199, 201
    challenges, 111
    dynamic contracts, 111
    exercises, 112
    resource balancing and,
        125
    semantic invariants, 125
    vs. test-driven develop-
        ment, 108
    testing, 220–230
    using, 103–112
Design Patterns, 44
diagnostic tools, enabling,
    222
Dinosaur Brains, 24
diversification in knowledge
    portfolios, 15
do no harm, 7, 286
documentation
    agility and, 260
    of assumptions, 199, 201
    building in, 23
    as communication, 23
    DRY principle, 34
    orthogonality in, 45
    presentation of, 22–23
    project glossaries, 241,
        251
    prototypes and, 57
    requirements, 249
    semantic invariants, 111
    user stories, 250
    version control of, 85
dodo, 167

domain languages
    challenges, 64
    external, 62
    internal, 62
    using, 27, 59–65
don't outrun your headlights,
    104, 125–127, 213
Don't Panic, 89, 255
doodling, 100, 194
DRY principle
    about, 27
    beyond code, 31
    comments, 23, 34
    communication, 19, 38,
        267
    compared to orthogonali-
        ty, 45
    in documentation, 34
    incremental approach,
        126
    knowledge, 37
    maintenance, 30–38, 267
    refactoring for, 211
    teams, 267
    understanding, 30–38
Dumpty, Humpty, 187
duplication, see also DRY
    principle
    code examples, 32–34
    code vs. knowledge dupli-
        cation, 34
    in documentation, 34
    knowledge, 31, 34–35, 37
    between programmers,
        37
    in prototyping, 58
    refactoring for, 211
    representational, 36
    as sign of structural
        problems, 44
    in tests, 217
    types of, 31–38
dynamic contracts, 111
dynamic data structures and
    resource allocation, 124

E

eXtreme Programming (XP),
    216, 257, 273, 282
Easier to Change principle,
    see ETC principle
editors
    challenges, 81, 83
    ETC message popup, 30
    extensions, 82
    using, 74, 81–83
Eiffel, 105, 107, 109

EJB (Enterprise Java Beans), 43

Elixir
  actor model, 186
  as domain language, 62
  failing fast, 114
  guard clauses, 106
  macros, 156
  parallelism, 173
  pattern matching, 155
  pipe operator (|>), 151
  transformations example, 150–157
  wrapping values in transformations, 154–157

Elm
  debugger, 94
  pipe operator (|>), 151

email, 25

-enableassertions flag, 115

encrypting, data, 232, 235

end-to-end design, 218

engineering daybooks
  ETC principle, 29
  hard problems, 29, 255
  using, 74, 100

English, as another programming language, 19

Eno, Brian, 248

Enterprise Java Beans (EJB), 43

entropy
  avoiding, 1, 6–8, 265
  challenges, 8
  failing tests and, 222
  manual procedures, 279
  naming things, 242
  refactoring and, 212–213
  teams, 265

environments
  assertions in production environment, 117
  changing in knowledge portfolios, 16
  exploring shells, 80
  test environments, 275

Erlang
  processes, 186
  supervision, 114, 186

errors
  assertions vs. error handling, 115
  coupling in error handling, 113

failing fast, 104, 109, 112–114
reading error message, 92, 113
taking responsibility for, 3–5
transformations and error handling, 154–157
undocumented errors and accidents of implementation, 198

estimating
  algorithm speed, 191, 203–209
  fortune telling, 126
  model building, 66–68
  schedules, 69
  time, 28, 65–71, 204

ETC principle, 19, 27–30, 242

ethics, 285–287

Eton College, xxii

events
  asynchronous, 143, 146
  defined, 137
  exercises, 146
  finite state machines, 138–141, 146
  observer pattern, 138, 142
  publish/subscribe strategy, 138, 143
  reacting to, 129, 137–147
  reactive programming, 138, 143–147
  streams, 138, 143–147

exceptions
  antipatterns, 123
  design by contract, 109
  raising all, 113
  reading error message, 92, 113
  resource deallocation, 122–123
  resource transactions, 177, 179
  security of reporting, 234
  semaphores, 177

exercises
  about, xvi
  answers to, xvi, 293–306
  assertions, 118
  balancing resources, 125
  blackboards, 190
  changeability, 146
  design by contract, 112
  domain languages, 64

estimating algorithms, 209
estimating time, 71
events, 146
finite state machines, 146
orthogonality, 46
programming by coincidence, 202
property-based testing, 230
prototypes, 59
requirements, 252
tests, 230
text manipulation, 99
transformations, 157

expectations vs. requirements, 281

expiring assets, 14

exponential algorithms, 204, 206

extensions, editor, 82

external domain languages, 62

F

F#, pipe operator (|>), 151

facial expressions, 20

fads, avoiding, 49, 266, 271

failing fast, 104, 109, 112–114

fatigue, start-up, 9

fear
  of blank page, 193
  of making mistakes, 194
  symptom of coupling, 131

feature bloat, 13, 251

feature switches, 222, 273

feedback
  agile processes, 260–262
  assertions as, 117
  communication, 20, 22, 126
  debugging, 117
  good-enough software, 12
  incremental approach, 126
  instinct and, 194
  in modeling estimates, 68
  from requirements, 246, 249–250, 261
  sources of, 126
  testing as, 126, 192, 214–223

tracer bullets, 50–51, 54, 268
trying new development ideas, 271

files
file comparison tools, 76
file completion in shell, 80
finally clause, 122
finish what you start, 118
finite state machines (FSM), 138–141, 146
"Five Whys", 18
flaming, 25
formatting details, in configuration data, 166
FORTRAN, 240
fortune telling, 126
forums, 38
four-dots problem, 253, 306
Fowler, Martin, 2, 210, 213
FSM (finite state machines), 138–141, 146
function pipelines
about, 129, 151
vs. chains, 135
coupling from, 135
deferring, 156
pipe operator (|>), 151
transformations with, 150–157
using if assignments in languages without, 153
functional languages
concurrency and, 180
design by contract, 107
orthogonality exercise, 46
functions
accessor, 36
aliasing shell functions, 80
bind functions, 157
design by contract, 105, 107
orthogonality, 44
pipelines, 129, 135, 150–157
future of programming, 126, 285–287

G

gardening metaphor, 210
gates, 268
Gelernter, David, 188
The Gift of Fear, 192

global data, 44, 131, 134–135
glossary, project, 241, 251
goals
delighting users, 280
delivery as real goal, 272
knowledge portfolios, 15
learning, 16, 19
Golden Rule, 286
good-enough software, 1, 11–13, 269
guard clauses, 106
GUI interfaces
disadvantages, 78
GUI wars, 127
orthogonality challenge, 46
testing challenge, 280

H

handoffs, 268
harm
do no, 7, 286
Stone Soup strategy, 10
Haskell, pipe operators, 151
headlights, avoiding outrunning, 104, 125–127, 213
heapsort, 204
Heisenbugs, 116
heuristics, 206
hex, 156
hints, password, 236
Holland, Ian, 133
hopelessness, 6
Hopper, Grace, 9, 88
hosting, repositories, 87
hot-code loading, 186
HTML, as plain text, 75
Hypothesis tool, 225

I

i for loop variable, 240
IDEs
automatic refactoring, 213
limits of, 73, 78
if assignments, using as pipelines, 153
if statements, assertions, 117
image processing blackboard exercise, 190
implementation
accidents of, 198
modular, 199

implicit assumptions, 200
imposter syndrome, 194
incremental approach
don't outrun your headlights, 104, 125–127, 213
end-to-end functionality, 218
modular implementation, 199
need for, 126
refactoring, 210, 213
teams, 268
tracer bullets as, 53
individuality, xxii, 260
inertia, *see* Boiled Frogs
infinite loops, 105
inheritance
alternatives to, 161–165
avoiding, 129, 158–166
building types with, 160
challenges, 46, 166
decoupling, 131, 136, 160–166
vs. delegation, 46
history of, 158
multiple, 161
inner loops, 207
inquisitiveness, xx
instincts, 193–196
integrated circuits, 219
integration testing, 219, 275–276
interfaces
as alternative to inheritance, 161, 166
multiple, 46
prototyping, 58
internal domain languages, 62
invariants
class invariants and design by contract, 105, 107, 109
testing with, 224–230
investments, knowledge portfolios as, 14
IP addresses, in configuration data, 166
Isobelle/ML, 151
isolation
branches in version control, 86
orthogonality, 40–41, 43
isolation, programmer, 16

issue management, repository hosting tools, 87
iterations, estimating project schedules, 70

J

Jack of all trades, xxi
jargon
    in this book, xvii
    consistency in, 241
    knowledge portfolios, 16
Java
    assertions, 115, 117
    inheritance, 159
    pipe operator (|>), 151
    resource allocation, 125
JavaScript
    actor model example, 182
    inheritance, 159
JavaSpaces, 188
Jeffries, Ron, xviii, 217
JSON
    as external language, 63
    as plain text, 75
    static configuration with, 166
    text manipulation exercise, 99

K

Kafka, 189
kaizen, xxii
Kanban, 273
Kay, Alan, 159
Kernighan, Brian, 98
key sequences, 81, 222
    editor, 83
key/value data structures, 37
keys
    in configuration data, 166
    security of, 235
knowledge
    as base material, 74
    DRY principle, 31, 34–35, 37
    as expiring assets, 14
    keeping in plain text, 74–75
    portfolio, 1, 13–19, 266
    project librarians, 38
    refactoring for, 211
    teams, 266
Knuth, Donald, 208

L

laissez faire concurrency, 187
Lakos, John, 10
Langr, Jeff, xviii
languages
    challenges, 19, 64
    domain languages, 27, 59–65
    English as another programming language, 19
    ETC principle, 30
    exercises, 46, 64
    functional languages, 46, 107, 180
    goals for learning, 16, 19
    mini-languages, 64
    naming conventions and culture, 240
    object-oriented languages, 46, 122, 158
    orthogonality exercise, 46
    pattern languages, 241
    procedural languages, 124
    scripting languages, 57, 65
    support for exclusive access, 180
    text manipulation languages, 74, 97–100
Law of Demeter, 43, 133
Lawn maintenance, xxii
Lean, 273
learning
    from debugging, 96
    goals, 15
    knowledge portfolio, 1, 13–19, 266
    opportunities for, 17
    programmer agency and, 3
    prototyping as, 57
    taking responsibility for, 3
    teams, 266
    text manipulation languages, 98
librarians, project, 38
libraries
    coupling symptoms, 131
    design by contract, 109
    DRY principle, 36
    orthogonality, 43
license keys, in configuration data, 166
Linda, 188

linear algorithms, 204, 209
listening, 22
lizard brain, 191–197
loading, hot-code, 186
locking, semaphores, 176–178
logarithmic algorithms, 204, 206
logs
    actor trace ids, 190
    debugging, 94
    logging function, 144
    logging levels in configuration data, 166
    resource allocation, 122
    as test windows, 222
loops
    estimating speed with Big-O notation, 203, 206–207
    i for loop variable, 240
    infinite, 105
    inner, 207
    nested, 206

M

macros
    C/C++, 115
    Elixir, 156
    shell advantages, 78
mailboxes, actor model, 181
maintenance
    design by contract and, 108
    DRY principle, 30–38, 267
    fortune telling, 126
    global data, 44
    as ongoing, 30
    orthogonality, 44–45
    team involvement, 266
Manifesto for Agile Software Development, 243, 259–261
manual procedures, avoiding, 279
Markdown, 45
matrice multiplication, 204
meetings
    communication in, 20–21
    standup, 38, 270
    as symptom of coupling, 131
    team presence, 267
meetups, 16

memory
    allocation in dynamic da-
        ta structures, 124–125
    estimating consumption
        by running program,
        207
    estimating consumption
        with Big-O notation,
        204
    memory leaks, 125
    shared state and, 175
memory leaks, 125
merging branches, 85, 87
messages
    actor model, 181–186
    logs, 222
messaging systems, using like
    blackboards, 189
metadata, policy as, 248
methods
    chaining vs. transforma-
        tions, 158
    delegation, 162
    design by contract, 105
    train wrecks from chain-
        ing, 131–135
Meyer, Bertrand, 36, 105,
    107, 209
mini-languages, 64
mistakes, fear of, 194
mixins, 46, 161, 164–166
mixology, 171
mob programming, 256, 258
mockups, gathering require-
    ments with, 247
model building for estimates,
    66–68
modules
    coupling symptoms, 131
    parallelism, 173
    prototyping, 58
    unit testing, 219–221
Monad library, 156
monitors (for resources), 180
Motif, 127
mouse, 82–83
multiple inheritance, 46
multiple interfaces, 46
multiplication, matrice, 204
mutexes, 180
mutual exclusion strategies,
    176–181
The Mythical Man-Month, 24,
    269, 285

N
Nact library, 182
naming
    challenges, 242
    consistency in, 241
    ETC principle, 28
    importance of, 238
    projects, 240, 267, 269
    renaming, 241
    strategies for, 192, 238–
        242
    teams, 240, 267, 269
    variables, 240
National Cyber Security Cen-
    tre, 236
NATS, 189
nested loops, 206
nesting resource allocations,
    121
Netflix, 277
network monitoring black-
    board exercise, 190
news, following for knowledge
    portfolios, 16
NIST, 236
Norvig, Peter, 218
Novobilski, Andrew J., 219
NULL, 125

O
object-oriented languages
    balancing resources, 122
    inheritance, 158
    orthogonality exercise, 46
*Object-Oriented Software
    Construction*, 36, 105, 209
objects
    extending with mixins,
        164–166
    object stores and black-
        boards, 170
observables, observer pattern,
    142
observer pattern, 138, 142
observers, observer pattern,
    142
obsolescence, plain text and,
    75
officers, quality, 265
online communication, 25
OpenAPI, 37
OpenLook, 127
optimal packing container
    problems, 206

optimization, premature, 208
options vs. excuses, 4
order
    blackboard data, 189
    nesting resource alloca-
        tions, 121
orthogonality, 27, 39–46, 211
overembellishment, 12
overrefinement, 12
overspecification in require-
    ments, 250
ovicide, 187

P
P (semaphores), 176
pair programming, 256–259,
    282
parallelism
    activity diagrams, 171
    challenges, 174
    defined, 169
    Elixir compiler, 173
    opportunities for, 173
parameterization, configuring
    for, 166–168
parameters
    checking, 96
    in configuration data,
        166
    in model-building, 68
    resource balancing with,
        120
parsing
    external domain lan-
        guages, 63–64
    frameworks, 63
    generators, 63, 65
    log messages, 222
    trace messages, 94
partitioning, algorithm run-
    times, 204, 206
passwords, security, 235–237
paste functionality and pass-
    words, 236
pattern languages, 241
pattern matching
    blackboards, 188–189
    Elixir, 155
    function pipelines, 155–
        158
patterns
    analyzing other people's
        code, 196
    Decorator Pattern, 43

exceptions antipatterns, 123

observer pattern, 138, 142

password antipatterns, 236

phantom, 199

Singleton pattern, 44

Strategy pattern, 44

PEG parsers, 63, 65

Peopleware, 24

performance
algorithm speed, 191, 203–209
assertions and, 116–117
DRY principle, 35
programming by coincidence, 198
prototyping and, 57
refactoring for, 211
testing, 275–276
version control advantages, 85

persistence frameworks, 37

PERT, estimating with, 69

phantom patterns, 199

Phoenix, 61–62

Pike, Rob, 98

pipe operator (|>), 151

pipelines
about, 129, 151
vs. chains, 135
coupling from, 135
deferring, 156
pipe operator (|>), 151
transformations with, 150–157
using if assignments in languages without, 153

piña colada, 171

plain text, 74–78, 99, 173

plans, using, 201

plugins, editors, 83

policy
as metadata, 248
vs. requirements, 110, 248

polymorphism, 162

ports, in configuration data, 166

Post-it notes, 27, 58

postconditions, design by contract, 105, 109

The Practice of Programming, 98

Pragmatic Bookshelf
example of design for concurrency/parallelism, 173
text manipulation examples, 98

preconditions, design by contract, 105, 109–110

prefix classes, 158

premature optimization, 208

presentation
communications, 21, 25
documentation, 22–23
email, 25
orthogonality in, 45

pride in work, 263, 282

principle of least privilege, 232, 234

priorities in programming deliberately, 201

privacy, 286

privilege, principle of least, 232, 234

problem solving
debugging as, 89
programmer's role, 281

procedural languages, semantic invariants for resource allocation, 124

process of elimination in debugging, 95

processes, 170, 181, 186

production environment, assertions in, 117

productivity
orthogonality and, 40
tracer bullets advantages, 53

Program Evaluation Review Technique, *see* PERTThe ii tag should not be here.

programmers, *see also* responsibility, programmer; teams
agency of, 1–2
change resistance, 1–2
change strategies, 1, 9–11
characteristics of, xx–xxi, 1
community participation, 16, 19
duplication of efforts, 37
ethics, 285–287
individuality, xxii, 260

knowledge portfolio, 1, 13–19, 266

mob programming, 256, 258

pair programming, 256–259, 282

as problem solvers, 281

role, xix

role in defining requirements, 244–251

signing work, 263, 282

starter kit, 273–280

working together, 243, 256–259

programming
by coincidence, 108, 191, 197–202, 223
as continuous process, xxii
as craft, xix, xxi–xxii
deliberately, 197–202
ethical, 285–287
future of, 126, 285–287
individuality in, xxii
mob programming, 256, 258
pair programming, 256–259, 282
paradigms and ETC principle, 30
reactive, 138, 143–147
signing work, 263, 282
starter kit, 263
as therapy, 245
transformations, 129, 147–158
working together, 243, 256–259

project glossaries, 241, 251

project librarians, 38

projects, *see also* requirements
cargo cults, 263, 270–273
delighting users, 263, 280–281
expectations, 280
glossaries, 241, 251
measuring success, 263, 280–281
naming, 240, 267, 269
parameterizing with configuration, 166–168
pride in, 263, 282
signing work, 263, 282
solving puzzles, 243, 252–256

starter kit, 263, 273–280
version control for project
  management, 87
prompt, configuring shell, 79
proofreading, 25
property-based testing, 108,
  192, 224–230, 278
protocols, as alternative to
  inheritance, 161, 166
prototypes
  about, 27
  defined, 54
  as disposable, 54, 58,
    195
  exercises, 59
  gathering requirements
    with, 247
  to get past blocks, 195
  vs. tracer code, 54, 56,
    58
  using, 56–59
publish/subscribe
  blackboards, 170
  events strategy, 138, 143
publishers, publish/sub-
  scribe strategy, 143
Pugh, Greg, 94
puzzles, solving, 243, 252–
  256
Python
  property-based testing
    example, 225–229
  text manipulation exam-
    ples, 98

Q
quality
  good-enough software, 1,
    11–13, 269
  officers, 265
  in requirements discus-
    sions, 12
  teams and, 265, 269
  version control advan-
    tages, 85
questions
  ethical, 286
  involving audience in
    communications, 22
  as opportunities for
    learning, 17
  programmer inquisitive-
    ness, xx
  puzzle-solving, 255
  for requirements, 245
  for users, 280

quicksort, 204, 206
quotes in email and social
  media, 25

R
R, %>% operator, 151
React, 144
reactive programming, 138,
  143–147
readability, 76, 192
readers, involving, 22
reading
  critical thinking and, 17
  goals for knowledge port-
    folios, 16–19
realism, as programmer
  characteristic, xxi
recipient list, checking, 25
record-keeping
  for debugging, 92
  engineering daybooks,
    29, 74, 100, 255
  estimates, 68, 71
  resource allocation, 122
recovery, version control and,
  86, 88
recursion, estimating speed,
  203
Refactoring, 212
refactoring
  automatic, 213
  defined, 210
  need for, 191, 209
  for orthogonality, 44
  as redesign, 212
  scheduling, 201, 212
  strategies for, 209–213
  when to refactor, 211
reflection and refinement,
  teams, 266
regressions
  binary chop, 93
  regression tests, 229, 274
  release, 93
regular expressions, time
  parser exercise, 65
releases
  debugging strategies, 93
  regression, 93
  version control and, 85,
    274
REPL, results as feedback,
  126
replaceability
  ETC principle, 29

incremental approach,
  126
programming deliberate-
  ly, 201
reporting
  bugs, 90
  repository hosting tools,
    87
  security and, 234
repositories
  APIs, 37, 190
  central, 37, 85, 190
  hosting, 87
  for message formats, 190
  storing main on network
    or cloud drive, 84
representations in transformation wrappers, 154
requirements
  about, 243
  blackboards, 189
  challenges, 252
  creep, 251, 265
  difficulty of gathering,
    244
  documentation, 249
  domain language chal-
    lenge, 64
  exercises, 252
  vs. expectations, 281
  as feedback, 246, 249–
    250, 261
  finding transformations
    with, 149
  good-enough software, 12
  metrics on new, 265
  myths, 244
  overembellishment, 12
  overspecification, 250
  vs. policy, 110, 248
  as a process, 246
  team and, 265, 268
  tracer bullets, 27, 50–55,
    249, 268
  understanding, 244–252
  user stories, 250
  users reading, 61, 249
resources
  balancing, 104, 118–125
  challenges, 125
  checking usage, 124
  coupling in allocation,
    119
  DRY principle, 37
  encapsulating in classes,
    122
  estimating algorithm
    speed, 203–209

as global data, 136
language support for ex-
clusive access, 180
nesting allocation, 121
shared state in, 179
transactional, 177–180
wrapping, 124
resources for this book
algorithms, 208
code files, xvii, 185
communication, 24
trust, 4
UML diagrams, 171
responsibility, component
design by contract, 110
ETC principle, 28
prototyping, 58
responsibility principle
and orthogonality, 41
responsibility, programmer
ethical, 285–287
pride in work, 282
taking, 1, 3–5, 265
teams, 265
responsive applications
finite state machines,
138–141
observer pattern, 138,
142
publish/subscribe strate-
gy, 138, 143
reactive programming,
138, 143–147
writing, 137–147
restructuring, 210
reusability
decoupling and, 135
DRY principle, 38
global data and, 135
orthogonality and, 41
reversibility, 27, 47–50
review in knowledge portfolios, 15
reviews, code, 38
risk
knowledge portfolios, 15
orthogonality benefits, 41
programming by coinci-
dence, 198
prototypes, 56
responsibility and, 4
robustness in prototyping, 57
RSpec, using domain lan-
guage, 60, 62–63

rubber ducking
avoiding programming by
coincidence, 201
debugging with, 94
with engineering day-
books, 101
listening to lizard brain,
194
puzzle-solving, 255
Ruby
as domain language, 62
inheritance, 159
tainted data in, 232
text manipulation exam-
ples, 98
rules engines, 189
rules vs. values, 28
runtime systems, design by
contract, 109
Rust
data ownership, 180
estimating algorithms ex-
ercise, 209

S
saboteurs, 277
scheduling
estimating schedules, 69
refactoring, 201, 212
team learning and im-
provement, 266
upgrades, 95
Schrödinger's cat, 50
scope, resource balancing
and, 120, 122
scope, project
estimating time, 67
increases in, 251, 265
in requirements discus-
sions, 12
scripting languages
prototypes, 57
time parser exercise, 65
scripts, central spot for, 38
Scrum, 38, 273
search, algorithm runtimes,
204, 206
secrets
encrypting, 235
security of, 235
security
authentication, 237
cryptography, 237
data, 232–233, 235
denial of service attacks,
233

encryption, 232
ethical questions, 286
minimizing attack surface
area, 232–234
obscurity and, 231
passwords, 235–236
principle of least privi-
lege, 232, 234
repository hosting tools,
87
secure defaults, 232, 234
strategies for, 192, 231–
237
updates, 232, 235
sed, 98
Sedgewick, Robert, 208
"select is broken", 95
semantic invariants
design by contract, 110
requirements vs. policy,
110
resource allocation, 124–
125
semaphores, 176–178
sequential search, algorithm
runtimes, 204
services and security, 233
sets
algorithm runtimes, 204,
206
partitioning, 204, 206
shared directories vs. version
control, 84
shells
advantages, 74, 78
challenges, 46, 80
customizing, 79
using, 78–80
Ship of Theseus, xv
Shrier, Kim, xviii
side effects, assertions, 116
signature function example,
149–157
signing work, 263, 282
Simula 67, 158
single responsibility principle,
28
Singleton pattern, 44
singletons, 44, 136
situational awareness, 11
Smalltalk, 159, 212

snake_case
    naming conventions and culture, 241
    text manipulation exercise, 100
social media, 25, 285
soft skills, 16
software rot, *see* entropy
solutions
    puzzle solving, 253
    to exercises, xvi, 293–306
sorting, algorithm runtimes, 204, 206, 209
special characters in passwords, 236
specs in Clojure, 106
spelling, checking, 22, 25
square law algorithms, 204, 206
stacks, debugging in, 92
standup meetings, 38, 270
start-up fatigue, 9
starter kit, 263, 273–280
starting, fears/blocks to, 193
state
    actor model, 170, 181–186, 190
    design by contract, 107
    finite state machines, 138–141, 146
    mutual exclusion strategies, 176–181
    nonatomic updates, 175
    passing in transformations, 153
    processes, 170, 181, 186
    semaphores, 176–178
    shared, 170, 174–181
    test coverage, 277
    transactional resources, 177–180
Stone Soup, 1, 9–11
Strategy pattern, 44
streams, 138, 143–147
stress testing, 276
Stroop effect, 238, 242
Structured Design, 40
style
    communications, 21
    in prototyping, 57
style sheets, 22, 45
subclassing, *see* inheritance
subscribers, publish/subscribe strategy, 143

success, measuring, 280–281
supervision, 114, 186
supervisor trees, 114
supervisors, 114
surprise
    in debugging, 96
    in property-based testing, 229
Swift, pipe operator (|>), 151
synchronization bar, 171

T

tainted data, 232
Taleb, Nassim Nicholas, 127
TDD (test-driven development), 108, 216–218, 222
teams
    about, 263
    agility, 243, 259–262, 266
    automation, 269
    branding, 267, 269
    challenges, 269
    code ownership, 282
    communicating presence, 267
    communication, 38, 257, 267
    Conway's Law, 257
    culture of testing, 222
    DRY principle, 37, 267
    individuality in, xxii
    knowledge portfolio, 266
    naming, 240, 267, 269
    pride in work, 282
    size of, 264, 269
    strategies for, 264–269
    tracer bullets, 268
    trust and taking responsibility, 3
technical debt, *see* entropy
Tell, Don't Ask principle, 132
temporal coupling, 169–174
test coverage, 217, 277
test windows, 221, 234
test-driven development (TDD), 108, 216–218, 222
Test-First Development, 216
testing
    ad hoc testing, 221
    algorithmic estimates, 207
    assumptions and programming by coincidence, 200–201

    assumptions with assertions, 104, 115–118, 201
    assumptions with property-based testing, 224–230
    automated, 275, 278, 280
    benefit in thinking about code, 192, 214, 216, 223–224, 229
    boundary conditions, 91
    challenges, 230, 280
    chips, 219
    to code, 192, 214–224
    continuous, 275–278
    with contracts, 108, 220–230
    Cucumber tests, 60, 62
    culture of, 222
    decoupling and, 135, 223
    after deployment, 221
    exercises, 230
    failing tests before fixing bugs, 91
    as feedback, 126, 192, 214–223
    finding bugs only once, 278
    global data, 135
    integration, 219, 275–276
    under load, 276
    need for, 214
    orthogonality and, 40–41, 44
    performance, 275–276
    plain-text advantages, 75, 77
    project management with, 263, 274–278
    property-based testing, 108, 192, 224–230, 278
    redundancy in, 217
    refactoring and, 211, 213
    regression tests, 229, 274
    repository hosting tools, 87
    stress testing, 276
    test coverage, 217, 277
    test data, 225, 276
    Test During, 222
    test environments, 275
    Test First, 222
    Test Never, 222
    test windows, 221, 234
    test-driven development (TDD), 108, 216–218, 222

testing tests, 277
tests as first user of code, 215, 229
tracer bullets advantages, 53
usage patterns, 91
version control and, 93, 274
text
editors, 74, 81–83
manipulation, 74, 97–100
plain text, 74–78, 99, 173
themes, shell, 79
therapy, programming as, 245
thinking
analyzing other people's code, 196
benefits of testing code, 192, 214, 216, 223–224, 229
critical thinking in knowledge portfolio, 17
critical thinking, need for, xxi
critical thinking, questions for, 18
design by contract and, 107, 111
externalizing issues, 194
instincts, 193–196
listening to lizard brain, 191–197
naming things, 192, 238–242
need for, xxi, 1, 191
outside the box, 252–256
as programmer characteristic, xxi, 1
programming by coincidence, 191, 197–202, 223
refactoring and, 191, 209–213
security, 192, 231–237
test to code, 192, 214–224
time
Big-O notation, 204
communications timing, 21
as design element, 170
editor fluency and, 81
estimating, 28, 65–71, 204
for learning, 3, 17
orthogonality benefits, 40

parsing time specification exercise, 65
prototypes, 56, 59
for refactoring, 212
scope creep, 265
team size, 269
temporal coupling, 169–174
text manipulation languages, 98
in tracing statements,.94
UTC, 199
time bombs, 221
timestamps, reactive event handling example, 144
tips, about, xvi
tools, see also editors; version control
approach to, 73
combining in shell, 78
diagnostic, 222
hosting repositories, 87
orthogonality, 43, 46
plain-text advantages, 75–76
prototyping, 57
tool building skills, 269
top-down design, 218
trace ids, 190
tracer bullets
about, 27
identifying requirements with, 50–55
vs. prototypes, 56, 58
requirements with, 249
teams, 268
tracing statements, 94, 222
trackpad, 82–83
train wrecks, 131–135
traits, as alternative to inheritance, 161, 164–166
transactional resources, 177–180
transformations, 129, 147–158
transitions, finite state machines (FSM), 139–141
traveling salesman problem, 204, 206
trolls, 25
trust, 3
Trust and team performance, 4
try...catch blocks, 122
turtle graphics exercise, 64

type checking, 154
types, inheritance and, 160
The Tyranny of Metrics, 259
T Spaces, 188

U
UML, 171
Unicode, 241
Uniform Access principle, 36
unit testing
with contracts, 108, 220–223
decoupling and, 135
defined, 276
as feedback, 126
global data, 135
orthogonality and, 44
project management with, 275
with property-based testing, 229
strategies for, 219–221
tests as first user of code, 215, 229
Unix
philosophy and plain text, 77
transformations example, 147
unlocking, semaphores, 176–178
upgrades, scheduling, 95
upper bounds, Big-O notation, 204, 207
URLs, for test window, 222
user groups, 16
user interfaces
prototyping, 57
repository hosting tools, 87
user stories, 250
users
access patterns, 276
agility and, 260
buy-in, 53
deleting old/unused, 233
delighting, 263, 280–281
involvement in coding, 256–258
involvement in communications, 22
involvement in debugging, 90
involvement in end-to-end building, 218

involvement in good-enough software trade-offs, 11
principle of least privilege, 232, 234
questions for judging success, 280
reading of Cucumber features, 61
reading requirements, 60–61, 249
refactoring for, 211
role in defining requirements, 245–248
security, 233
shadowing, 247
testing usage patterns, 91
tests as first user, 215, 229
tracer bullets advantages, 53

UTC, 199

utility routines, central spot for, 38

V

V (semaphores), 176

validations
in configuration data, 166
with mixins, 164
testing in build, 275–276
validation suites, 37

Valim, José, xviii

values
changing pipeline functions from calls to values, 156

in model-building, 68
vs. rules, 28
wrapping in transformations, 154–157

variables, names, 240

vendors
flexibility in, 48
orthogonality and, 41
responsibility and, 4
reversibility and, 47–49

verification, 275–276

version control
advantages, 84–85
challenges, 88
debugging and orthogonality, 44
defined, 85
importance of, 74, 85, 263, 274
plain-text advantages, 76
project management with, 87, 263, 274
security, 235
vs. shared directories, 84
testing and, 93, 274
testing specific releases, 93
using, 84–88

Vue.js, 144

W

When good-enough software is best, 11

windows, see broken windows; test windows

with (Elixir), 156

workflow
analyzing for concurrency in, 171–174
analyzing for parallelism in, 171
with blackboards, 189
test-driven development (TDD), 216–218
version control advantages, 86–87
workflow systems, 189

wrapping
actor model example, 185
configuration, 167
global data, 136
resources, 124
values in transformations, 154–157

X

XP (eXtreme Programming), 216, 257, 273, 282

Y

YAML
Ansible with, 61
as external language, 63
as plain text, 75
static configuration with, 166
text manipulation exercise, 99

Yourdon, Ed, 11

Notes and Doodles

Notes and Doodles

Notes and Doodles

Notes and Doodles

Notes and Doodles

Register Your Product at informit.com/register

Access additional benefits and **save 35%** on your next purchase

- Automatically receive a coupon for 35% off your next purchase, valid for 30 days. Look for your code in your InformIT cart or the Manage Codes section of your account page.

- Download available product updates.

- Access bonus material if available.*

- Check the box to hear from us and receive exclusive offers on new editions and related products.

*Registration benefits vary by product. Benefits will be listed on your account page under Registered Products.

InformIT.com—The Trusted Technology Learning Source

InformIT is the online home of information technology brands at Pearson, the world's foremost education company. At InformIT.com, you can:

- Shop our books, eBooks, software, and video training
- Take advantage of our special offers and promotions (informit.com/promotions)
- Sign up for special offers and content newsletter (informit.com/newsletters)
- Access thousands of free chapters and video lessons

Connect with InformIT—Visit informit.com/community

the trusted technology learning source

Addison-Wesley • Adobe Press • Cisco Press • Microsoft Press • Pearson IT Certification • Que • Sams • Peachpit Press

 Pearson

*Dave Thomas and Andy Hunt are internationally recognized
as leading voices in the software development community.
They consult and speak around the world. Together, they founded the
Pragmatic Bookshelf, publishing award-winning, leading-edge books fo
software developers. They were two of the authors of the Agile Manifesto*

*Dave currently teaches college, turns wood, and plays
with new technology and paradigms.*

*Andy writes science fiction, is an active musician,
and loves to tinker with technology.*

But, most of all, they're both driven to keep learning.

pragdave.me

toolshed.com

79. Policy Is Metadata 248
Don't hardcode policy into a system; instead express it as metadata used by the system.

80. Use a Project Glossary 251
Create and maintain a single source of all the specific terms and vocabulary for a project.

81. Don't Think Outside the Box—Find the Box 254
When faced with an impossible problem, identify the real constraints. Ask yourself: "Does it have to be done this way? Does it have to be done at all?"

82. Don't Go into the Code Alone 259
Programming can be difficult and demanding. Take a friend with you.

83. Agile Is Not a Noun; Agile Is How You Do Things 259
Agile is an adjective: it's how you do something.

84. Maintain Small Stable Teams 264
Teams should be small and stable, where everyone trusts each other and depends on each other.

85. Schedule It to Make It Happen 266
If you don't schedule it, it's not going to happen. Schedule reflection, experimentation, learning and skills improvement.

86. Organize Fully Functional Teams 268
Organize Around Functionality, Not Job Functions. Don't separate UI/UX designers from coders, frontend from backend, testers from data modelers, design from deployment. Build teams so you can build code end-to-end, incrementally and iteratively.

87. Do What Works, Not What's Fashionable 271
Don't adopt a development method or technique just because other companies are doing it. Adopt what works for your team, in your context.

88. Deliver When Users Need It 273
Don't wait weeks or months to deliver just because your process demands it.

89. Use Version Control to Drive Builds, Tests, and Releases . 274
Use commits or pushes to trigger builds, tests, releases. Use a version control tag to deploy to production.

90. Test Early, Test Often, Test Automatically 275
Tests that run with every build are much more effective than test plans that sit on a shelf.

91. Coding Ain't Done 'Til All the Tests Run 275
'Nuff said.

92. Use Saboteurs to Test Your Testing 277
Introduce bugs on purpose in a separate copy of the source to verify that testing will catch them.

93. Test State Coverage, Not Code Coverage 278
Identify and test significant program states. Testing just lines of code isn't enough.

94. Find Bugs Once 278
Once a human tester finds a bug, it should be the last time a human tester finds that bug. Automatic tests should check for it from then on.

95. Don't Use Manual Procedures 279
A computer will execute the same instructions, in the same order, time after time.

96. Delight Users, Don't Just Deliver Code 281
Develop solutions that produce business value for your users and delight them every day.

97. Sign Your Work. 282
Artisans of an earlier age were proud to sign their work. You should be, too.

98. First, Do No Harm. 286
Failure is inevitable. Make sure no one will suffer because of it.

99. Don't Enable Scumbags 287
Because you risk becoming one, too.

100. It's Your Life. 287
Share it. Celebrate it. Build it. *And Have Fun!*
Enjoy this amazing life we have, and do great things.

Connect with InformIT: Visit informit.com/community

- Study groups! How about checking off each tip as you finish discussing them?
- Feel free to copy and share this card

the trusted technology learning source

Addison-Wesley • Adobe Press • Cisco Press • Microsoft Press • Pearson IT Certification • Que • Sams • Peachpit Press

Pearson

51. Don't Pay Inheritance Tax 161
Consider alternatives that better fit your needs, such as interfaces, delegation, or mixins.

52. Prefer Interfaces to Express Polymorphism. 162
Interfaces make polymorphism explicit without the coupling introduced by inheritance.

53. Delegate to Services: Has-A Trumps Is-A 163
Don't inherit from services: contain them.

54. Use Mixins to Share Functionality 165
Mixins add functionality to classes without the inheritance tax. Combine with interfaces for painless polymorphism.

55. Parameterize Your App Using External Configuration . . 166
When code relies on values that may change after the application has gone live, keep those values external to the app.

56. Analyze Workflow to Improve Concurrency 171
Exploit concurrency in your user's workflow.

57. Shared State Is Incorrect State 174
Shared state opens a large can of worms that can often only be fixed by rebooting.

58. Random Failures Are Often Concurrency Issues 180
Variations in timing and context can expose concurrency bugs, but in inconsistent and irreproducible ways.

59. Use Actors For Concurrency Without Shared State . . . 182
Use Actors to manage concurrent state without explicit synchronization.

60. Use Blackboards to Coordinate Workflow 189
Use blackboards to coordinate disparate facts and agents, while maintaining independence and isolation among participants.

61. Listen to Your Inner Lizard 194
When it feels like your code is pushing back, it's really your subconscious trying to tell you something's wrong.

62. Don't Program by Coincidence. 200
Rely only on reliable things. Beware of accidental complexity, and don't confuse a happy coincidence with a purposeful plan.

63. Estimate the Order of Your Algorithms 207
Get a feel for how long things are likely to take before you write code.

64. Test Your Estimates 208
Mathematical analysis of algorithms doesn't tell you everything. Try timing your code in its target environment.

65. Refactor Early, Refactor Often. 212
Just as you might weed and rearrange a garden, rewrite, rework, and re-architect code when it needs it. Fix the root of the problem.

66. Testing Is Not About Finding Bugs 214
A test is a perspective into your code, and gives you feedback about its design, api, and coupling.

67. A Test Is the First User of Your Code 216
Use its feedback to guide what you do.

68. Build End-To-End, Not Top-Down or Bottom Up 218
Build small pieces of end-to-end functionality, learning about the problem as you go.

69. Design to Test 221
Start thinking about testing before you write a line of code.

70. Test Your Software, or Your Users Will 223
Test ruthlessly. Don't make your users find bugs for you.

71. Use Property-Based Tests to Validate Your Assumptions . 224
Property-based tests will try things you never thought to try, and exercise your code in ways it wasn't meant to be used.

72. Keep It Simple and Minimize Attack Surfaces 234
Complex code creates a breeding ground for bugs and opportunities for attackers to exploit.

73. Apply Security Patches Quickly 235
Attackers deploy exploits as quick as they can, you have to be quicker.

74. Name Well; Rename When Needed 242
Name to express your intent to readers, and rename as soon as that intent shifts.

75. No One Knows Exactly What They Want 244
They might know a general direction, but they won't know the twists and turns.

76. Programmers Help People Understand What They Want 245
Software development is an act of co-creation between users and programmers.

77. Requirements Are Learned in a Feedback Loop 246
Understanding requirements requires exploration and feedback, so the consequences of decisions can be used to refine the initial ideas.

78. Work with a User to Think Like a User 247
It's the best way to gain insight into how the system will really be used.

22. Program Close to the Problem Domain 60
Design and code in the language of the problem domain.

23. Estimate to Avoid Surprises 66
Estimate before you start. You'll spot potential problems up front.

24. Iterate the Schedule with the Code 70
Use experience you gain as you implement to refine the project time scales.

25. Keep Knowledge in Plain Text 75
Plain text won't become obsolete. It helps leverage your work and simplifies debugging and testing.

26. Use the Power of Command Shells 79
Use the shell when graphical user interfaces don't cut it.

27. Achieve Editor Fluency 81
An editor is your most important tool. Know how to make it do what you need, quickly and accurately.

28. Always Use Version Control 85
Version control is a time machine for your work; you can go back.

29. Fix the Problem, Not the Blame 89
It doesn't really matter whether the bug is your fault or someone else's—it is still your problem, and it still needs to be fixed.

30. Don't Panic 89
This is true for galactic hitchhikers and for developers.

31. Failing Test Before Fixing Code 91
Create a focussed test that reveals the bug before you try fixing it.

32. Read the Damn Error Message 92
Most exceptions tell both what failed and where it failed. If you're lucky you might even get parameter values.

33. "select" Isn't Broken 95
It is rare to find a bug in the OS or the compiler, or even a third-party product or library. The bug is most likely in the application.

34. Don't Assume It—Prove It 96
Prove your assumptions in the actual environment—with real data and boundary conditions.

35. Learn a Text Manipulation Language 98
You spend a large part of each day working with text. Why not have the computer do some of it for you?

36. You Can't Write Perfect Software 102
Software can't be perfect. Protect your code and users from the inevitable errors.

37. Design with Contracts 107
Use contracts to document and verify that code does no more and no less than it claims to do.

38. Crash Early 113
A dead program normally does a lot less damage than a crippled one.

39. Use Assertions to Prevent the Impossible 115
If it can't happen, use assertions to ensure that it won't. Assertions validate your assumptions. Use them to protect your code from an uncertain world.

40. Finish What You Start 118
Where possible, the function or object that allocates a resource should be responsible for deallocating it.

41. Act Locally 121
Keep the scope of mutable variables and open resources short and easily visible.

42. Take Small Steps—Always 126
Small steps always; check the feedback; and adjust before proceeding.

43. Avoid Fortune-Telling 127
Only look ahead as far as you can see.

44. Decoupled Code Is Easier to Change 131
Coupling ties things together, so that it's harder to change just one thing.

45. Tell, Don't Ask 132
Don't get values from an object, transform them, and then stick them back. Make the object do the work.

46. Don't Chain Method Calls 134
Try not to have more than one dot when you access something.

47. Avoid Global Data 136
It's like adding an extra parameter to every method.

48. If It's Important Enough To Be Global, Wrap It in an API . 136
…but only if you really, really want it to be global.

49. Programming's About Code, But Programs Are About Data 149
All programs transform data, converting an input into an output. Start designing using transformations.

50. Don't Hoard State; Pass It Around 153
Don't hang on to data within a function or module. Take one down and pass it around.

See more at **pragprog.com**

The Pragmatic Programmer
20th Anniversary Edition

1. Care About Your Craft . . . . **xxi**
Why spend your life developing software unless you care about doing it well?

2. Think! About Your Work . . . . **xxi**
Turn off the autopilot and take control. Constantly critique and appraise your work.

3. You Have Agency **2**
It's your life. Grab hold of it and make it what you want.

4. Provide Options, Don't Make Lame Excuses **4**
Instead of excuses, provide options. Don't say it can't be done; explain what can be done.

5. Don't Live with Broken Windows **7**
Fix bad designs, wrong decisions, and poor code when you see them.

6. Be a Catalyst for Change **9**
You can't force change on people. Instead, show them how the future might be and help them participate in creating it.

7. Remember the Big Picture **10**
Don't get so engrossed in the details that you forget to check what's happening around you.

8. Make Quality a Requirements Issue **12**
Involve your users in determining the project's real quality requirements.

9. Invest Regularly in Your Knowledge Portfolio **15**
Make learning a habit.

10. Critically Analyze What You Read and Hear **17**
Don't be swayed by vendors, media hype, or dogma. Analyze information in terms of you and your project.

11. English is Just Another Programming Language **20**
Treat English as Just Another Programming Language. Write documents as you would write code: honor the DRY principle, ETC, automation, and so on.

12. It's Both What You Say and the Way You Say It. **22**
There's no point in having great ideas if you don't communicate them effectively.

13. Build Documentation In, Don't Bolt It On **23**
Documentation created separately from code is less likely to be correct and up to date.

14. Good Design Is Easier to Change Than Bad Design . . . **28**
A thing is well designed if it adapts to the people who use it. For code, that means it must adapt by changing.

15. DRY—Don't Repeat Yourself **31**
Every piece of knowledge must have a single, unambiguous, authoritative representation within a system.

16. Make It Easy to Reuse **38**
If it's easy to reuse, people will. Create an environment that supports reuse.

17. Eliminate Effects Between Unrelated Things **40**
Design components that are self-contained, independent, and have a single, well-defined purpose.

18. There Are No Final Decisions **48**
No decision is cast in stone. Instead, consider each as being written in the sand at the beach, and plan for change.

19. Forgo Following Fads **49**
Neal Ford says, "Yesterday's Best Practice Becomes Tomorrow's Antipattern." Choose architectures based on fundamentals, not fashion.

20. Use Tracer Bullets to Find the Target **51**
Tracer bullets let you home in on your target by trying things and seeing how close they land.

21. Prototype to Learn **57**
Prototyping is a learning experience. Its value lies not in the code you produce, but in the lessons you learn.

See more at **pragprog.com**